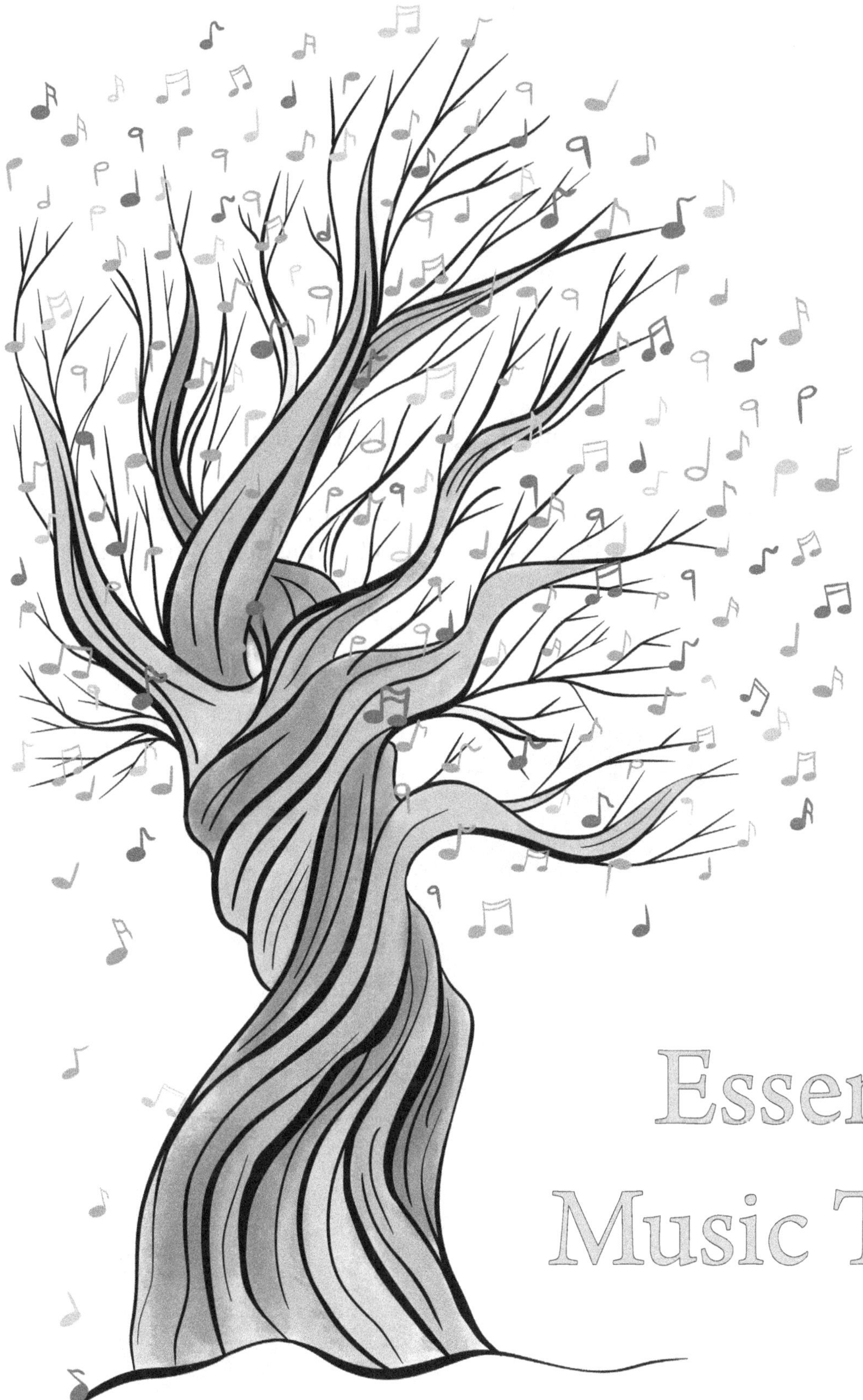

Essential Music Theory

4-6

Mark Sarnecki

San Marco Publications

Elementary Music Theory © 2023 by San Marco Publications. All rights reserved.

All right reserved. No part of this book may be reproduced in any form or by electronic or mechanical means including Information storage and retrieval systems without permission in writing from the author.

ISBN: 9781896499383

Contents

Lesson 1: **Music Notation** — 1

Lesson 2: **Time** — 13

Lesson 3: **Major Scales** — 55

Lesson 4: **Minor Scales** — 77

Lesson 5: **Intervals** — 98

Lesson 6: **Chords** — 122

Lesson 7: **Cadences** — 147

Lesson 8: **Transposition** — 153

Lesson 9: **Melody** — 165

Lesson 10: **History** — 187

Lesson 11: **Music Analysis** — 227

Music Terms and Signs — 244

Practice Examinations — 249

This volume covers Levels 4 to 6 of Essential Music Theory. The abbreviations for these levels are ❹, ❺, and ❻ and they appear in the left margin of the page. These symbols indicate the level of the material being covered. The number ❹ refers to Level 4; the number ❺ refers to Level 5; and the number ❻ refers to Level 6. Level 4 material is required for the Level 5; Level 4 and 5 material is required for Level 6.

1

Music Notation

Music existed for a long time before it was written down. Initially it was handed down by rote, which means melodies and songs were taught from generation to generation. There was no written music; people just copied the sounds. Some people still learn music this way. Developing a system of notating music meant that it could be shared far away. It could be played or sung by a musician who could read the lines and symbols created by someone they have never met. In this lesson, we are going to review some of the basic rules of music notation.

The Staff

A single staff never has a left barline. A **double barline** at the end of a measure or line indicates the end of a section. It is used to clarify the end of a section such as a **da capo** section. Note that the key signature is placed between the clef and the time signature.

Figure 1.1

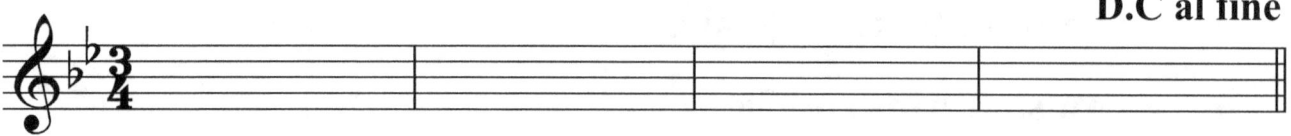

The grand staff begins with a **systemic barline**. A systemic barline joins two or more staves together. It goes through both staves to create the grand staff. The grand staff also begins with a brace in front of the systemic barline. A ***final double barline*** at the end consists of a thin line and a thick line. This marks the end of a composition or the end of a movement of a larger work.

Figure 1.2

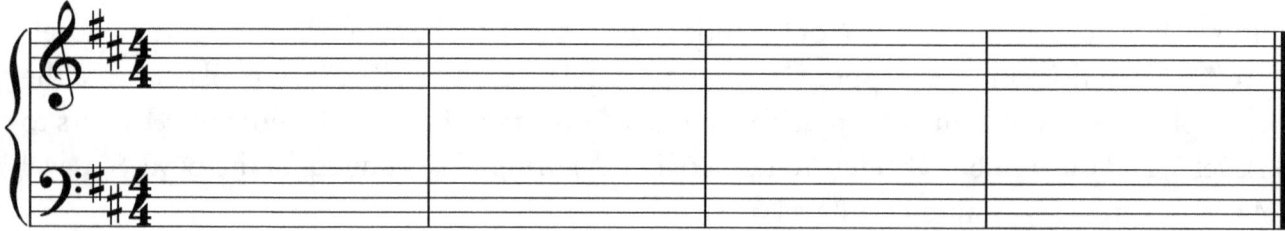

Notes and Note Stems

Notes are placed on the lines and in the spaces. The normal length of a single stem is usually one octave (3½ spaces). Flags for eighth and sixteenth notes always go on the right side of the note. Groups of eighth or sixteenth notes are joined with beams.

Figure 1.3

Stem Direction for Beamed Groups

Notes below the middle line have stems that go up, and notes above the middle line have stems that go down. Stems of notes on the middle line can go either way.

For two beamed notes, stem direction is determined by the note that is farthest away from the middle line as shown in Figure 1.4. If the note is farther above, the stems go down. If it is farther below, the stems go up.

Figure 1.4

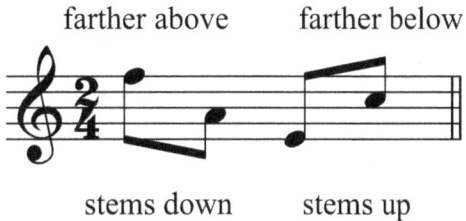

For groups of three or more beamed notes if the majority of notes are **on or above** the middle line the stems go down as in Figure 1.5 a and b. If the majority of the notes are **below** the middle line the stems go up (Figure 1.5 c). If the number of notes **above and below the middle line are equal**, the note farthest from the middle line dictates the stem direction (Figure 1.5 d).

Figure 1.5

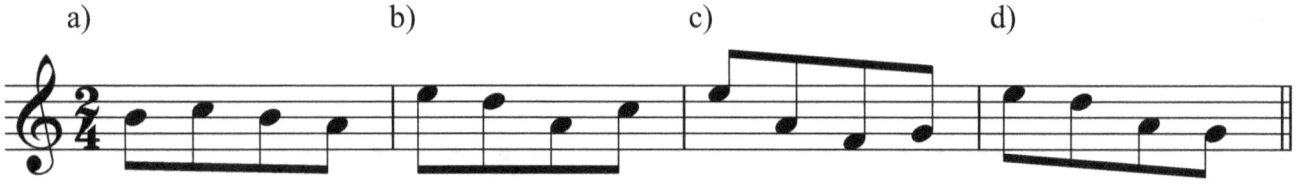

Rests

Placement of rests on the staff is important. The whole rest (Figure 1.6 a) is used to indicate a whole measure of rest. It hangs from the fourth line and is placed in the center of the measure. The half rest (Figure 1.6 b) is placed on top of the third line. The quarter rest is positioned as shown in Figure 1.6 c. The bottom hook of this rest goes through the second staff line. The hook of the eight rest is placed in the third space (Figure 1.6 d). The two hooks of the sixteenth rest are placed in the second and third space of the staff. (Figure 1.6 e).

Figure 1.6

❹ 1. Add stems to the following note heads.
❺
❻

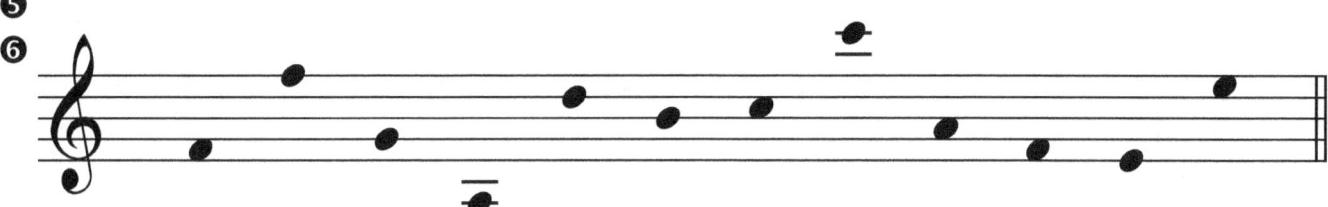

2. Add stems to the following groups of four eighth notes.

3. Circle any notes or groups of notes that have wrong stem direction.

Ledger Lines

Ledger lines are used to extend the range of the staff. Ledger lines are spaced the same distance vertically as the lines of the staff.

Figure 1.7

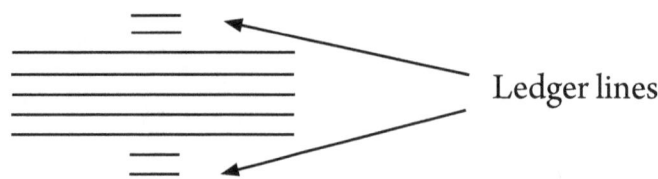

Stems of all notes above and below the first ledger line must extend to the middle staff line (Figure 1.8).

Figure 1.8

In this level we will study notes up to four ledger lines above and below the staff. Figure 1.9 shows these ledger line notes on the treble staff.

Figure 1.9

1. Write the following notes using ledger lines below the treble staff.

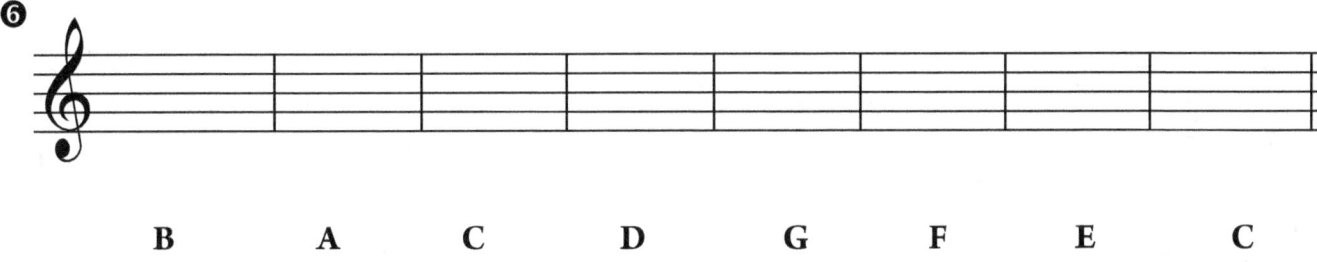

     B   A   C   D   G   F   E   C

2. Write the following notes using ledger lines above the treble staff.

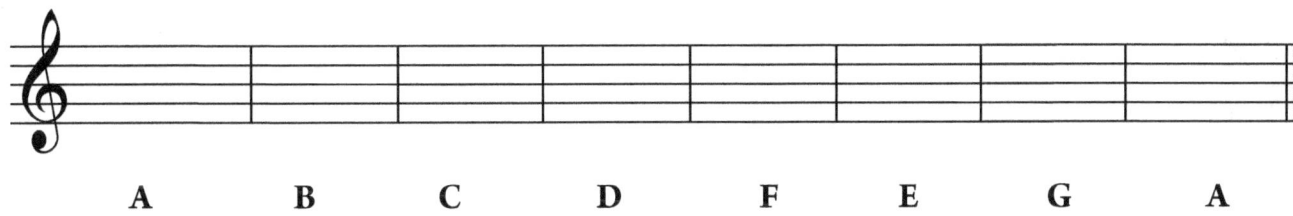

     A   B   C   D   F   E   G   A

Figure 1.4 shows the ledger line notes on the bass staff.

Figure 1.4

3. Write the following notes using ledger lines below the bass staff.

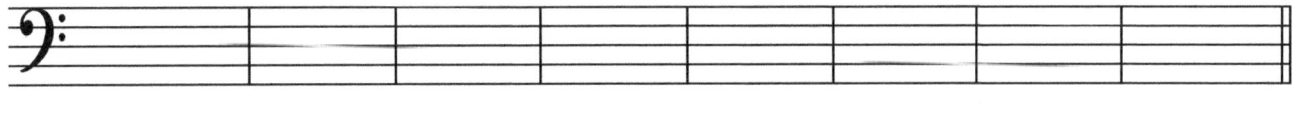

     A   B   D   C   E   G   F   E

4. Write the following notes using ledger lines above the bass staff.

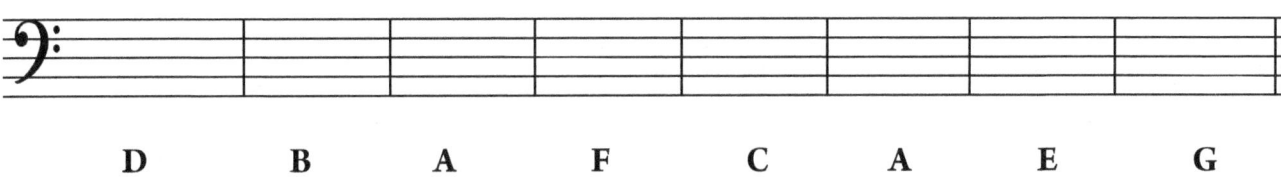

     D   B   A   F   C   A   E   G

5. Name the following notes and then write them at the same pitch in the other clef.

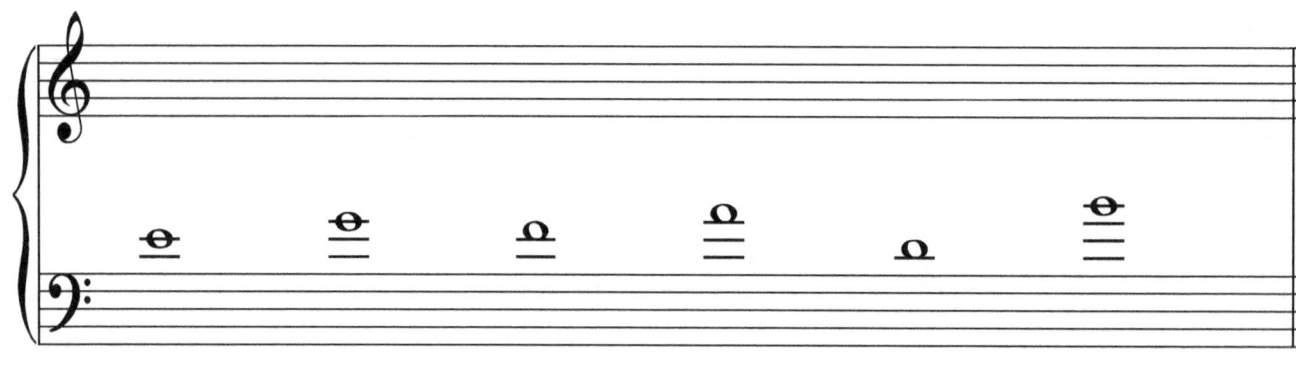

6. Rewrite the following melodies in the other clef without changing the pitch.

Jean Sibelius
Symphony No. 3, III

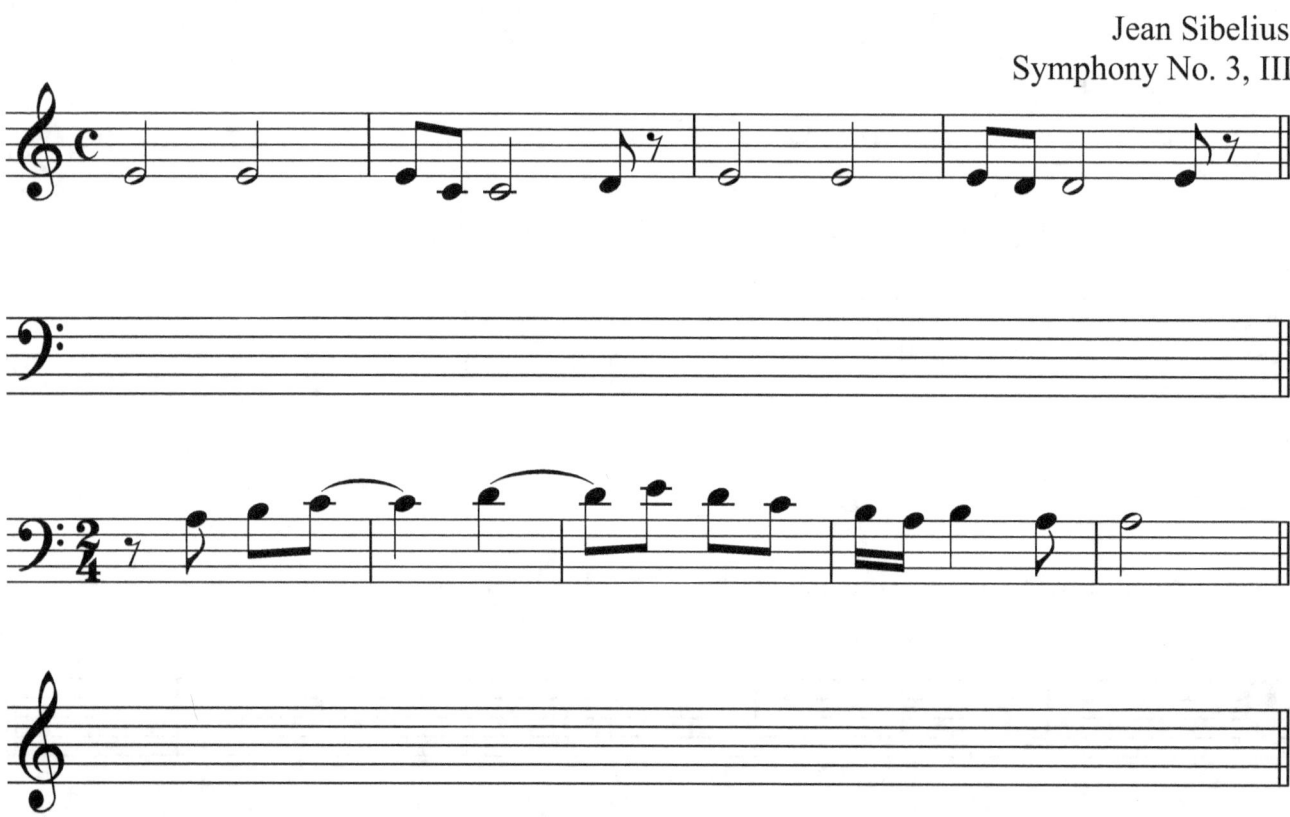

Enharmonic Equivalents

Each black key on the keyboard has both a sharp name and a flat name. When notes have the same pitch but different names they are said to be *enharmonic equivalents*. Enharmonic basically means "same note different name". They are the same note, but they have different meanings. It's like the words there, their, and they're. They sound the same but mean something different. There are many reasons why we call some notes by alternate names, and we will learn more about that when we study scales and keys.

Figure 1.10 shows some of the enharmonic notes on the keyboard. Some of the white keys may have more than one name. B♯ is also C and B is also C♭. E♯ is also F and E is also F♭.

Figure 1.10

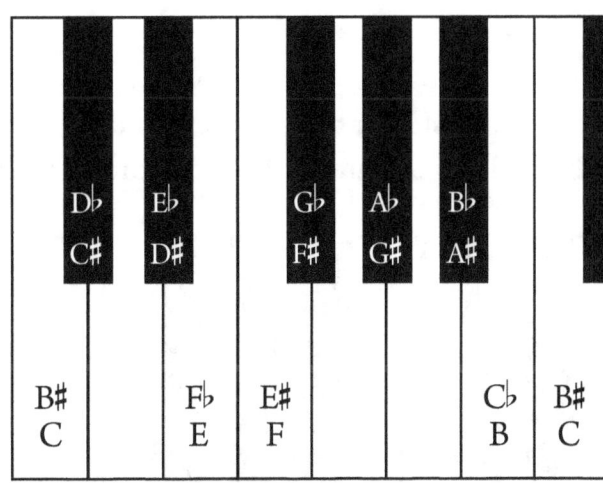

1. Give the enharmonic equivalents for the following notes.

F♯ _____   A♯ _____   F _____

B♭ _____   B _____   G♭ _____

C♯ _____   G♯ _____   D♭ _____

D♯ _____   C _____   A♭ _____

E♯ _____   B♭ _____   E♭ _____

Accidentals

Notes are altered by the use of signs called accidentals. Accidentals raise or lower the pitch of a note.

Sharp	♯	Double-sharp	𝄪
Flat	♭	Double-flat	♭♭
Natural	♮		

The Double Sharp

A ***double-sharp*** raises a note by a whole step or two half steps and looks like this: x . Double sharps are not very common but are sometimes required to spell a chord or interval correctly.

Figure 1.11

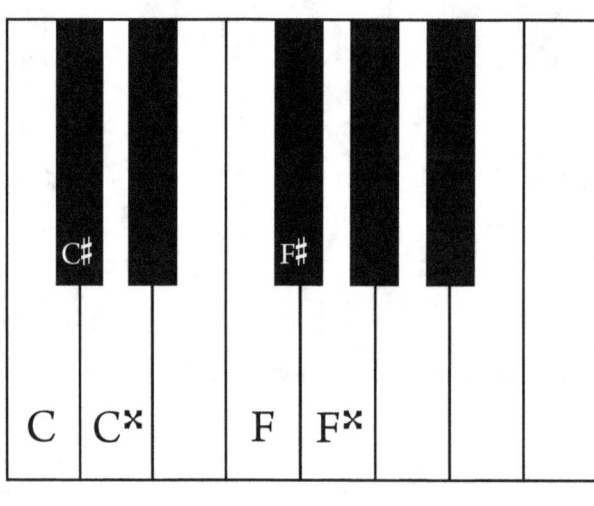

1. Apply double-sharps to each note

The Double Flat

A *double-flat* lowers a note by a whole step or two half steps and looks like this: ♭♭. Like double-sharps, double-flats occur rarely.

Figure 1.12

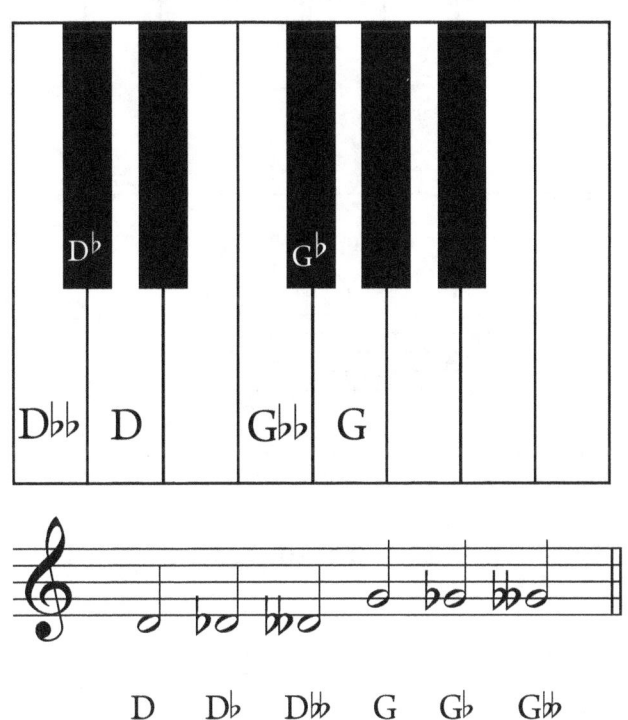

2. Apply double-flats to each note

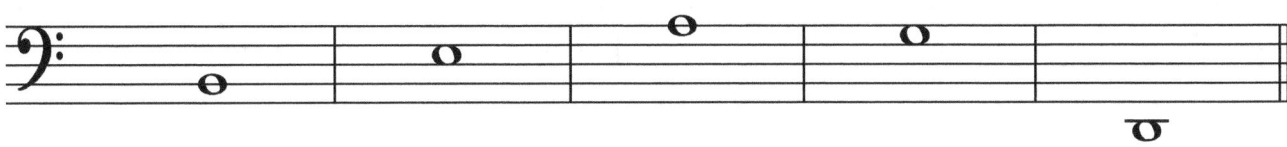

Enharmonic Equivalents

With the use of double-sharps and double-flats, every note except G♯/A♭ can have three names.

Figure 1.13 illustrates that the note G can be G, F𝑥, or A♭♭. These notes are considered *enharmonic equivalents*. This means that they are the same pitch but have different names, like F♯ and G♭.

Figure 1.13

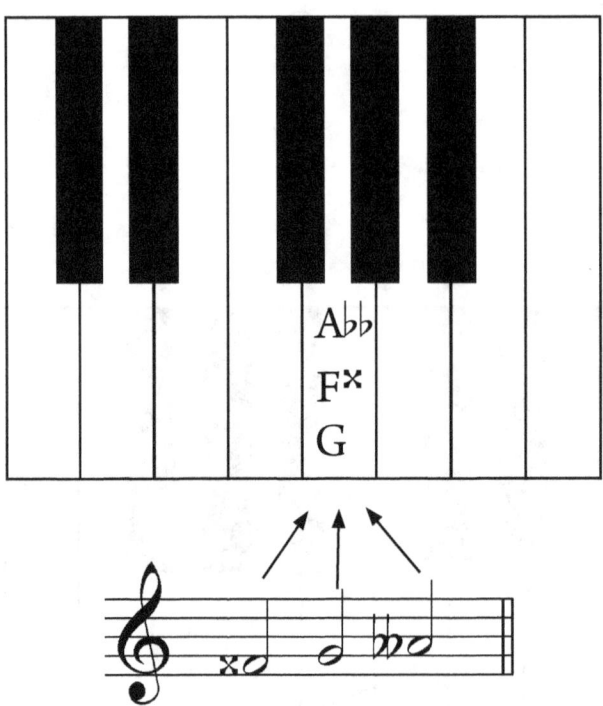

1. Write two enharmonic equivalents for each of the following notes.

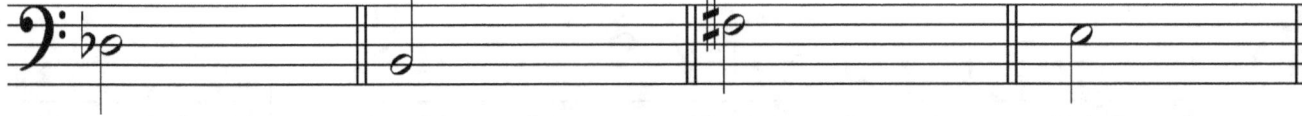

❻ 2. Rewrite the following melodies in the other clef without changing the pitch.

2 Time

❹
❺
❻

Simple Time Review

Previous levels covered the time signatures 2/4, 3/4, and 4/4. The bottom number of the time signature tells us that the quarter note receives one beat and the top number tells us how many beats are in each measure. Time signatures with 2, 3, or 4 as the top number are in *simple time*.

Figure 2.1

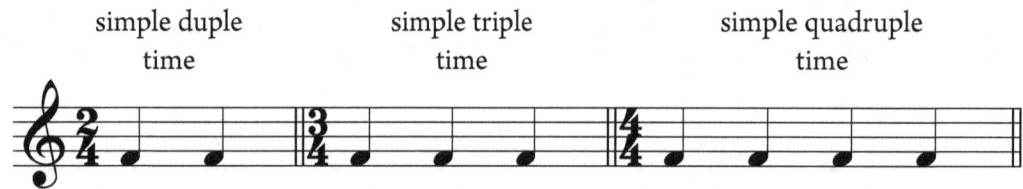

Chart of Relative Note Values

❹ 1. Add one note to complete each measure.
❺
❻

2. Add time signatures at the beginning of each line.

The Triplet

When the beat is divided into three equal parts the result is a *triplet*. Triplets fall into a category of notes we call *tuplets*. A tuplet is a group of notes that do not follow the normal rules of counting. In this lesson, we are going to cover triplets.

The Eighth Note Triplet

The most common triplets are eighth note triplets. The three notes of this triplet are beamed together and there is a small "3" over the beam indicating that it is a triplet. This triplet often occurs in 2/4, 3/4, and 4/4 time where it represents one complete beat. Figure 2.2 contains eighth note triplets. When writing eighth note triplets, the number must be positioned avoiding staff lines if possible. The number is placed in the middle of the beam no matter what the stem direction.

Figure 2.2

Triplets are played in the time of two notes of the same value. An eighth note triplet consists of three eighth notes played in the time of two eighth notes. In this case, one beat. Essentially, an eighth note triplet is equal to a quarter note or one beat in quarter time (2/4, 3/4, 4/4). Figure 2.3 shows triplet eighth notes with counting.

Figure 2.3

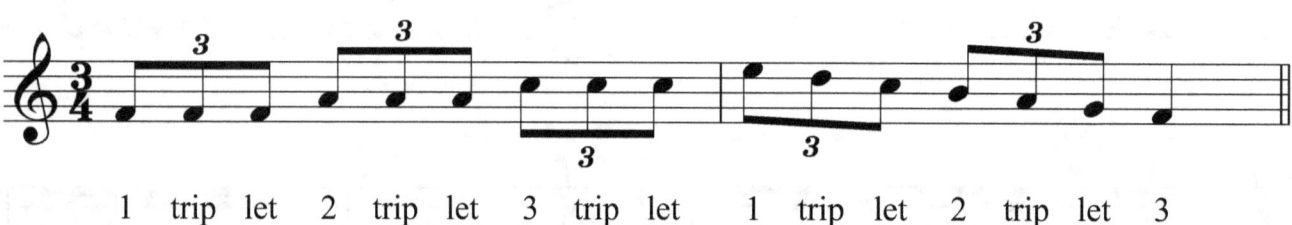

1. Add bar lines according to the time signatures.

2. Add time signatures to the following

Robert Schumann
Papillons Op. 2, No. 11

Joseph Haydn
Quartet, Op. 76, No. 5

Antonin Dvorak
Quartet in F

Ludwig van Beethoven
Symphony No. 5, III

More Simple Time Signatures

The time signature 2/8 is in *simple duple time*. The eighth note receives one beat and there are two beats in each measure. In other words, every measure is equal to two eighth notes.

Study Figure 2.4.

$\frac{2}{8}$ two beats in each measure

the eighth note receives one beat

Figure 2.4

3/8 is a *simple triple time* signature. There are three beats in each measure and the eighth note receives one beat. Study Figure 2.5.

$\frac{3}{8}$ three beats in each measure

the eighth note receives one beat

Figure 2.5

4/8 is a **simple quadruple time** signature. There are four beats in each measure and the eighth note receives one beat. Study Figure 2.6.

four beats in each measure

the eighth note receives one beat

Figure 2.6

1   2   3   4   1   2   3   4   1   2   3   4   1   2   3   4

❹1. Add the correct time signature at the beginning of each line.
❺
❻

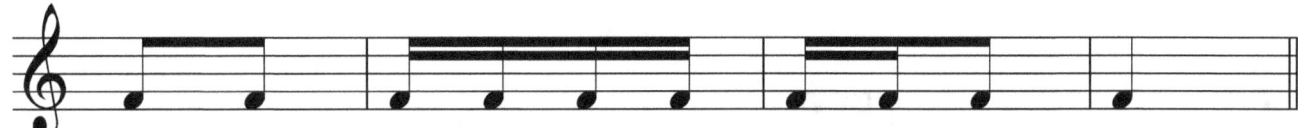

© San Marco Publications 2023

2. Add one note to complete each measure.

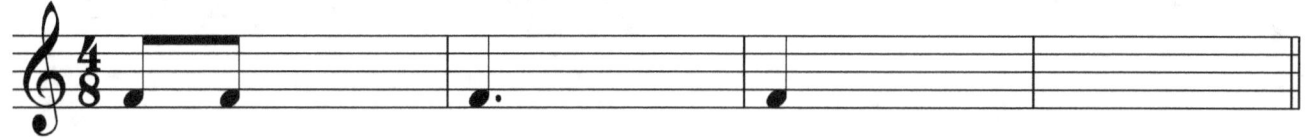

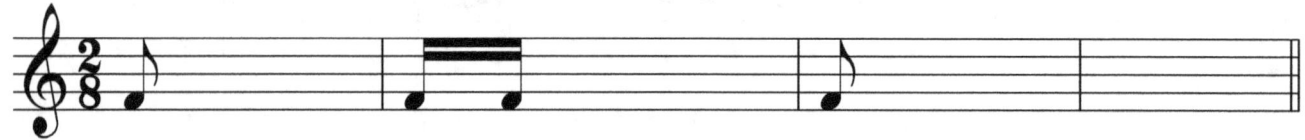

The Sixteenth Note Triplet

To determine the length of a sixteenth note triplet we follow the rule that a triplet's length is the same as two notes of the same value. A sixteenth note triplet is three sixteenth notes in the time of two sixteenth notes. This is equal to one eighth note. In 2/8, 3/8, and 4/8 time this means that triplet sixteenth notes are equal to one beat. Figure 2.7 contains triplet sixteenth notes.

Figure 2.7

1. Add bar lines according to the time signatures.

Syncopation

A lot of music follows a strict 4/4 tempo or four beats to every measure. The first beat of the measure is a strong beat and it is emphasized. Clap the rhythm of Figure 2.8 and count a steady 4 beats. Clap on each beat emphasizing the first beats. These are steady single beats.

Figure 2.8

Figure 2.9 is a syncopated rhythm. Clap the beats, but hold out beat 4 and don't clap on the next, or first, beat which is tied. Instead emphasize the 2nd beats.

Figure 2.9

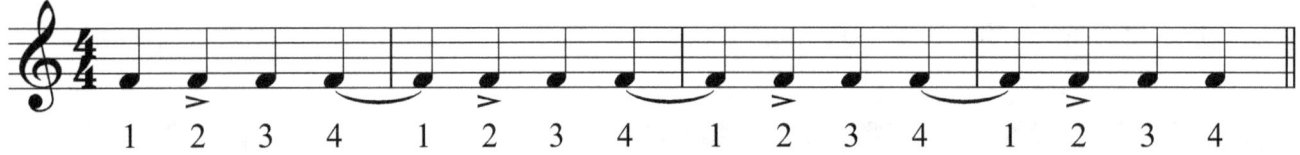

Often, the emphasis is given to the first beat of a measure. Syncopation means to shift the typical accent and emphasize what would normally be a "weak" beat. Not playing on the first beat creates a sense of anticipation and gives the music a jazzy feeling. Syncopation can also be created with longer notes in unexpected places as shown in Figure 2.10. Placing a half note on beat two in measure 2 emphasizes a weak beat by holding it longer. This also occurs with the quarter note on the second half of beat three in measure 3.

Figure 2.10

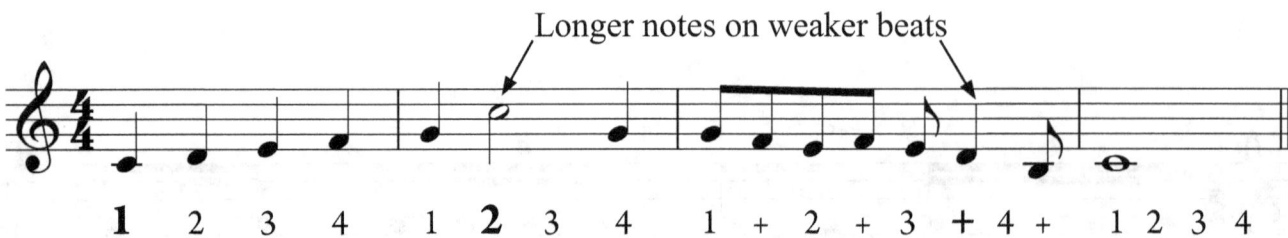

Rests in Simple Time

There are specific rules for adding rests to a measure in simple time. It is important to show each beat as clearly as possible. Each beat or each part of the beat must be completed before beginning the next beat. In Figure 2.11 measure 2, each eighth note beat is finished with an eighth note rest. In measures 3 and 4, the sixteenth note has a sixteenth rest to complete part of the beat and then an eighth rest to finish the remainder of the beat.

Figure 2.11

In Figure 2.12, measure 3, the incomplete sixteenth note beats are completed separately with sixteenth note rests. This shows each beat. Joining these rests into one eighth rest is wrong.

Figure 2.12

In simple triple time each beat or part of the beat should be completed first. Join beats 1 and 2, a strong and weak beat, into one rest. **Do not join beats 2 and 3, two weak beats, into one rest.** Never join two weak beats into one rest.

Figure 2.13

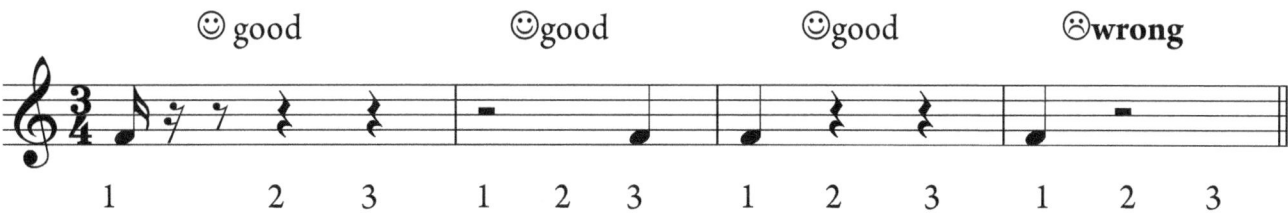

❹ We never use rests larger than one beat unless it is in the first half or last half of a measure in simple
❺ quadruple time (4/4, 4/8). Join beats 1 and 2 and beats 3 and 4 into one rest. **Never join beats 2**
❻ **and 3, a weak beat and a medium beat, into one rest.** As in all simple time signatures, finish any
incomplete beats first.

Figure 2.14

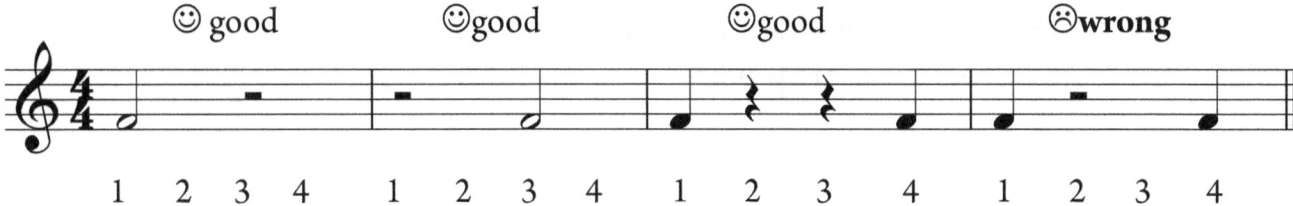

A whole rest represents a complete measure of silence in almost all time signatures.

Figure 2.15

❹❺❻ 1. Complete the following **single quarter note** beats by adding rests.

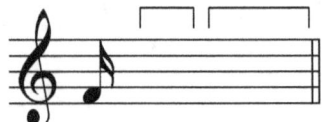   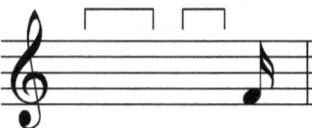

2. Add one rest under each bracket to complete the following measures.

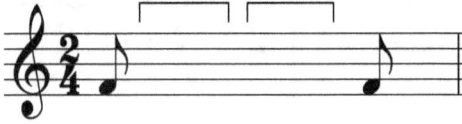   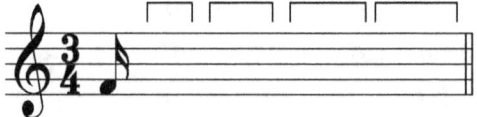

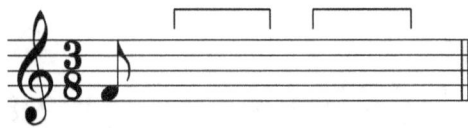   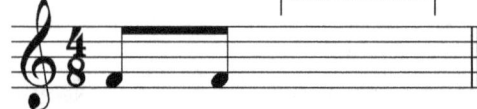

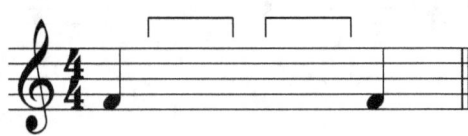   

© San Marco Publications 2023

3. Add the correct number of rests under each bracket to complete each measure.

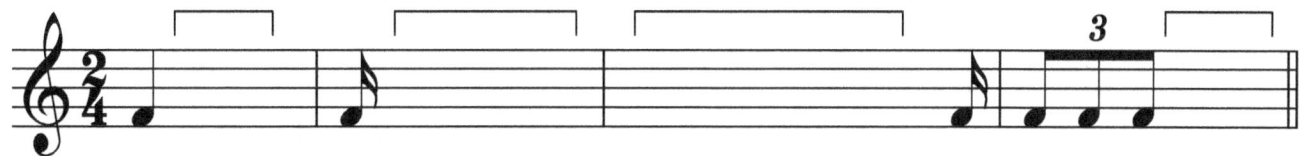

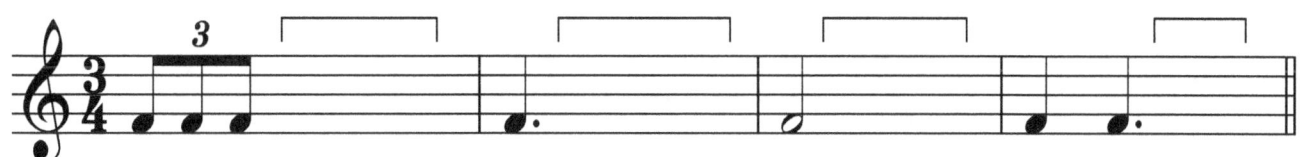

Simple Duple Time

In ***simple duple time*** the top number of the time signature is always 2. The time signature 2/4 is in simple duple time. Every measure is equal to 2 quarter notes.

Another simple duple time signature is 2/2. Here, the half note receives one beat and there are two beats in each measure. In other words, every measure is equal to two half notes. In all simple duple time signatures beat 1 is a *strong* beat and beat 2 is a *weak* beat. Study Figure 2.16.

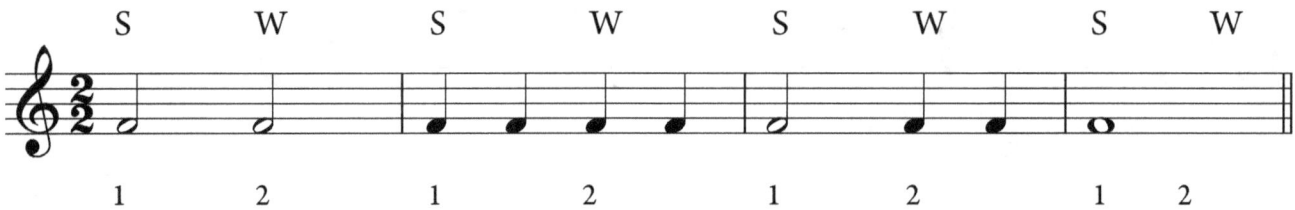

Figure 2.16

 This is an abbreviation for 2/2 time, sometimes called ***cut time*** or ***alla breve***.

Figure 2.17 is in 2/8 time. Here, there are two beats in each measure and the eighth note receives one beat. Every measure is equal to 2 eighth notes. Beat 1 is strong and beat 2 is weak.

Figure 217

1. Using 2/4, 2/2 or 2/8 add the correct time signatures to the following melodies.

Simple Triple Time

In ***simple triple time*** the top number of the time signature is always 3. The time signature 3/4 is in simple triple time. Every measure is equal to 3 quarter notes.

Another simple triple time signature is 3/2. Here, the half note receives one beat and there are three beats in each measure. In other words, every measure is equal to three half notes. In all simple triple time signatures beat 1 is a *strong* beat and beats 2 and 3 are a *weak* beats. Study Figure 2.18.

3/2   three beats in each measure

the half note receives one beat

Figure 2.18

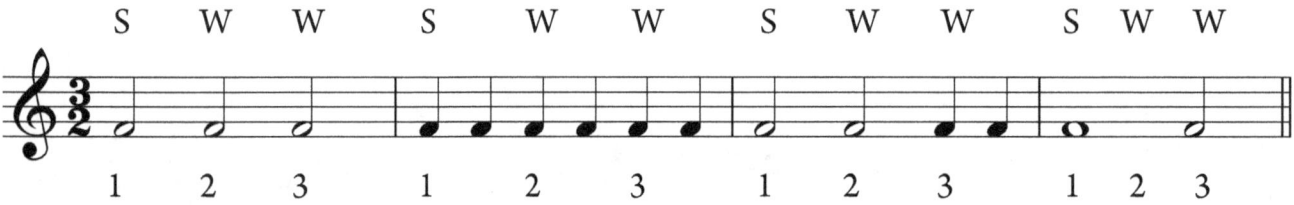

Figure 2.19 is in 3/8 time. Here, there are three beats in each measure and the eighth note receives one beat. Every measure is equal to 3 eighth notes. Beat 1 is strong and beats 2 and 3 are weak. *In 3/8 time all eighth and sixteenth notes are beamed into a complete bar.*

3/8   three beats in each measure

the eighth note receives one beat

Figure 2.19

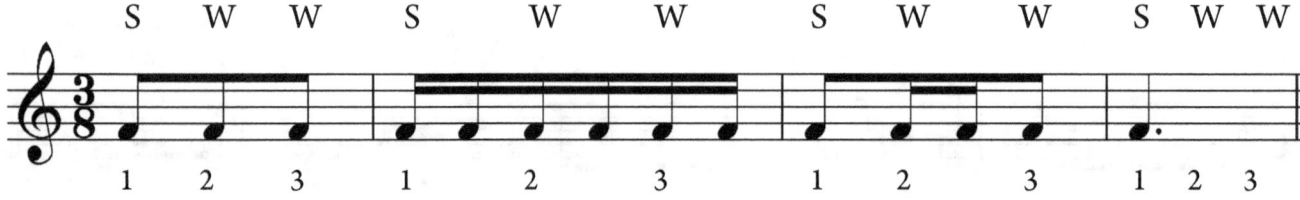

1. Add bar lines according to the time signatures.

⑤⑥ Simple Quadruple Time

In **simple quadruple time** the top number of the time signature is always 4. The time signature 4/4 is in simple quadruple time. Every measure is equal to 4 quarter notes.

Another simple quadruple time signature is 4/2. Here, the half note receives one beat and there are four beats in each measure. In other words, every measure is equal to four half notes. In all simple quadruple time signatures beat 1 is a *strong* beat, 2 is a *weak* beat, 3 is a *medium* beat, and beat 4 is a *weak* beat. Study Figure 2.20.

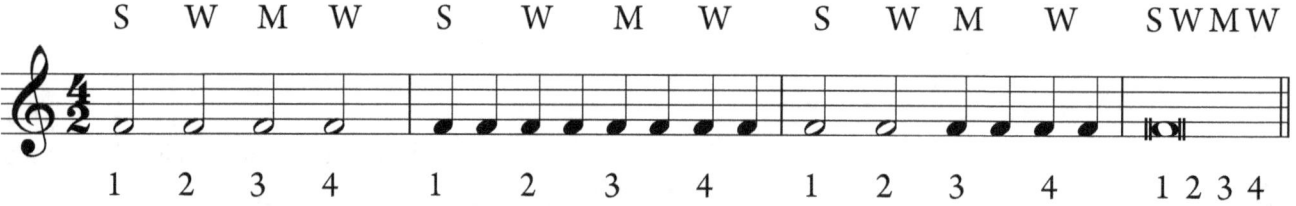

4/2 — four beats in each measure — the half note receives one beat

Figure 2.20

The **double whole note** and **double whole rest** equal 4 half notes. These are also called the **breve** and **breve rest**.

Note*** In 4/2 time a whole rest is not used for one complete measure of silence. Instead, the breve rest represents one complete measure of silence.

Figure 2.21 is in 4/8 time. Here, there are four beats in each measure and the eighth note receives one beat. Every measure is equal to 4 eighth notes.

4 four beats in each measure
8 the eighth note receives one beat

Figure 2.21

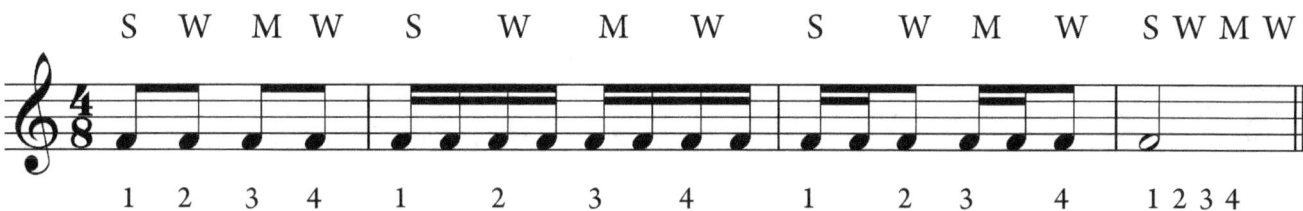

1. Add time signatures to the following melodies.

Girolamo Frescobaldi
Capriccio La Spagnoletta

Frederic Chopin
Nocturne Op. post.

Gustav Holst
Hymn Tune

Wolfgang Amadeus Mozart
Trio in C

© San Marco Publications 2023

Time

❺ 2. Add bar lines according to the time signatures.
❻

3. Add time signatures to the following lines.

❺❻ The Dotted Whole Note and Rest

A dot after a note or rest increases its value by half. A dotted whole note is worth 1 whole note and 1 half note. This is the equivalent of a full measure in 3/2 time.

Figure 2.22

Rest Review

Figure 2.23 contains all the rests we have studied.
In 4/2 time a breve rest is used to represent one complete measure of silence.

Figure 2.23

| Breve | Whole | Half | Quarter | Eighth | Sixteenth |

1. Add one note to complete each measure according to the time signature.

2. Add one rest to complete each measure according to the time signature.

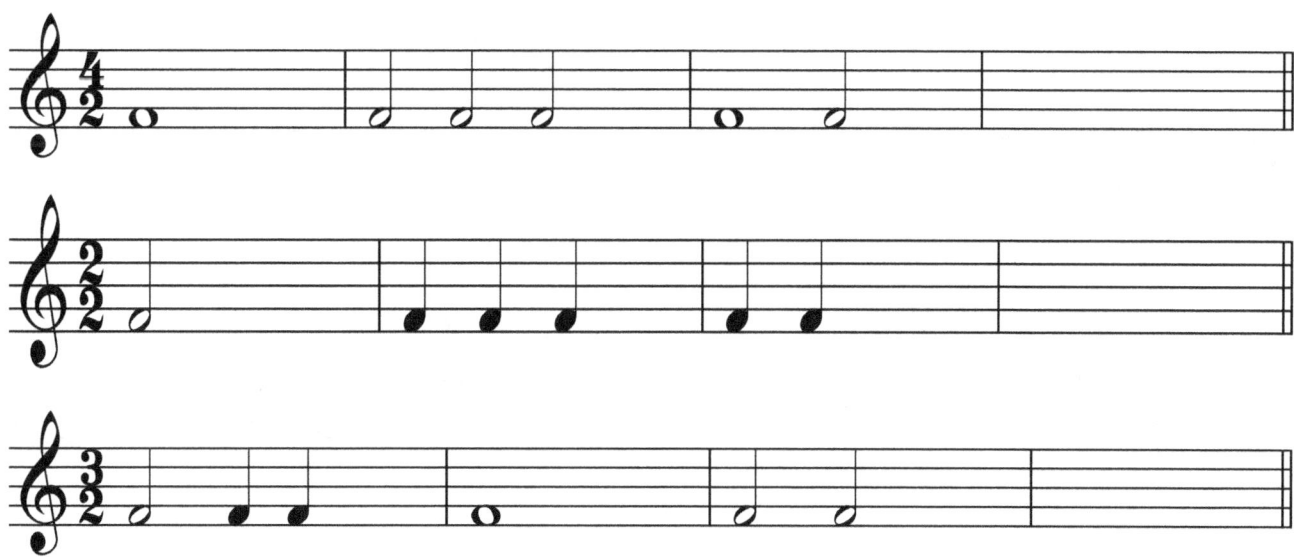

⑤⑥ Triplet Review

When the beat is divided into three equal parts the result is a *triplet*. Triplets fall into a category of notes we call *tuplets*. A tuplet is a group of notes that do not follow the normal rules of counting.

An eighth note triplet consists of three notes played in the time of two eighth notes (1 quarter note). A sixteenth note triplet consists of 3 sixteenth notes played in the time of 2 sixteenth notes (1 eighth note). Figure 2.24 contains the triplets presented in previous levels.

Figure 2.24

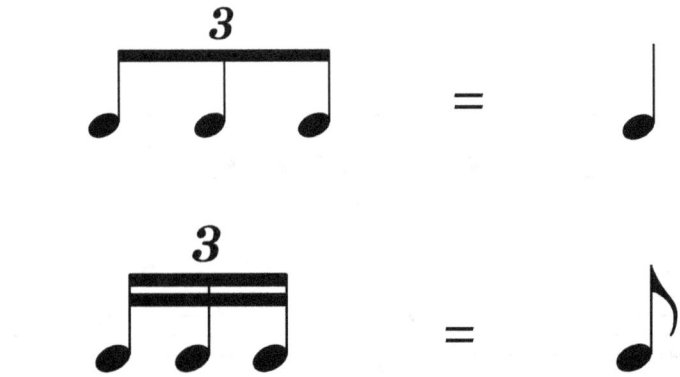

⑤⑥ 1. Add the correct time signature to each example.

The Quarter Note Triplet

The quarter note triplet follows the triplet rule of three notes in the time of two. In this case one quarter note triplet equals two quarter notes or one half note. This triplet represents one beat in 2/2, 3/2, and 4/2 time.

Figure 2.25 shows quarter note triplets. Quarter note triplets do not have a beam like eighth note triplets. When there is no beam a bracket is added and the number is centered within the bracket. If the notes go up or down sometimes the bracket is angled to match the direction of the notes.

Figure 2.25

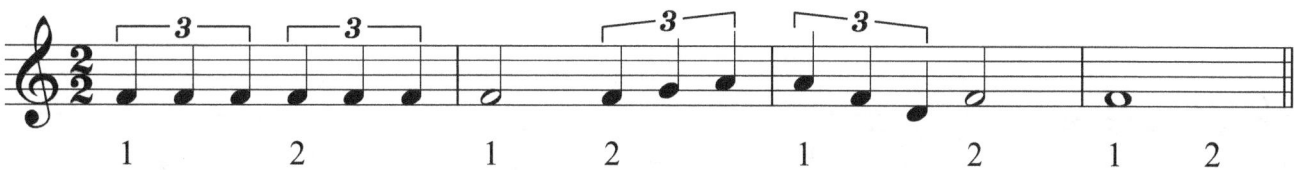

1. Add time signatures to the following lines. Write the beats under each measure.

2. Add the correct rests under each bracket to complete the following measures.

⁵⁄₆ Compound Time

In simple time the beat can be divided into 2 equal parts. The top number of the time signature is 2, 3, or 4.

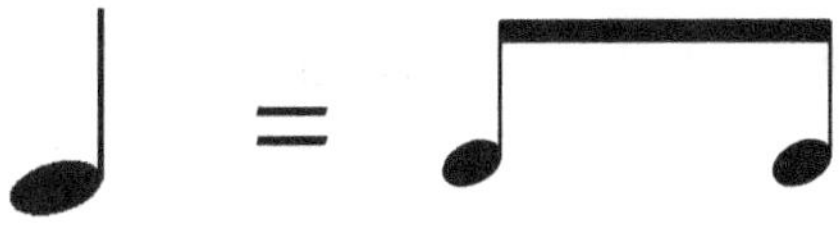

♩ = ♪♪   and   𝅗𝅥 = ♩ ♩

In simple time sometimes the beat can be divided into 3 equal parts using triplets.

♩ = ♪♪♪ (3)   and   𝅗𝅥 = ♩♩♩ (3)

In **compound time** the top number of the time signature is 6, 9, or 12. The beat is divided into 3 parts. The main beat is a dotted note.

♩. = ♪♪♪

A New Time Signature

6/8   In this time signature, every measure adds up to 6 eighth notes.

In 6/8 :

| ♪ = 1 | ♩ = 2 | ♩. = 3 | 𝅗𝅥. = 6 |

© San Marco Publications 2023

❺ In 6/8 time we do not say there are 6 beats in each measure.
❻ We say there are 2 beats in each measure and each measure contains 6 *pulses*.
   Every beat is a group of 3 pulses. Since there are 2 beats, 3 + 3 = 6 pulses.
   Therefore, 6/8 time is grouped into 2 groups of 3 pulses.
   6/8 time is **compound duple time**. **Compound** refers to each beat grouped in 3 pulses, and **duple** refers to two beats in each measure.

Figure 2.26 shows the difference in the way beats are grouped in 3/4 and 6/8. Both time signatures are equal to 6 eighth notes, but 3/4 is grouped into 3 groups of 2 eighth notes and 6/8 into 2 groups of 3 eighth notes.

The accent structure for 6/8 time is: **Strong** weak weak   **Medium** weak weak

Figure 2.26

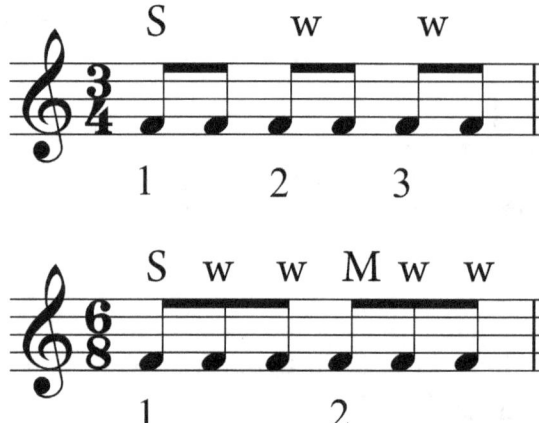

❺ 1. The following pieces are in 6/8 time. Circle the 2 main beats in each clef. Each beat consists of
❻   3 pulses.

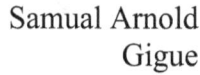
Samual Arnold
Gigue

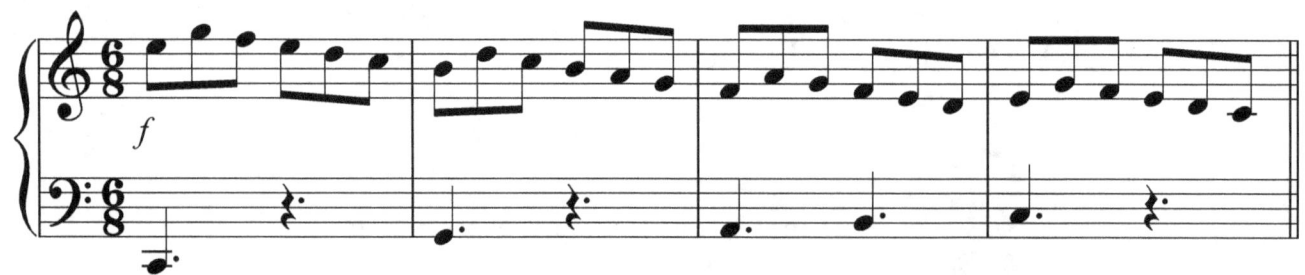

Ludvig Schytte
Etude

© San Marco Publications 2023

5 2. Add time signatures to the following lines.
6

3. Rewrite the following rhythms grouping them according to the time signatures.

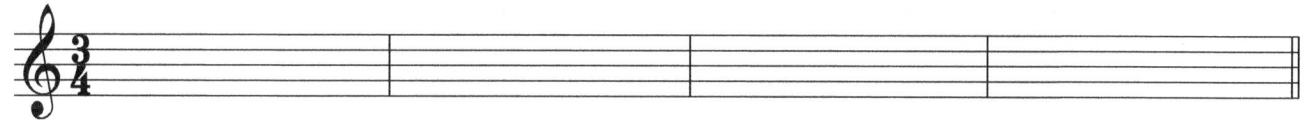

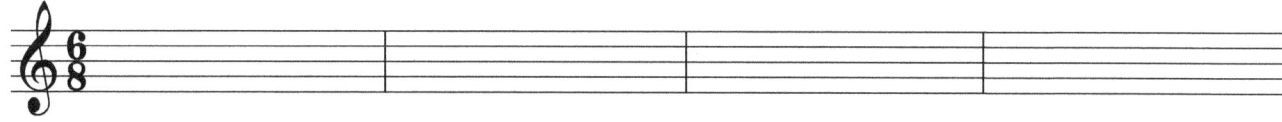

⁵⁄₆ Rests in Compound Time

In compound time a whole rest is used to indicate one complete measure of silence. Figure 2.27 shows a complete measure of silence in 6/8 time.

Figure 2.27

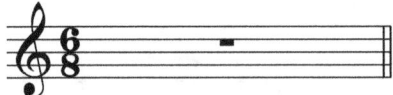

a. When adding rests to complete the first 2 pulses of a beat in 6/8 time, use one rest. In Figure 2.28 **a** one quarter rest is used to complete the first 2 pulses of the beat.
b. When adding rests to complete the last 2 pulses of a beat in 6/8 time, use 2 rests. In Figure 2.28 **b** 2 eighth rests are used to show pulses 2 and 3 of each beat.
c. Never join pulses 2 and 3 of a beat into one rest. This is wrong. Figure 2.28 **c**.
d. In 6/8 time single beats are usually represented by one dotted quarter rest Figure 2.28 **d**.
e. Although not that common, it is acceptable for a single beat to be written as a quarter rest followed by an eighth rest Figure 2.28 **e**.

Figure 2.28

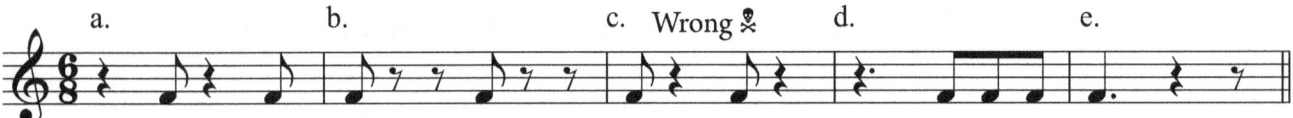

⁵⁄₆ 1. Add rests to complete each bar of 6/8 time.

2. Add rests under the brackets to complete each measure.

The Thirty-Second Note and Rest

A single thirty-second note is written with three flags (Figure 2.29). Thirty-second notes are grouped using three beams to join the notes (Figure 2.30). The thirty-second rest uses three hooks placed in the top three spaces of the staff (Figure 2.31). The thirty-second note is half the duration of a sixteenth note.

Figure 2.29

Figure 2.30

Figure 2.31

Figure 2.32

❻ A thirty-second note triplet is equal to one sixteenth note.

Figure 2.33

❻ 1. Name one note which lasts as long as the number of thirty second notes in each of the following.

   a. 2 thirty-second notes last as long as a _____ note.

   b. 4 thirty-second notes last as long as an _____ note.

   c. 16 thirty-second notes last as long as a _____ note.

   d. 12 thirty-second notes last as long as a _____ note.

   e. 32 thirty-second notes last as long as a _____ note.

   f. 8 thirty-second notes last as long as a _____ note.

2. Write the correct time signature for the following.

© San Marco Publications 2023

Time

❻ A dot placed next to a sixteenth note increases its value by half. A dotted sixteenth note is usually connected to a thirty-second note as seen on beats 1 and 3 in Figure 2.34.

Figure 2.34

❻ 1. Add the missing rest or rests under each bracket.

2. Add the bar lines to the following according to the time signatures.

⓺ More About Compound Time

A time signature that is in simple time has 2, 3, or 4 for the top number. A compound time signature has 6, 9, or 12 for the top number. Simple and compound time can be duple, triple or quadruple, depending on the number of beats in each measure.

Compound time breaks itself into groups of three. Compound duple time equals two groups of three, and the top number is 6. Compound triple equals three groups of three, and the top number is 9. Compound quadruple equals four groups of three, and the top number is 12. The main beat is a dotted note, since a dotted note can be divided into three equal parts. Let's examine the three types of compound time.

⓺ Compound Duple Time

Compound duple time has two beats in each measure. Each beat is equal to three pulses. In compound duple time, the upper number of the time signture is always 6. The lower number may be 8, 4, or 16.

Figure 2.35 shows three different compound duple time signatures. The first measure, in 6/8 time, contains six eighth note pulses. The main beat is a dotted quarter since it represents one group of three pulses.

In 6/4 time, there are six quarter note pulses in each measure. The main beat is a dotted half note since it represents one group of three quarter note pulses.

Figure 2.35

1. Add bar lines according to the time signatures. Circle each beat (group of 3 pulses).

Compound Triple Time

Compound triple time has 3 beats (3 groups of 3) in each measure. In 9/8 time there are 9 eighth notes in every measure. These are 9 pulses. There are 3 groups of 3 pulses which are considered 3 beats. Each beat is equal to a dotted note. In compound triple time the upper number of the time signature is always 9. The lower number may be 8, 4, or 16.

Figure 2.36

2. Add time signatures at the beginning of each line. Circle each beat (group of 3 pulses).

Compound Quadruple Time

Compound quadruple time has 4 beats (4 groups of 3) in each measure. In 12/8 time there are 12 eighth notes in every measure. We consider this 12 pulses. There are 4 groups of 3 pulses which are considered 4 beats. Each beat is equal to a dotted note. In compound quadruple time the upper number of the time signature is always 12. The lower number may be 8, 4, or 16.

Figure 2.37

❻ 3. Add bar lines according to the time signatures. Circle each beat (group of 3 pulses).

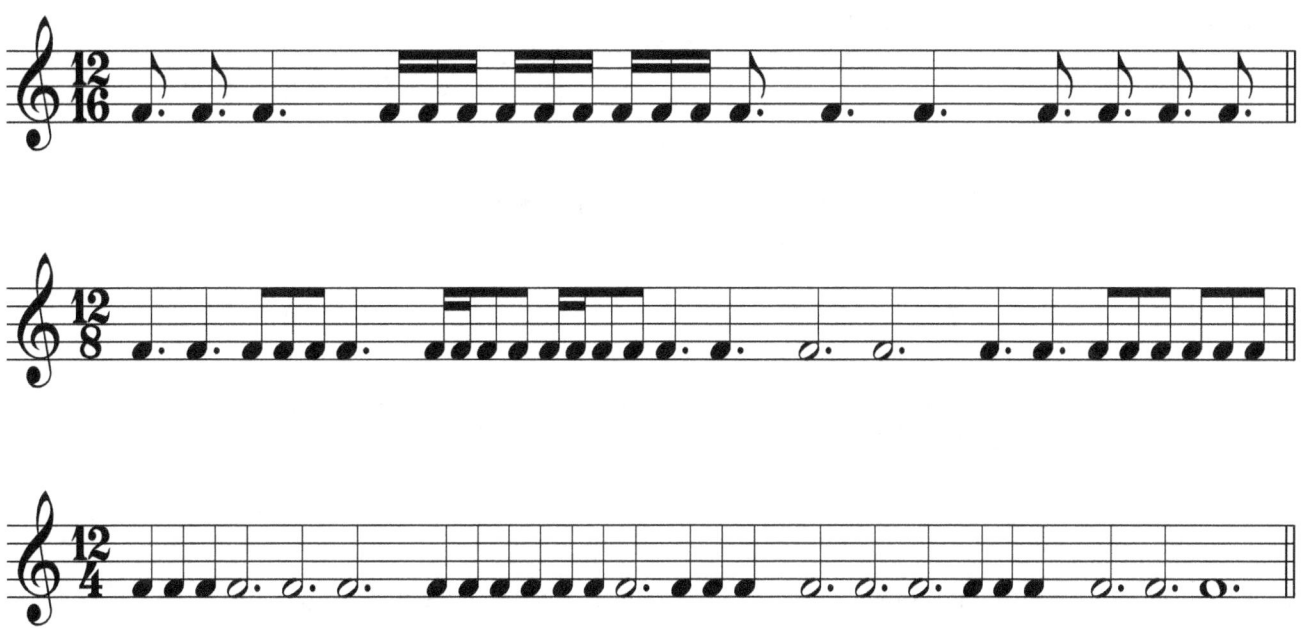

❻ Grouping Notes in Compound Time

In compound time notes and rests are grouped to show each beat as clearly as possible.

Figure 2.38 contains two measures of 9/8 time. In this time signature, the main beat is equal to a dotted quarter note. The notes in each measure are organized to reflect this. All notes belonging to one beat are placed together.

Figure 2.38

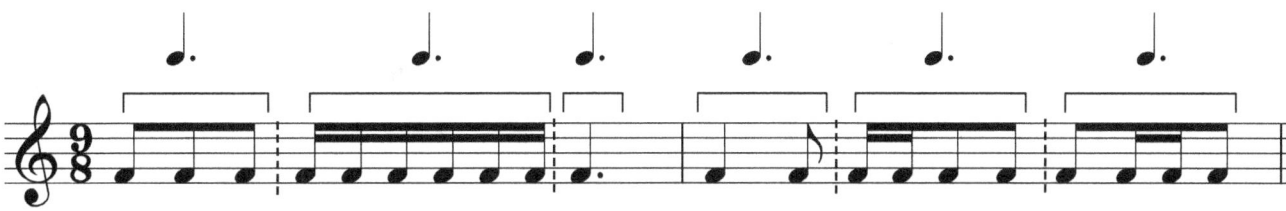

❻ Figure 2.39 illustrates the difference in note grouping between 6/8 and 3/4 time. 6/8 is compound *duple* time, and the notes are placed into two groups of three. 3/4 is simple *triple* time, and the notes are organized into three groups of two.

Figure 2.39

❻ 4. Rewrite the following passages grouping them according to the time signature.

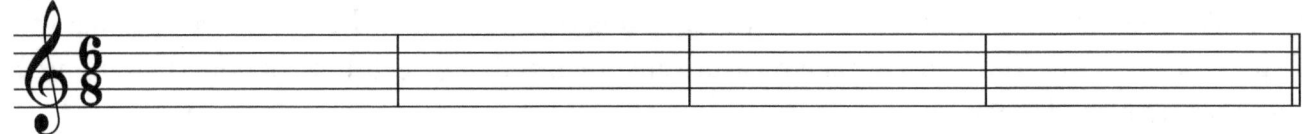

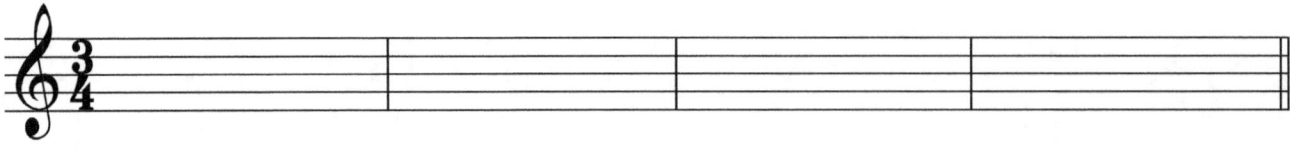

Rests in Compound Time

Dotted rests are not used in simple time. These rests are only used in compound time and represent one beat. Two beats may be joined into one dotted rest to represent the first half or the last half of a measure of compound quadruple time.

Figure 2.40

In compound time, each beat equals 3 pulses. The first 2 pulses of a beat should be joined into one rest as shown in Figure 2.41 a) and b). The last 2 pulses of a beat should use separate rests as shown in Figure 2.41 c) and d). Never join pulse 2 with pulse 3.

Figure 2.41

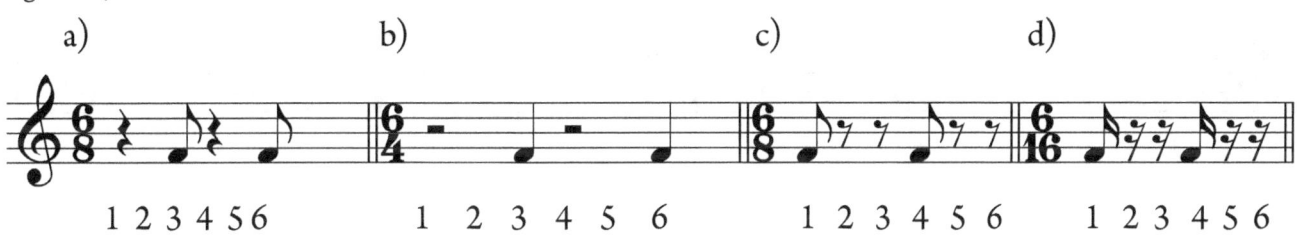

In compound triple time beats 1 and 2 may be joined into one rest. Do not join beats 2 and 3 into one rest.

Figure 2.42

❻ In compound quadruple time beats 1 and 2 should be joined into one rest. Beats 3 and 4 should be joined into one rest. Do not join beats 2 and 3 into one rest.

Figure 2.43

❻ 5. Add rests under the brackets to complete each measure.

6. Add the correct time signature to the following.

Ottorino Respighi
Pines of the Giancolo

Franz Liszt
Rhapsodie Espagnole

Franz Liszt
Sonata in B minor

Sergei Prokofiev
Sonata No. 3, V

6

Girolamo Frescobaldi
La Spagnoletta

Cesar Franck
Symphonic Variations

Joseph Haydn
Symphony in B flat, IV

Muzio Clementi
Sonata for 4 hands

Ludwig van Beethoven
Sonata Op. 31, No. 1

Albert Roussel,
Le Festin de L'Araignee

© San Marco Publications 2023   Time

Music Terms

Study the following music terms

ben, bene	well
col, coll', colla, colle	with
con	with
con brio	with vigor, spirit
con espressione	with expression
con fuoco	with fire
con grazia	with grace
con moto	with motion
e, ed	and
fortepiano, fp	loud then suddenly soft
grave	slow and solemn

3
Major Scales

Key Signatures

The first level of organization in a piece of music is the key. Music that uses a key signature is considered **tonal music**. Tonal music is centered around a specific tone called the **tonic**. A piece in C major is a tonal piece centered around the note C, the tonic.

A key signature is used to indicate the sharps or flats that are going to be played throughout a piece of music. Key signatures correspond to major and minor scales. We are going to study key signatures up to three sharps and three flats.

Not just any sharp or flat can appear in a key signature. Sharps and flats are placed in a specific order in a key signature. Here is the order of the first three sharps as they appear in a key signature:
F C G.

Figure 3.1 contains the key signatures up to three sharps on the grand staff.

Figure 3.1

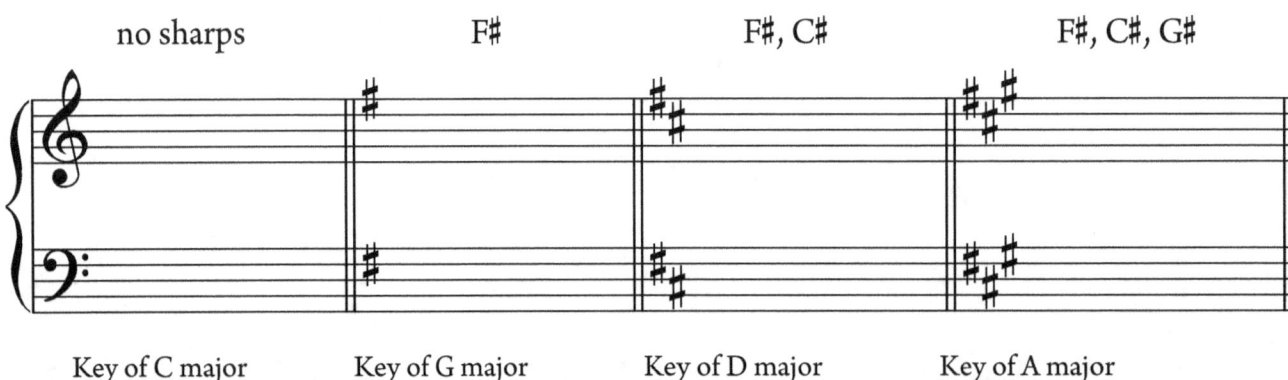

❹❺❻ 1. Write the following key signatures on the grand staff.

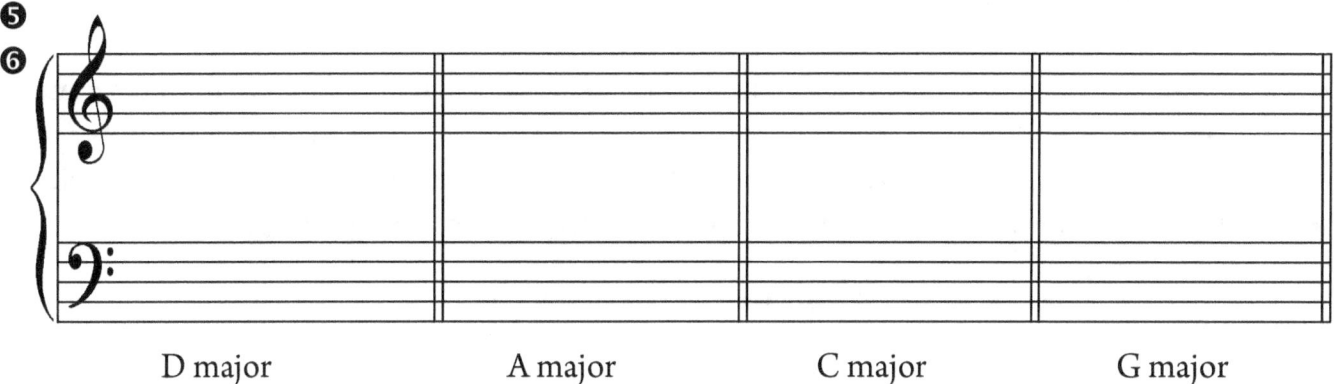

D major   A major   C major   G major

❹❺❻ The order of the first three flats as they appear in a key signature is: **B E A**.

Like sharps, flats always appear in a specific order. If there is one flat in a key signature it is always B♭. If there are two flats in a key signature they are always B♭ and E♭. Three = B♭, E♭, A♭, etc. You would never have a key signature with just a A♭. If you have an A♭, There must also be a B♭ and an E♭.

Figure 3.2 contains the key signatures up to three flats on the grand staff.

Figure 3.2

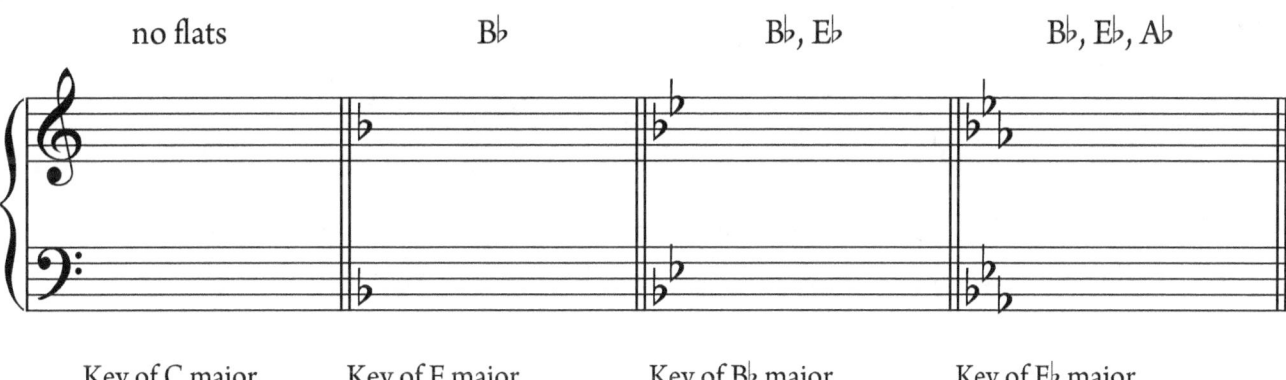

Key of C major   Key of F major   Key of B♭ major   Key of E♭ major

2. Write the following key signatures on the grand staff.

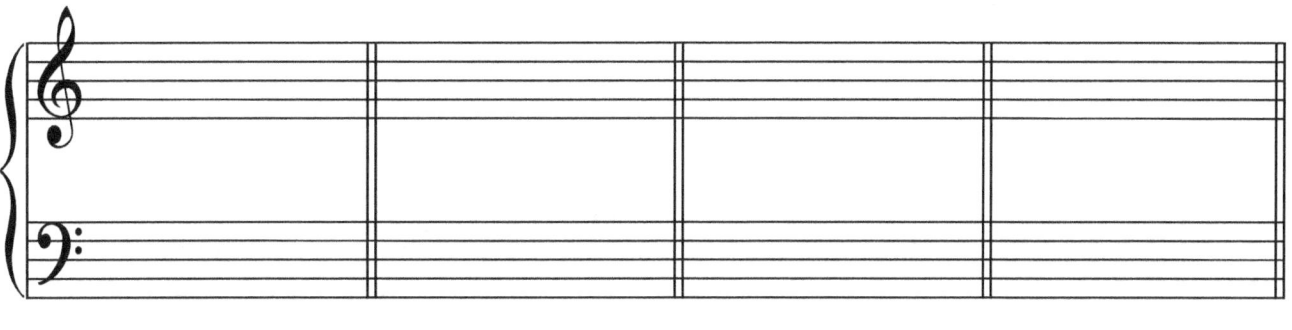

C major   E♭ major   B♭ major   F major

© San Marco Publications 2023

Major Scales

Major Scale Review

A major scale is a series of seven notes (eight with the repeated octave) that has a specific pattern of intervals. It starts and ends on the same note, the tonic. The tonic names the scale. If it starts and ends on G, the tonic is G, and it is the G major scale. Let's review the order of intervals in the major scale. Major scales are built on the following pattern of whole steps and half steps:

whole step - whole step - half step - whole step - whole step - whole step - half step

The scale can also be divided into two four note sections called tetrachords as shown in Figure 3.3. Each tetrachord is WWH with a W between the two (WWH W WWH).

Scale tones can be labeled with a number and a small sign called a **caret** on top ($\hat{1}$, $\hat{2}$, etc.). This indicates a *scale degree*. The first note of a scale is scale degree one ($\hat{1}$), The second is scale degree two ($\hat{2}$), etc.

Figure 3.3

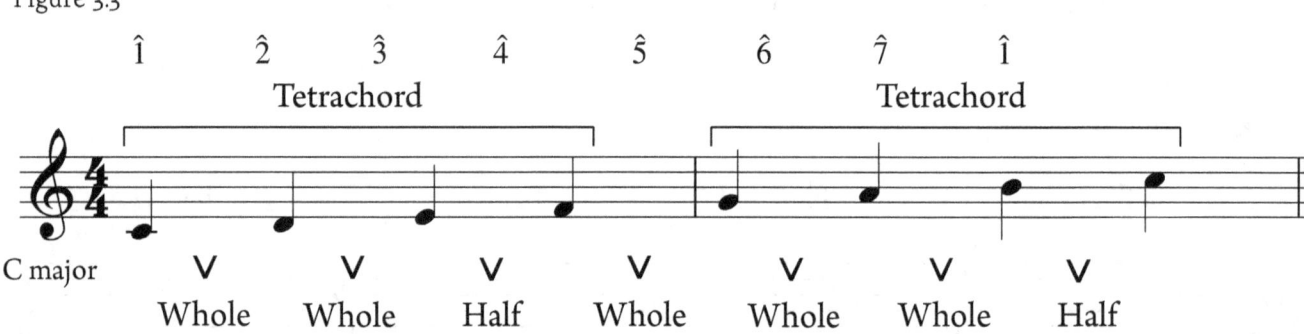

Figure 3.4 contains the A major scale ascending and descending written two different ways. The first uses accidentals instead of a key signature. The second uses a key signature.

Figure 3.4

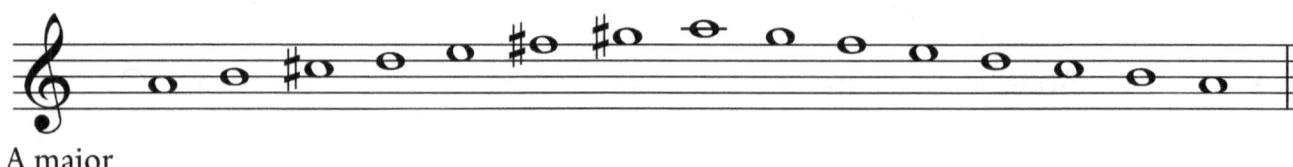

A major

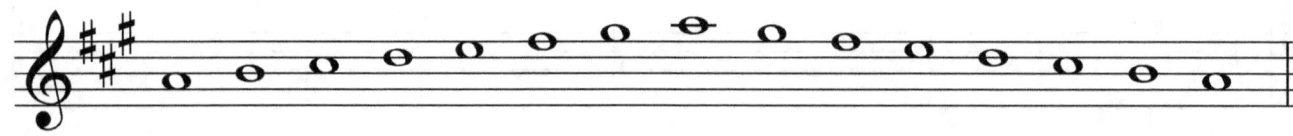

A major

❹
❺
❻ 1. Write the following scales ascending and descending using whole notes and a key signature.

A major

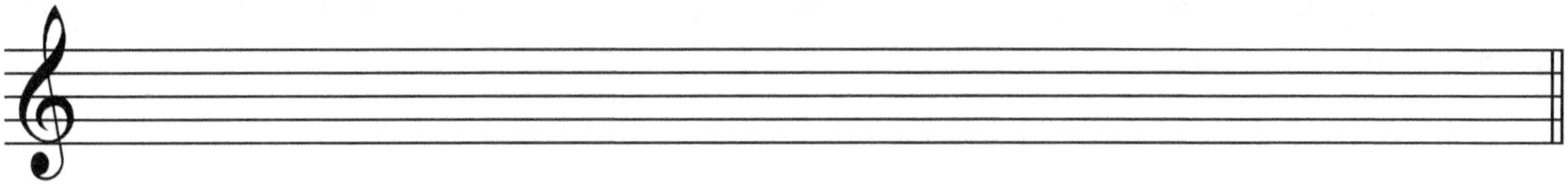

D major

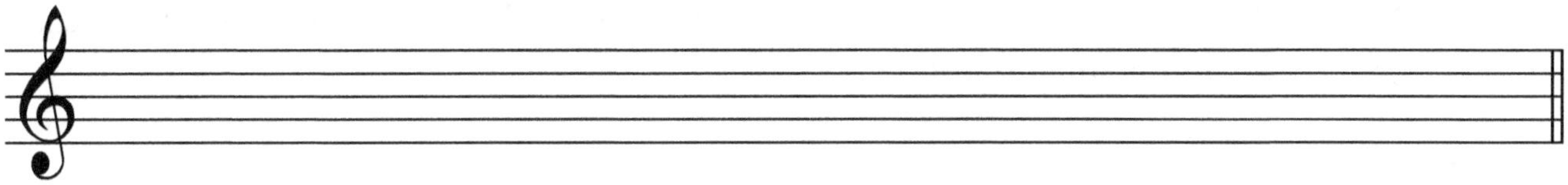

C major

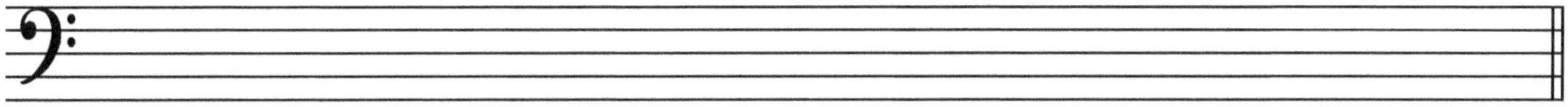

G major

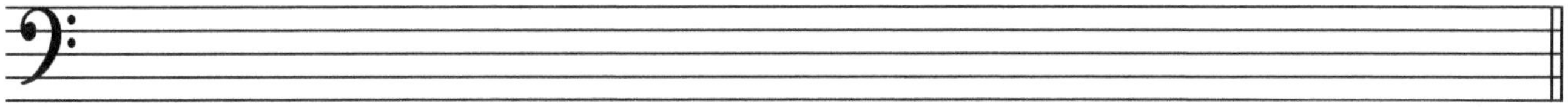

A major

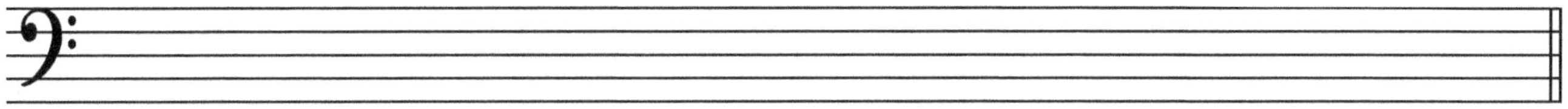

Technical Names for Scale Degrees

Each scale degree can have a technical name. This is a list of the names for four of the scale degrees covered in previous levels.

$\hat{1}$ tonic
$\hat{4}$ subdominant
$\hat{5}$ dominant
$\hat{7}$ leading tone

1. Write the following scales in half notes ascending and descending using a key signature. Label the tonic (T) and dominant (D) notes.

F major

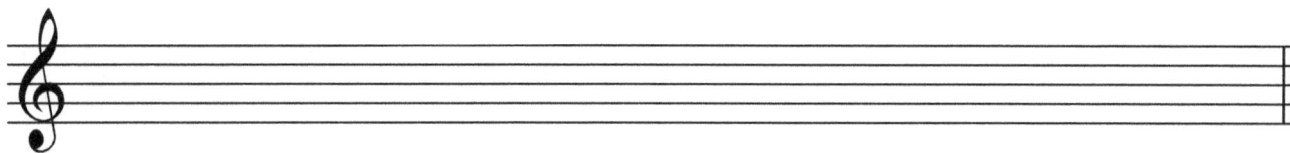

B♭ major

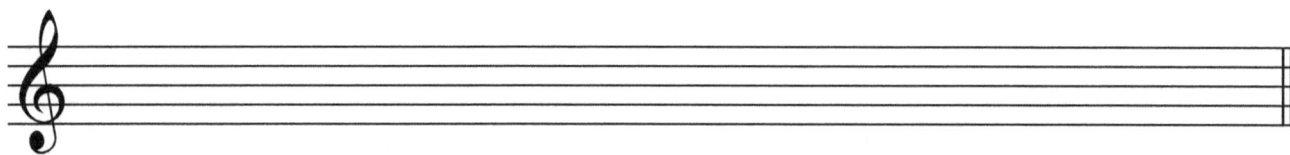

C major

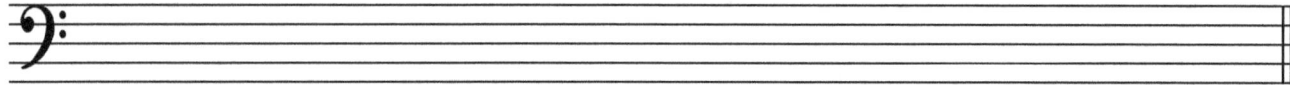

E♭ major

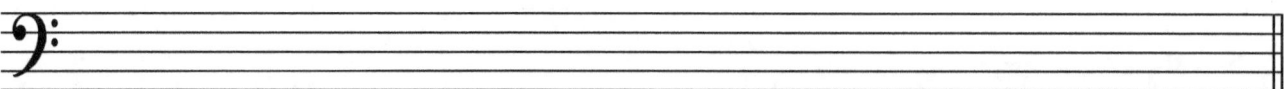

Major Scales

❹ 2. For the following scales: Add clefs and accidentals to create major scales. Label the leading
❺   tone(LT) for each. Do not duplicate scales.
❻

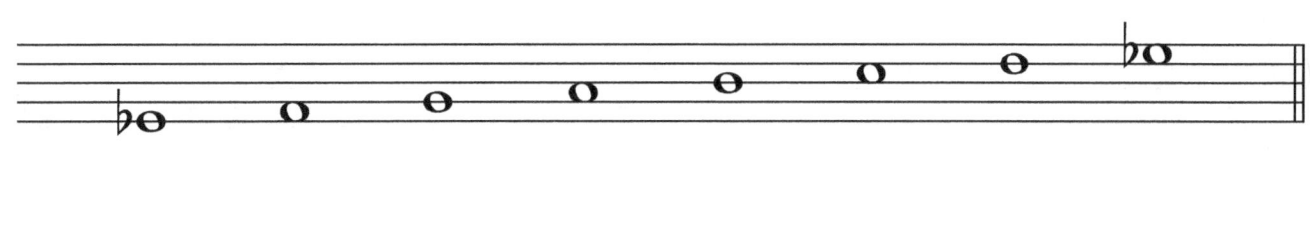

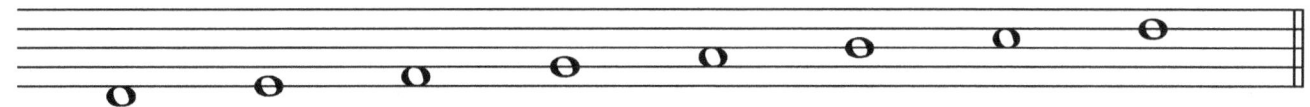

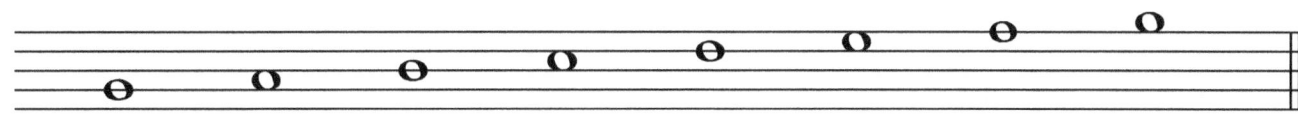

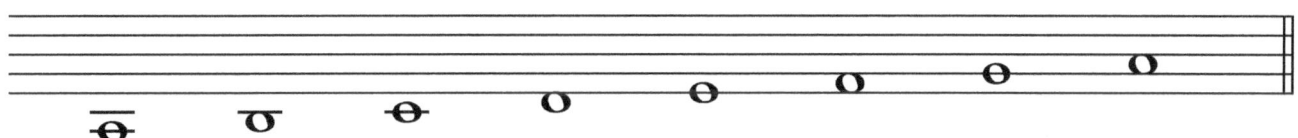

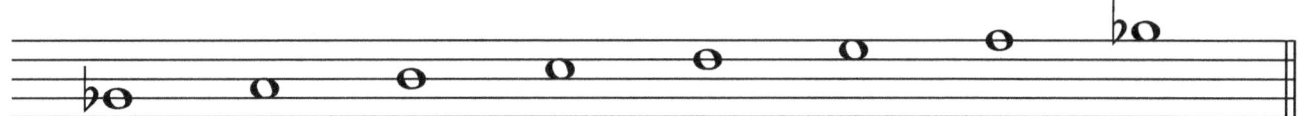

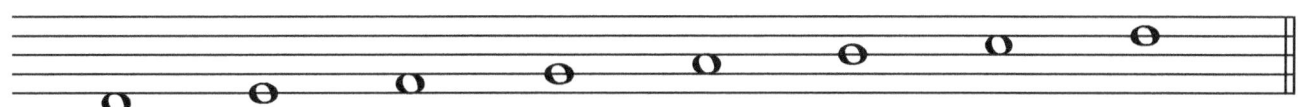

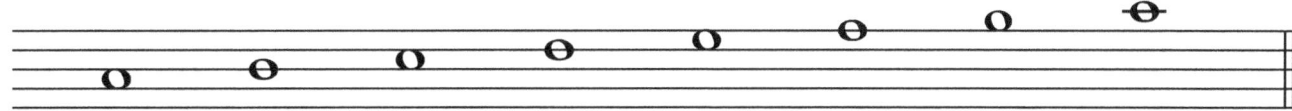

Major Scales

3. Write the following scales in quarter notes ascending and descending using key signatures.

The major scale with 3 sharps

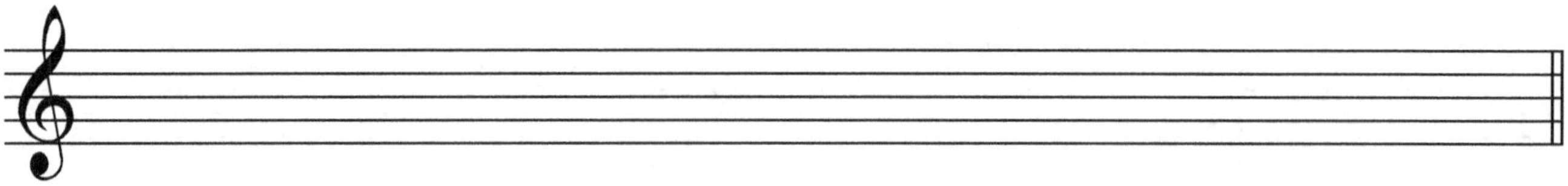

The major scale with 3 flats

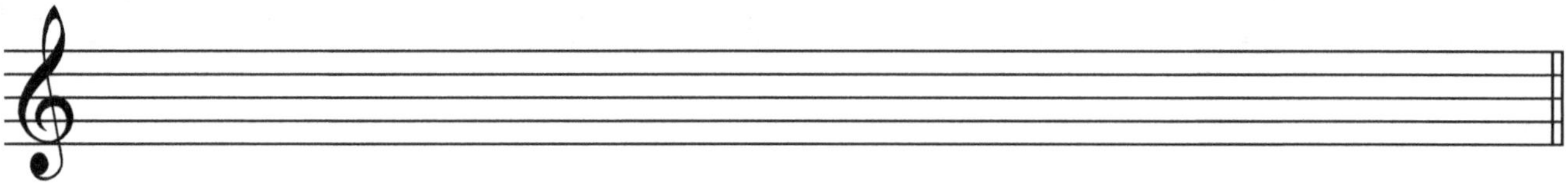

The major scale with 2 flats

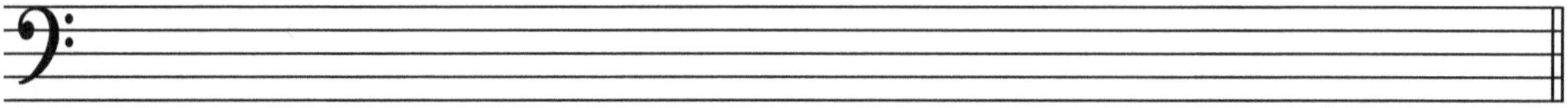

The major scale with F♯ as its leading tone

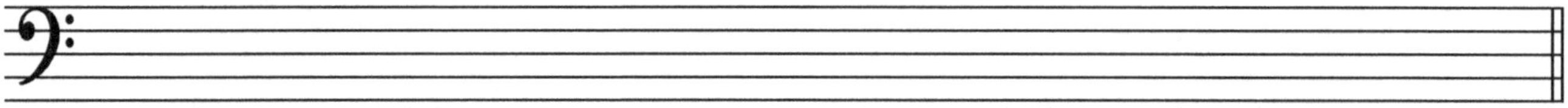

The major scale with A as its dominant

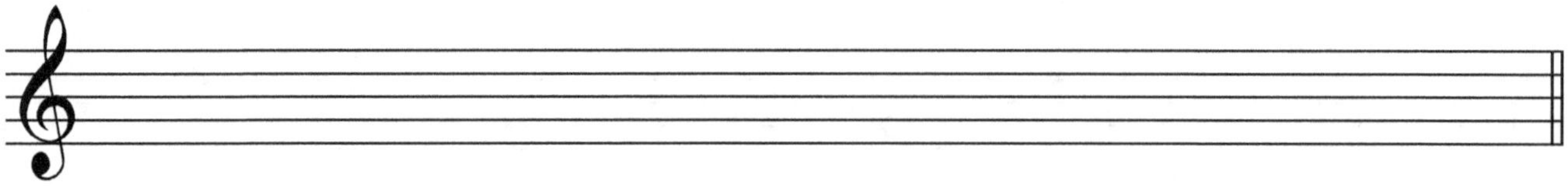

The major scale with F as its subdominant

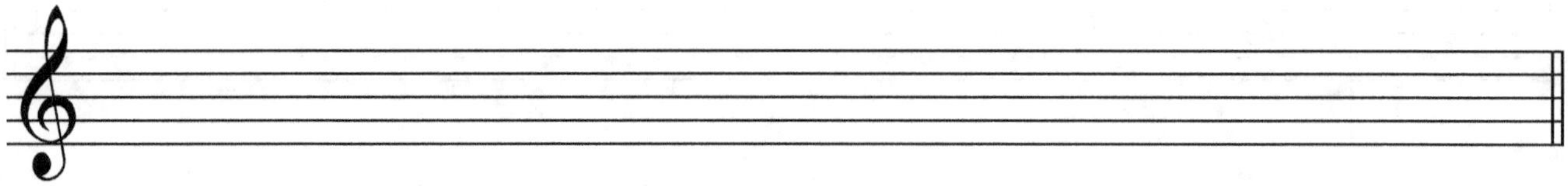

Music Terms and Signs

Terms

accelerando, accel.	becoming quicker
adagio	slow
prestissimo	as fast as possible
Tempo primo, (Tempo I)	return to the original tempo
vivace	lively, brisk
mano destra, M.D.	right hand
mano sinistra, M.S.	left hand

Signs

⊓	down bow	on a string instrument, play the note by drawing the bow downward
V	up bow	on a string instrument, play the note by drawing the bow upward
,	breath mark	take a breath or a small break

The Keys of E major and A flat Major

At this level we will learn two new major scales. E major has four sharps and A♭ major has four flats. These scales follow the same pattern of whole steps and half steps as all major scales.

Figure 3.5 contains the scales of E major and A♭ major.

Figure 3.5

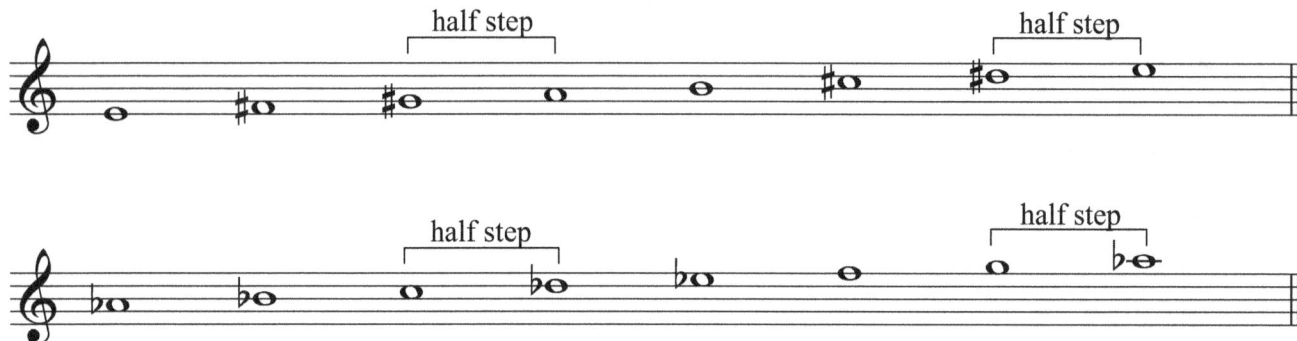

Key Signature Review

The first level of organization that a piece of music receives is the key. Music that uses a key signature is considered **tonal music**.

Each key signature is also the name of the major scale with the same name. For example, the key of A major will give you the correct accidentals for the scale of A major. This music is diatonic. This is music that is centered around a single tone or the **tonic**. A piece in A major is a tonal piece centered around the note A, the tonic.

Sharps and flats are placed in a specific order in a key signature. This is the order of the first four sharps as they appear in a key signature: **F C G D**.

Figure 3.6 contains the key signatures up to four sharps on the grand staff.

Figure 3.6

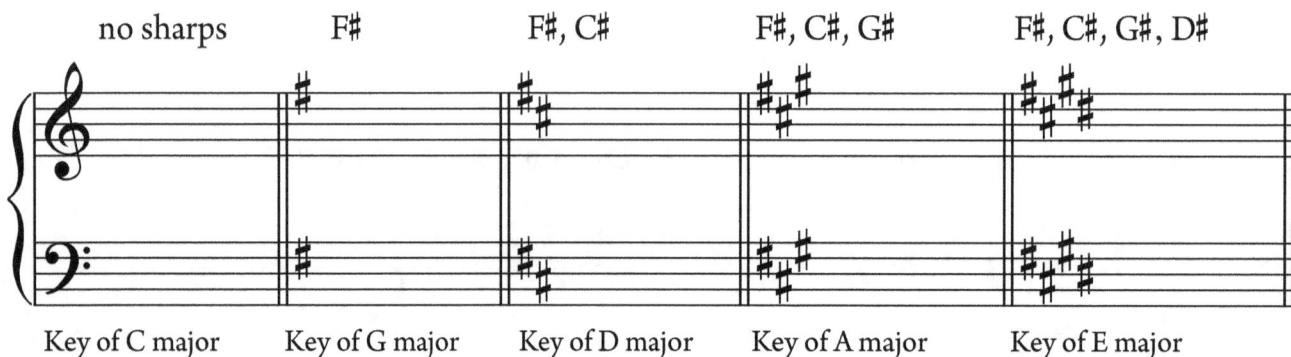

This is the order of the first four flats as they appear in a key signature: **B E A D**.

Figure 3.7 contains the key signatures up to four flats on the grand staff.

Figure 3.7

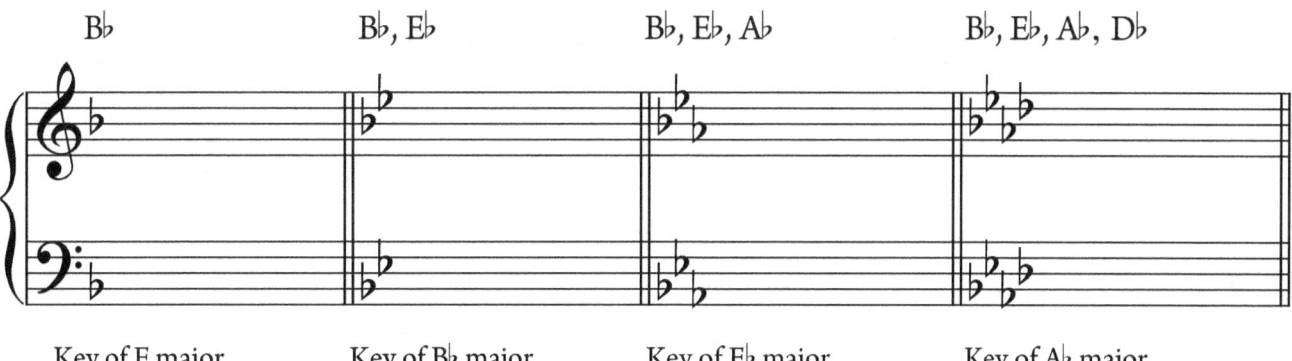

❺
❻ 1. Insert the necessary accidentals to the following melodies. The key is named for each.

Giuseppe Verdi
March from Aida

A♭ major

Gustav Mahler
Symphony No. 4, IV

E major

Francois Couperin
Concert Royal No. 2

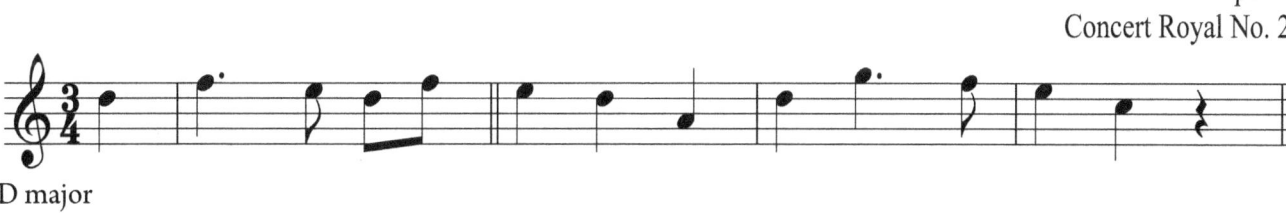

D major

Franz Schubert
Waltz Op. 50

A major

2. Write the following key signatures on the grand staff.

    D major   A major   E major   G major

    F major   A♭ major   B♭ major   E♭ major

These are the major key signatures covered in this level.

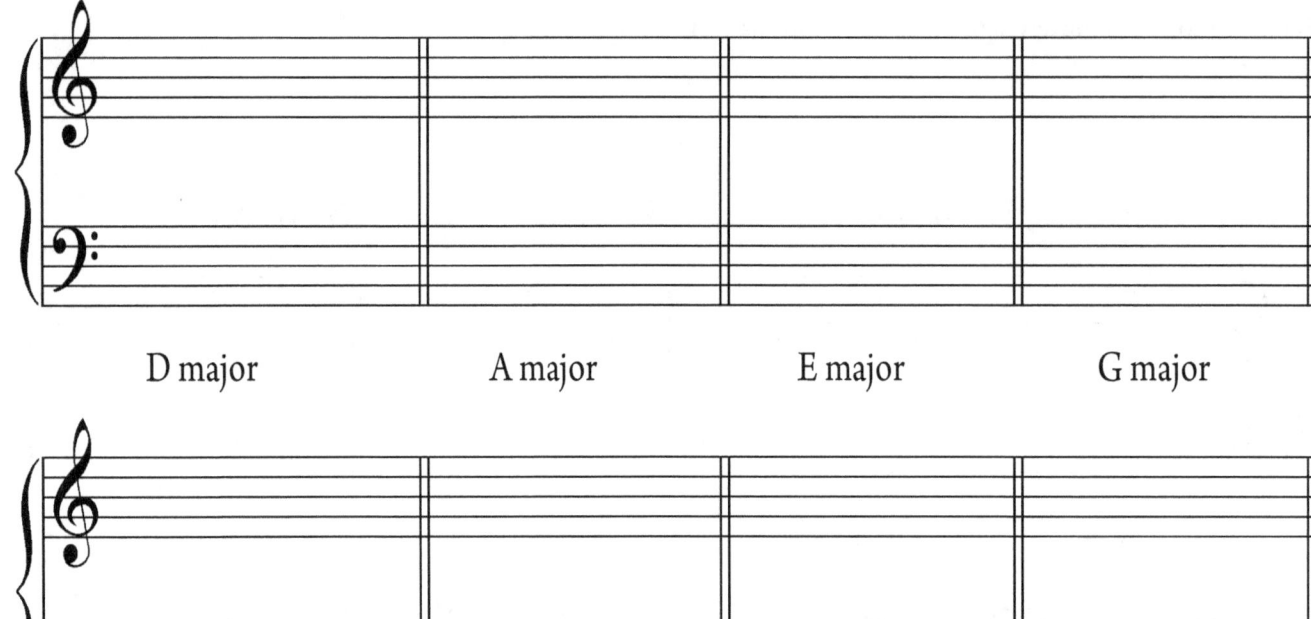

Major Scales	Key Signatures
C	no sharps or flats
G	F♯
D	F♯, C♯
A	F♯, C♯, G♯
E	F♯, C♯, G♯, D♯

Interval of a perfect 5th between the keys with sharps in the key signature → 5

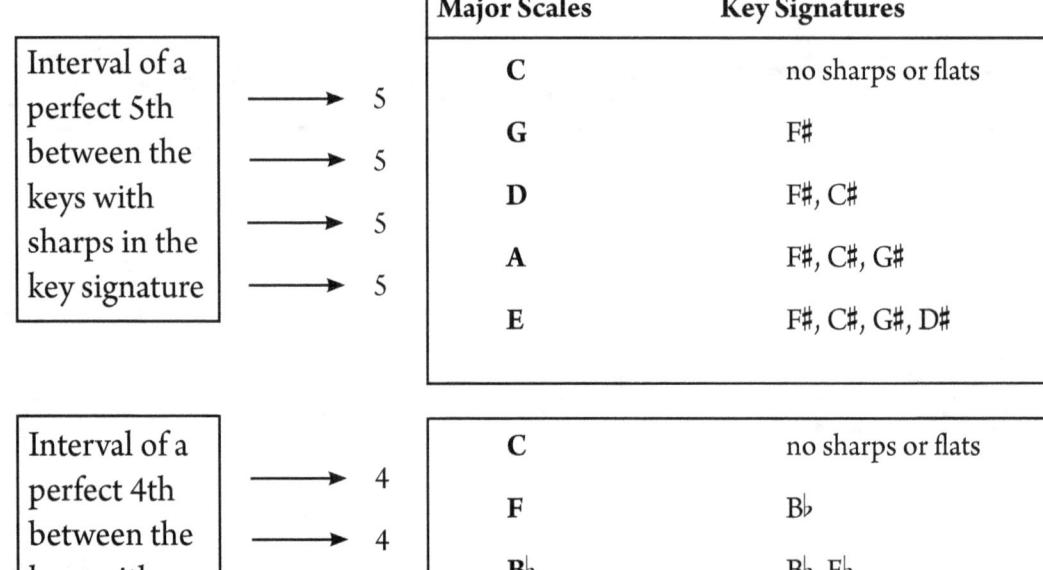

Major Scales	Key Signatures
C	no sharps or flats
F	B♭
B♭	B♭, E♭
E♭	B♭, E♭, A♭
A♭	B♭, E♭, A♭, D♭

Interval of a perfect 4th between the keys with flats in the key signature → 4

Major Scales

❺ 1. Write the following scales ascending and descending in wholes notes using a key signature for
❻   each.

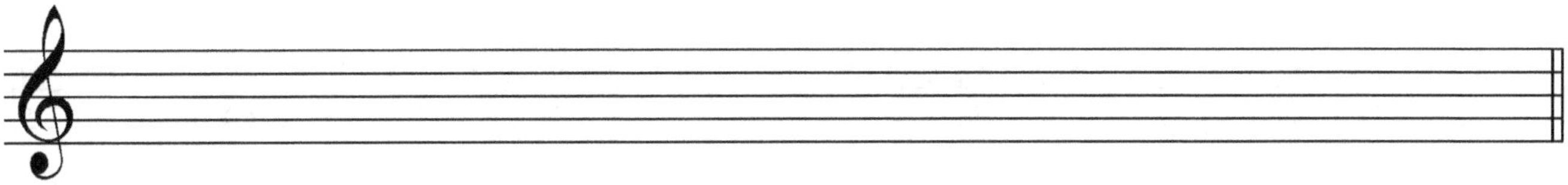

E major

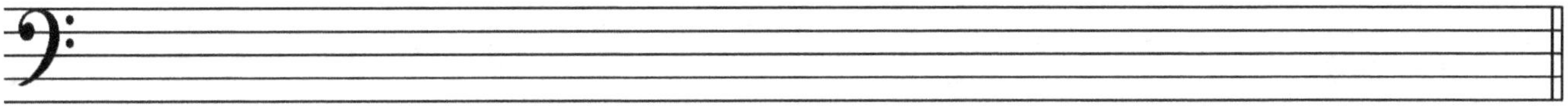

A♭ major

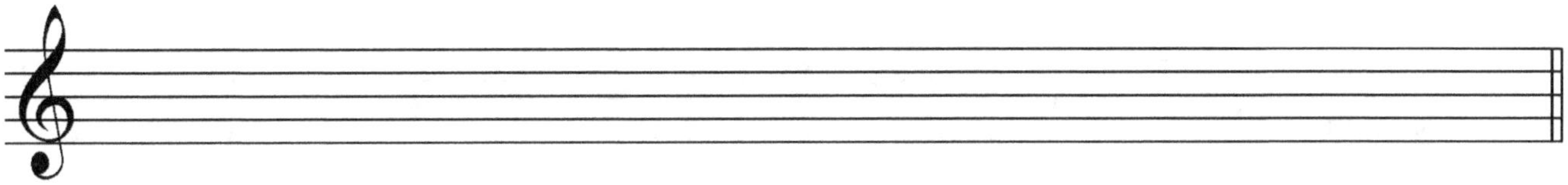

B♭ major

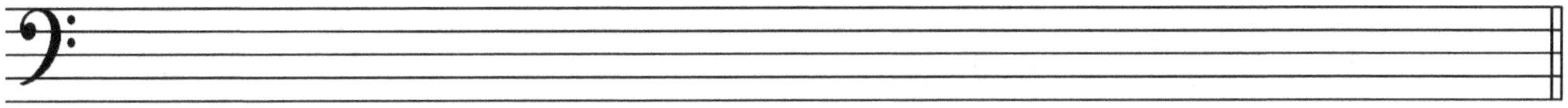

G major

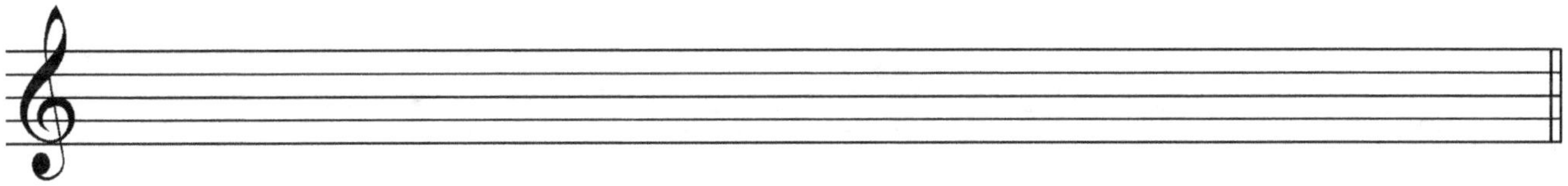

A major

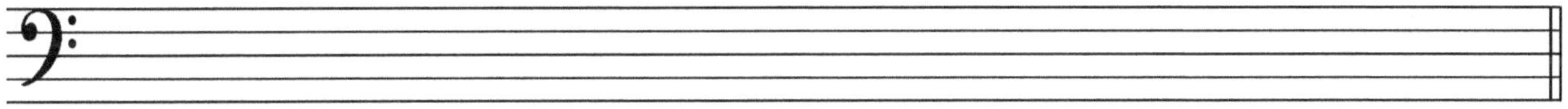

F major

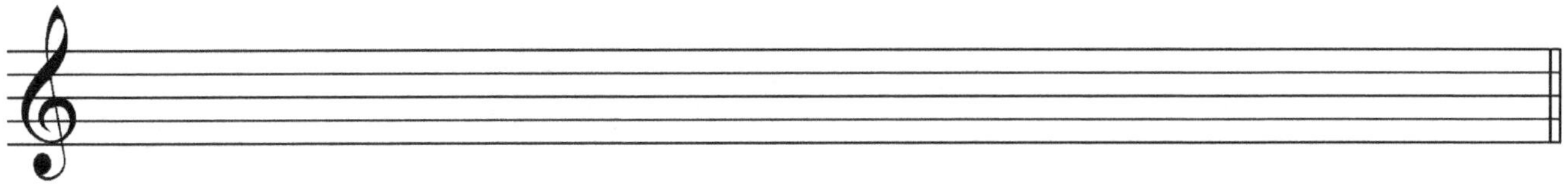

E♭ major

Major Scales

2. Add clefs and accidentals to create the following major scales.

E♭ major

A major

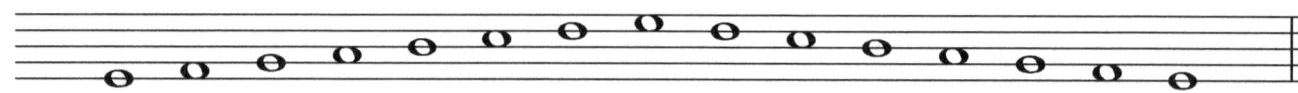

E major

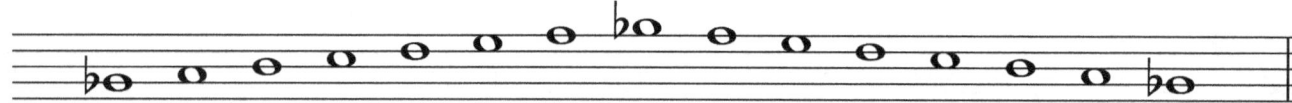

B♭ major

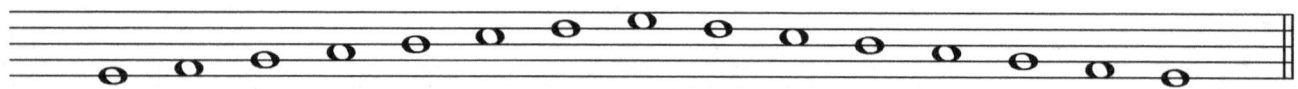

G major

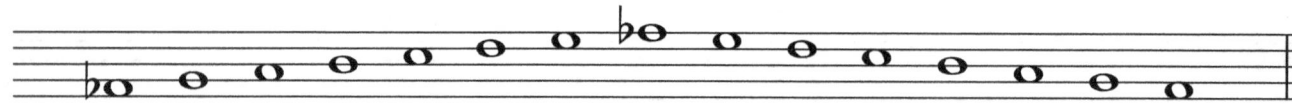

A♭ major

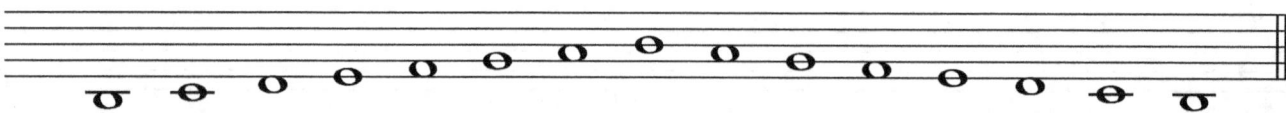

D major

❺ 3. Write the following scales using key signatures ascending and descending in half notes.
❻

The major scale with 4 flats

The major scale with D as the leading tone

The major scale with E as the dominant

The major scale with B♭ as the subdominant

The major scale with two sharps

The major scale with A as the subdominant

The major scale with F as the dominant

⁶Circle of Fifths

Figure 3.8 is the circle of 5ths. The circle of 5ths is a chart organizing all of the keys into a system that is used to relate them to one another. At the top, is the key of C major, which has no sharps or flats in its key signature. Each stop on the circle moving clockwise from C is a key with one more sharp than the previous key. Each stop moving down counter-clockwise from C is a key with one more flat than the last key. Each note is a perfect fifth away from another.

Figure 3.8

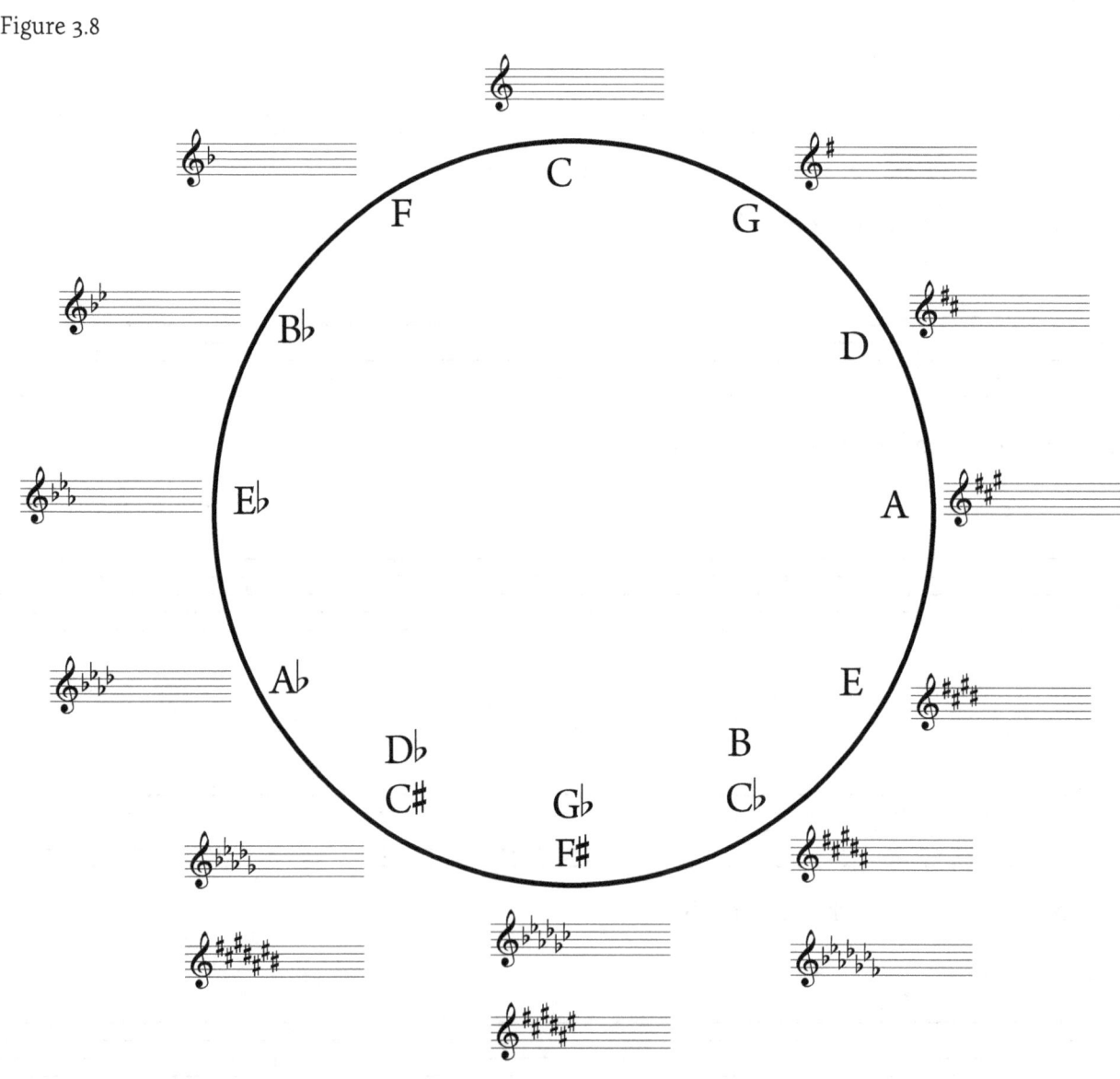

Major Scales

Sharp Keys

C major has no sharps or flats.

Figure 3.9 is a list of the sharp keys and where they are located on the staff. The order of sharps is **F C G D A E B**.

Here is a saying to help you remember the order of sharps:

Fat **C**ats **G**o **D**own **A**lleys **E**ating **B**irds.

Figure 3.9

Major Scales

Flat Keys

Flats within a key signature always follow a specific order.

Figure 3.10 is a list of the flat keys and where they are located on the staff. The order of flats is **B E A D G C F**.

Here is a saying to help you remember the order of flats:

Big **E**lephants **A**lways **D**rive **G**olf **C**arts **F**ast

Figure 3.10

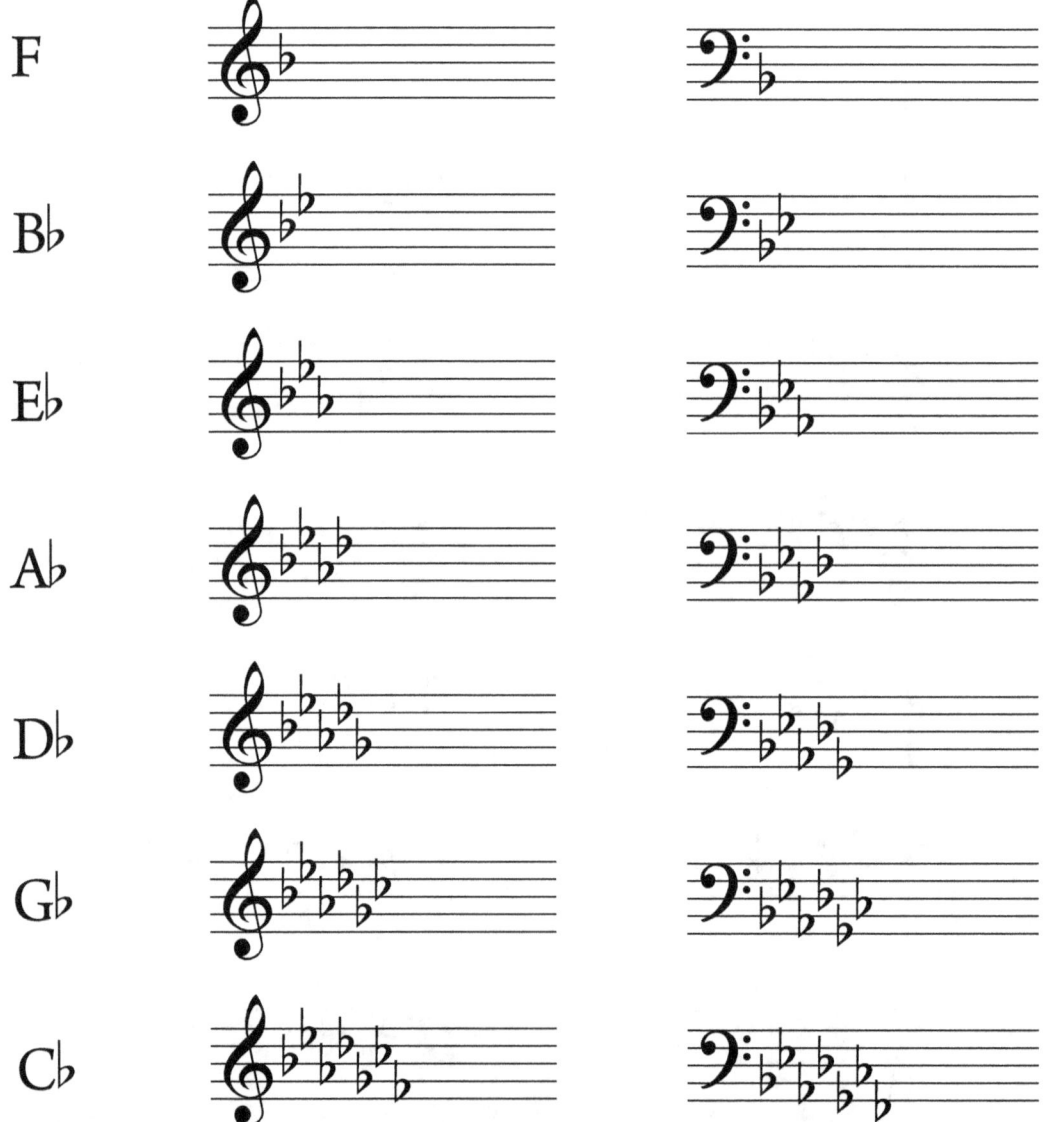

1. Name the following major keys and name the sharp and flats in each key.

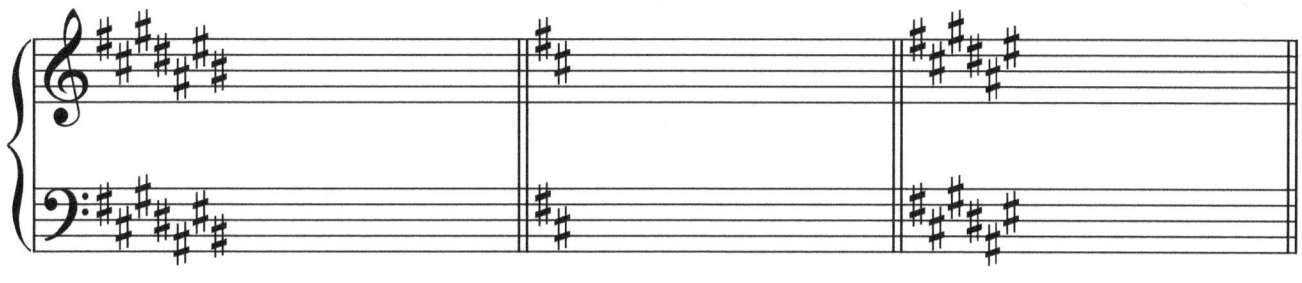

Key: _____   _____   _____

Sharps: _____   _____   _____

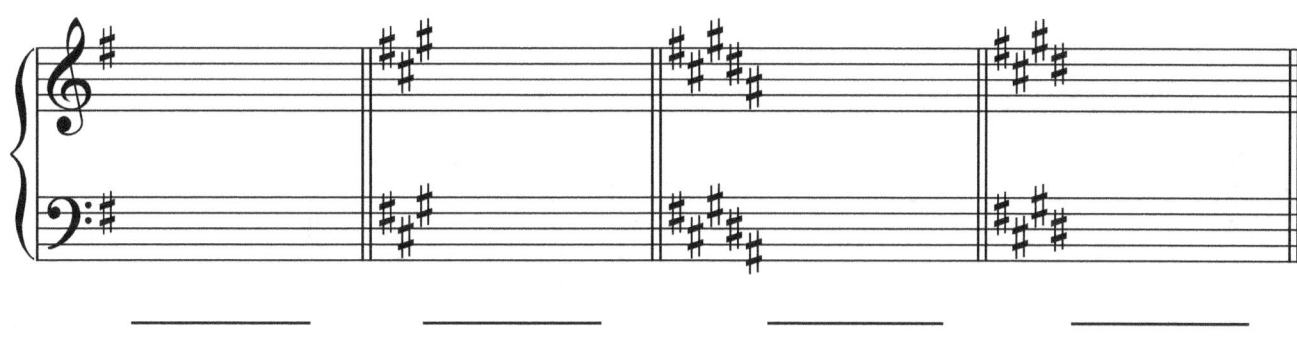

_____ _____ _____ _____
_____ _____ _____ _____

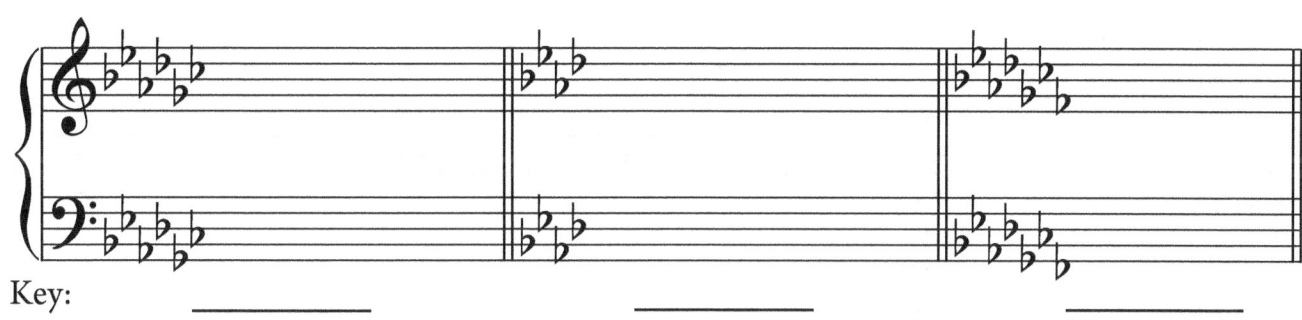

Key: _____   _____   _____

Flats: _____   _____   _____

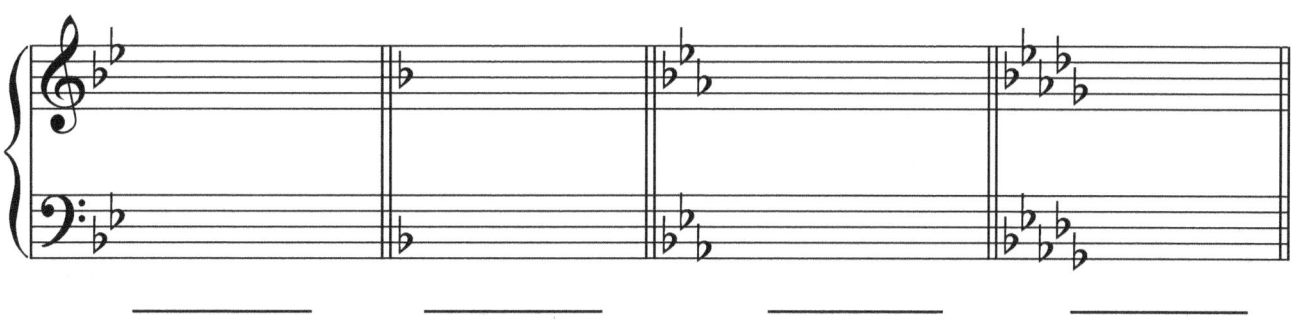

_____ _____ _____ _____
_____ _____ _____ _____

⁶Technical Names for Scale Degrees.

Every scale degree has a technical name. These are the names for each scale degree.

$\hat{1}$ Tonic
$\hat{2}$ Supertonic
$\hat{3}$ Mediant
$\hat{4}$ Subdominant
$\hat{5}$ Dominant
$\hat{6}$ Submediant
$\hat{7}$ Leading tone

1. Write the following major key signatures and notes on the grand staves.

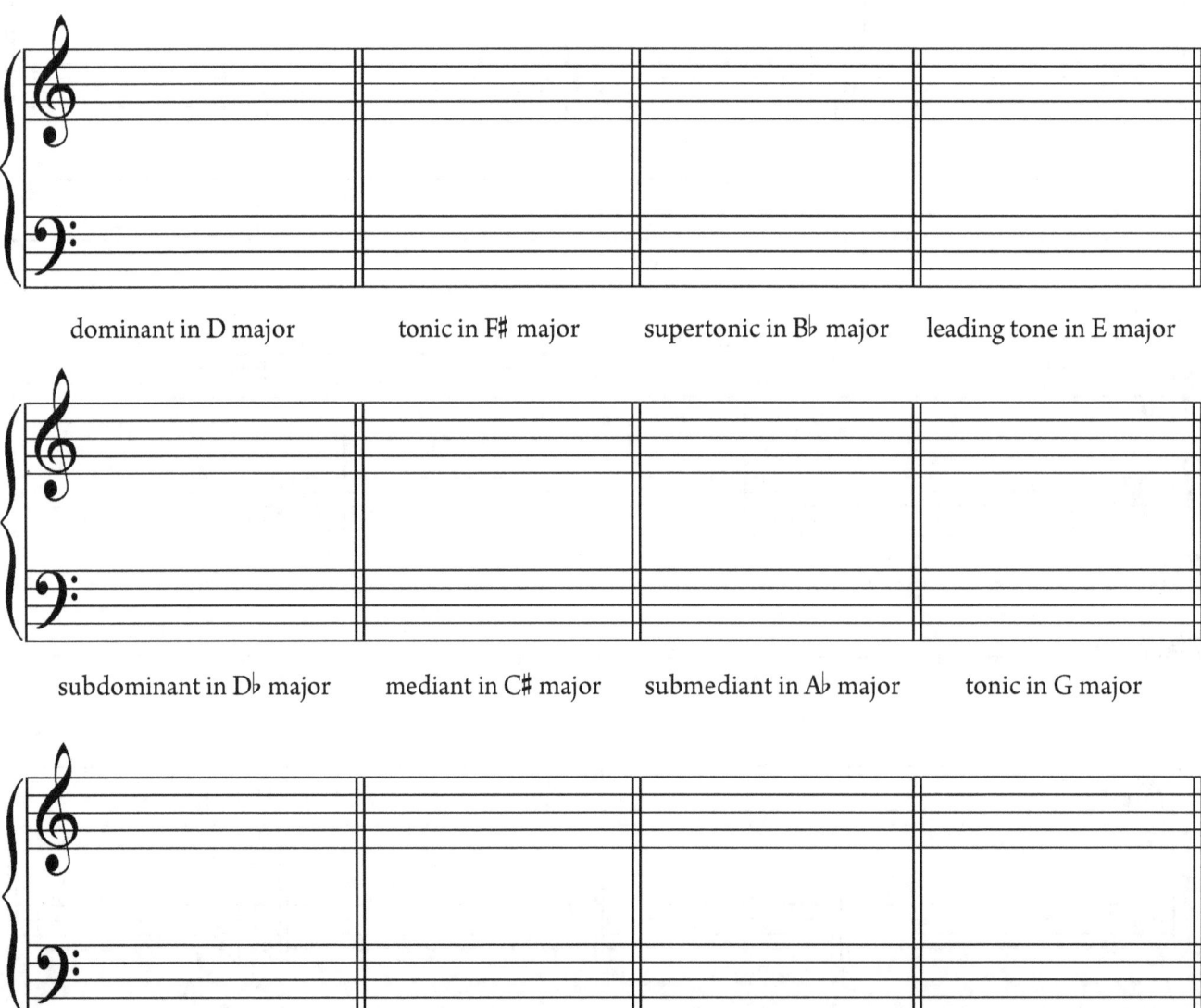

dominant in D major   tonic in F♯ major   supertonic in B♭ major   leading tone in E major

subdominant in D♭ major   mediant in C♯ major   submediant in A♭ major   tonic in G major

leading tone in B major   tonic in G♭ major   supertonic in E♭ major   dominant in A major

Major Scales

2. Write the following scales ascending and descending in wholes notes using a key signature for each.

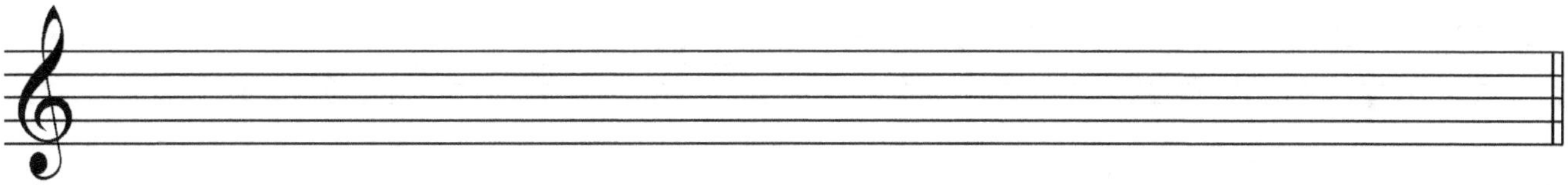

E major

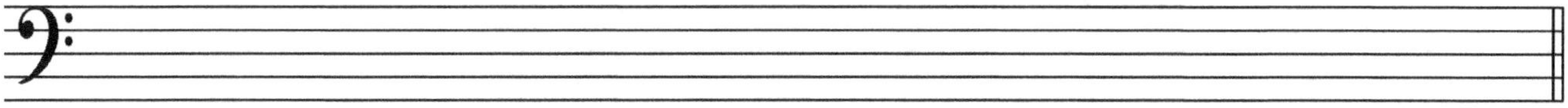

A♭ major

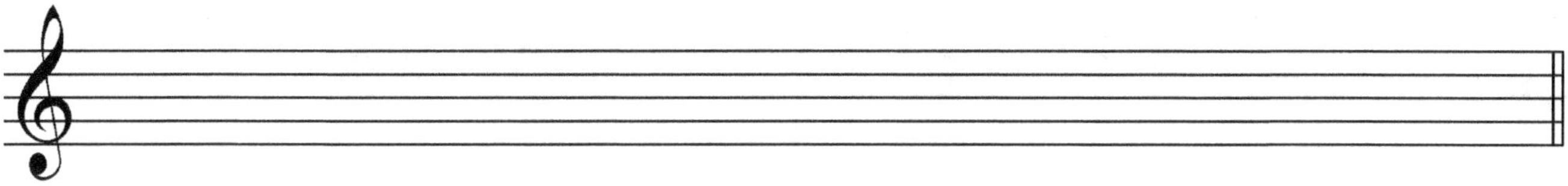

D♭ major

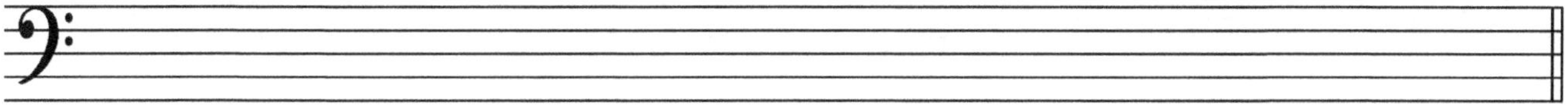

G major

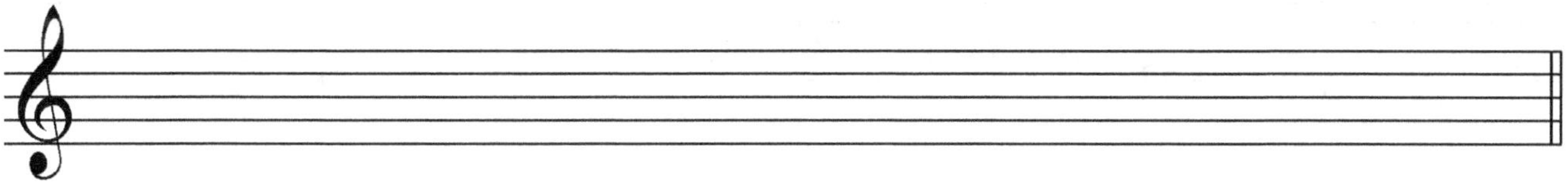

B major

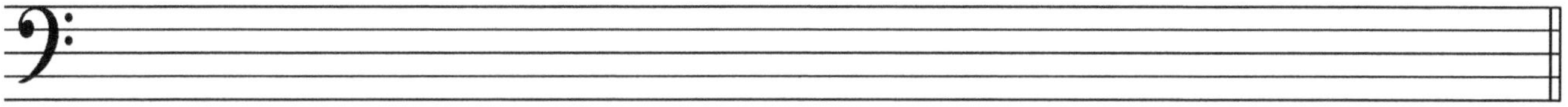

F major

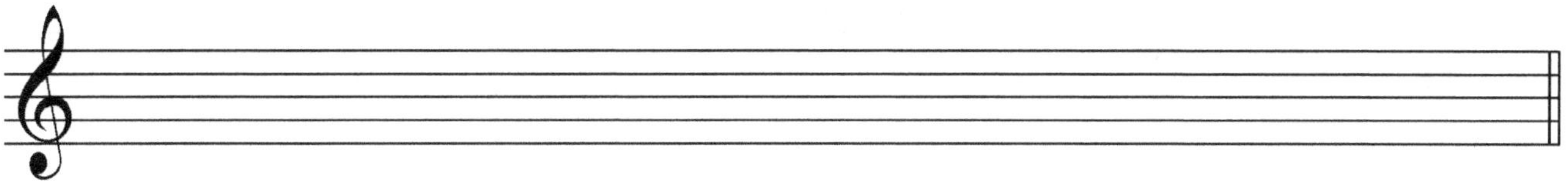

D major

3. Add clefs and accidentals to create the following major scales.

E♭ major

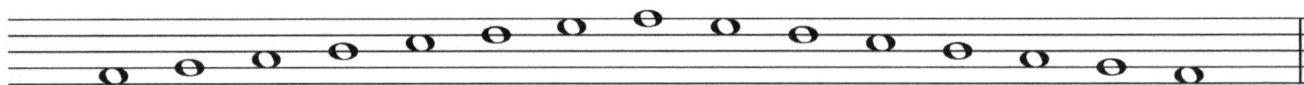

A major

F♯ major

B♭ major

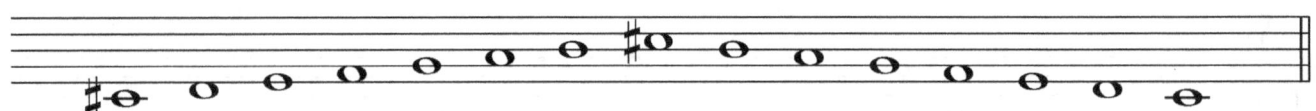

C♯ major

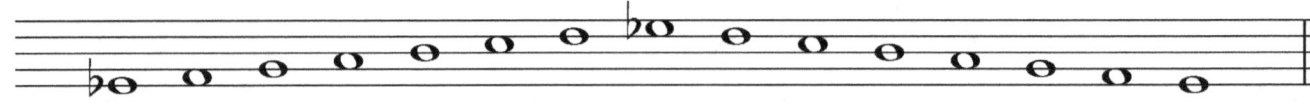

G♭ major

B major

4. Write the following scales ascending and descending using half notes.

The major scale with 5 flats

The major scale with D as the leading tone

The major scale with C♯ as the supertonic

The major scale with D♯ as the submediant

The major scale with one flat

The major scale with A as the subdominant

The major scale with F as the dominant

4
Minor Scales

❹
❺
❻

There are three types of minor scales: ***natural minor, harmonic minor***, and ***melodic minor***. Each of these minor scales has a different order of whole and half steps. Thankfully, it is not necessary to memorize these patterns to study minor scales.

Relative Major and Minor Keys

Major and minor scales are related by key signature. Every major key has a relative minor. They are related because they share the same key signature. C major and A minor have no sharps or flats. C major is the relative major of A minor and vice versa.

To determine a minor key signature:

1. Name the major key.

2. Count up six notes (or down three) to get the relative minor key.

The 6th note of the G major scale is E. E minor has the same key signature as G major, one sharp, F♯. Every key signature reflects two keys, one major and one minor.

Figure 4.1

G major scale

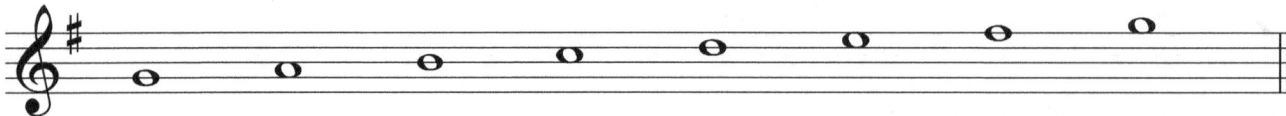

E natural minor scale

❹ Figure 4.2 is a chart of the relative major and minor keys up to three sharps and three flats.
❺
❻ Figure 4.2

Sharp Keys	Major	Minor
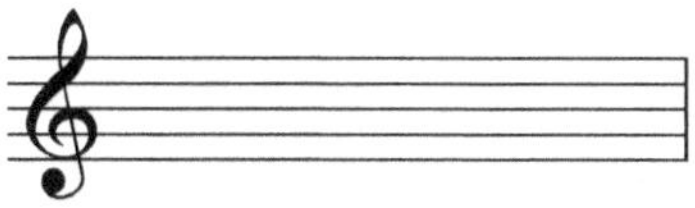 (no sharps)	C	A
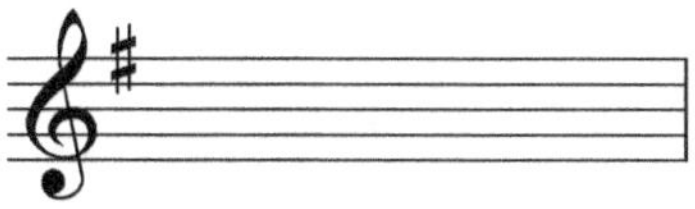 (1 sharp)	G	E
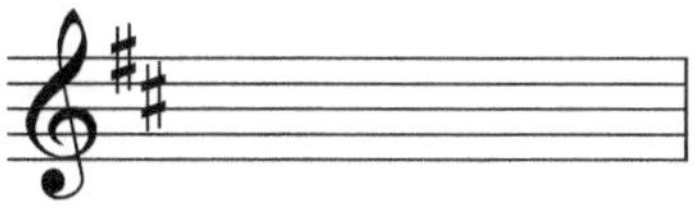 (2 sharps)	D	B
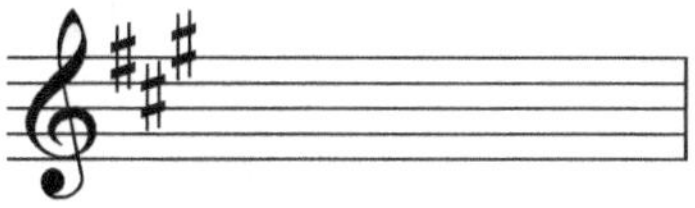 (3 sharps)	A	F#

Flat Keys	Major	Minor
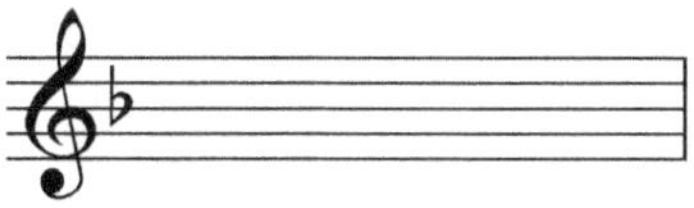 (1 flat)	F	D
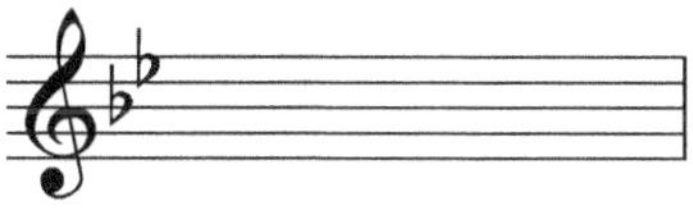 (2 flats)	B♭	G
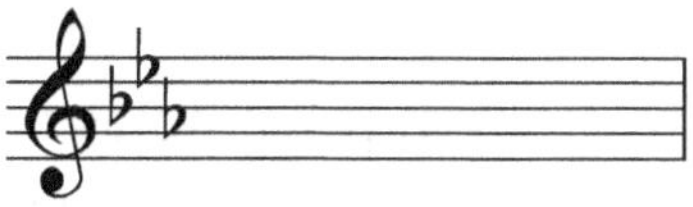 (3 flats)	E♭	C

❹ 1. Name the relative major or minor key of the following:
❺
❻

D minor _____   B♭ major _____

E minor _____   C major _____

B minor _____   D major _____

C minor _____   E♭ major _____

F♯ minor _____   A major _____

❹
❺ Parallel Major and Minor Keys
❻

Major and minor keys that share the same root or tonic are considered *parallel major and minor keys*. Sometimes they are called *tonic major and minor*. C major and C minor are parallel major and minor or tonic major and minor. This means they share the same tonic. Here are the notes of the C major scale:

C D E F G A B C

Here are the notes of the C natural minor scale:

C D E♭ F G A♭ B♭ C

The difference between these scales is three notes. From C major to C minor, three notes have been lowered to flats: E, A and B have been lowered to E♭, A♭ and B♭. In other words, $\hat{3}$, $\hat{6}$, and $\hat{7}$ have been lowered one half step to create the natural minor scale. This applies to all keys. If you lower $\hat{3}$, $\hat{6}$, and $\hat{7}$ of any major scale you get its parallel minor.

As we move through music theory studies we will see that many things can be derived from a major scale. This is simply another way to find the parallel minor scale.

Minor Scale Review

These are the three versions of the minor scale:

- The ***natural minor scale*** is the minor scale without any altered notes.
- The ***harmonic minor scale*** has raised $\hat{7}$ ascending and descending.
- The ***melodic minor scale*** has $\hat{6}$ and $\hat{7}$ raised ascending and lowered descending.

Figure 4.3 illustrates all three versions of the A minor scale.

Figure 4.3

A natural minor

A harmonic minor

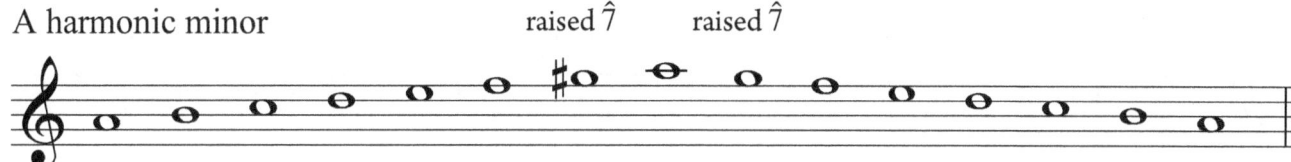

A melodic minor

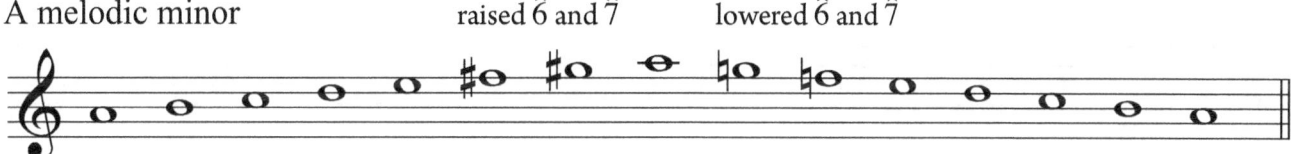

The Leading Tone and The Subtonic

Most of the time, minor keys require raised $\hat{7}$ in order for them to work harmonically in a composition. When we raise $\hat{7}$ it becomes a half step away from the tonic and this gives it a natural pull to the tonic. This is why it is called the ***leading tone***. It "leads" to the tonic.

If $\hat{7}$ is not raised, as in the natural minor scale, or the descending melodic minor scale, it does not have this pull to the tonic and is not called the leading tone. In this case it is a called the ***subtonic***. The subtonic only occurs in a minor key. In A minor, G♯ is the leading tone and G♮ is the subtonic. In major keys, there is no subtonic because $\hat{7}$ is always a semitone away from the tonic and it is always called the leading tone.

❹ 1. Write the following scales ascending and descending in whole notes using key signatures. La-
❺ bel the leading tone (LT) and the subtonic (ST) where applicable.

❻ B natural minor

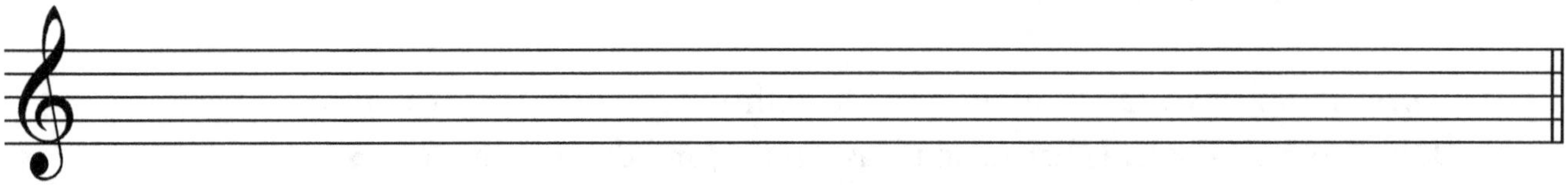

B harmonic minor

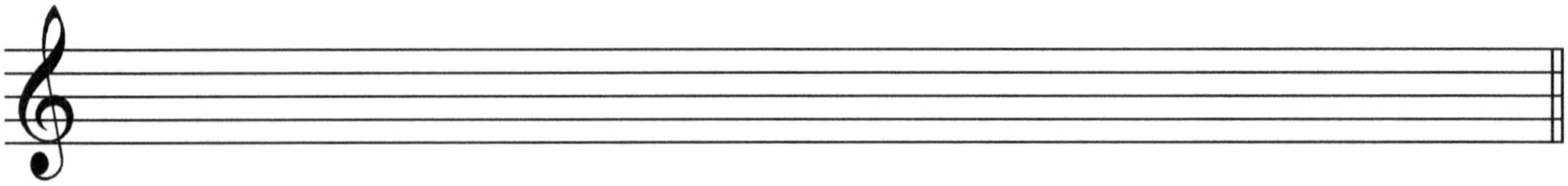

B melodic minor

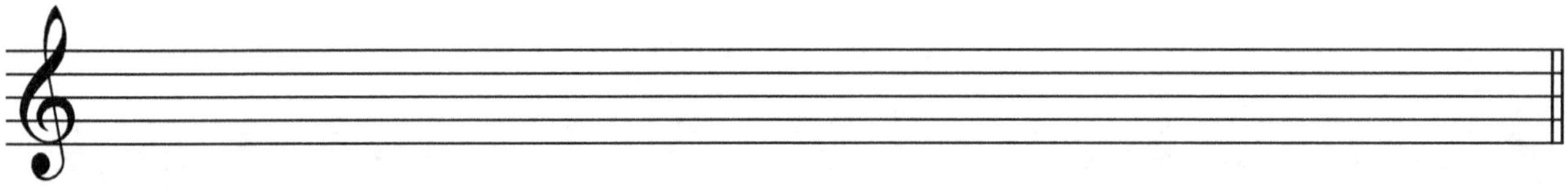

G natural minor

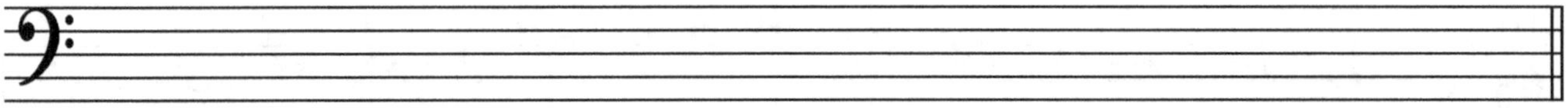

G harmonic minor

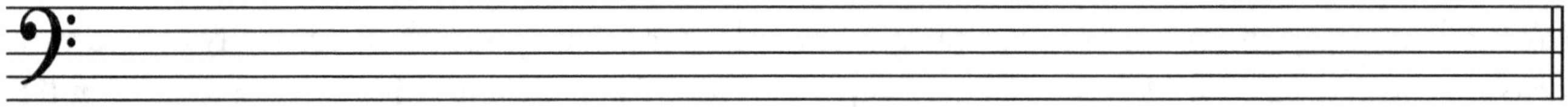

G melodic minor

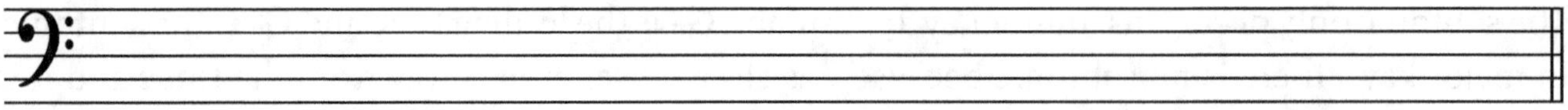

2. Identify the following minor scales.

_____

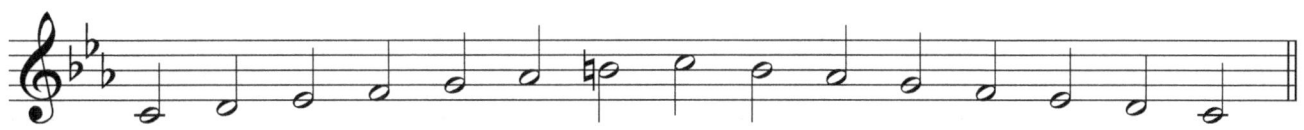
_____

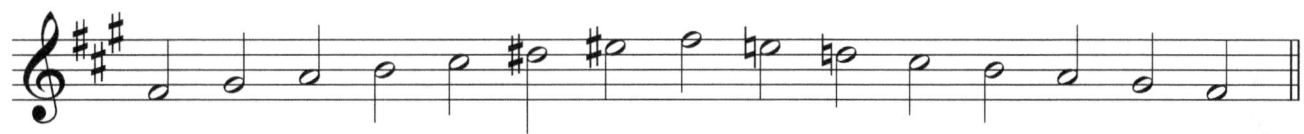
_____

_____

_____

_____

_____

❹
❺ 3. Write the following scales ascending and descending using a key signature in quarter notes.
❻ G harmonic minor

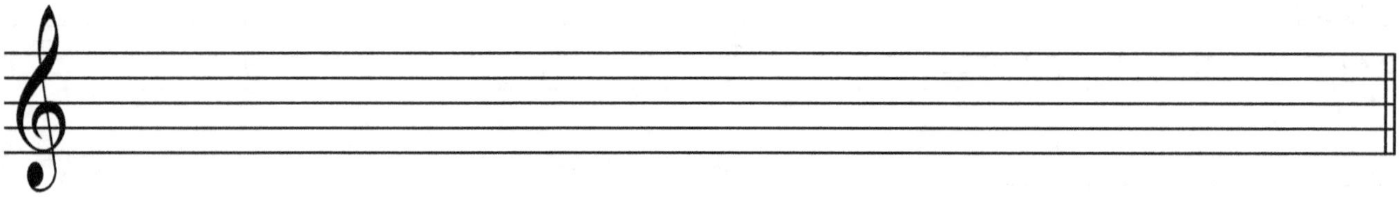

A natural minor

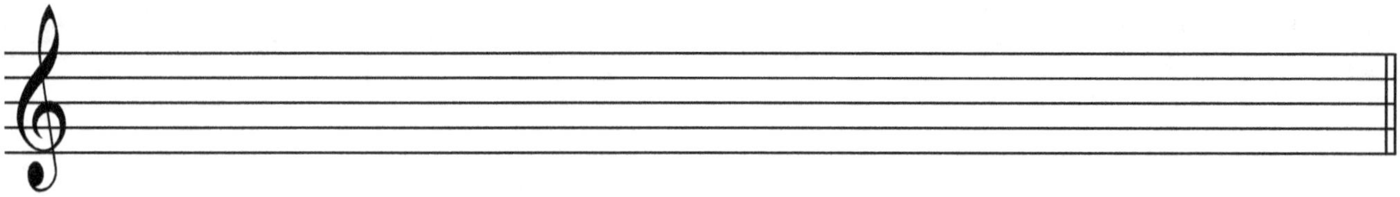

C melodic minor

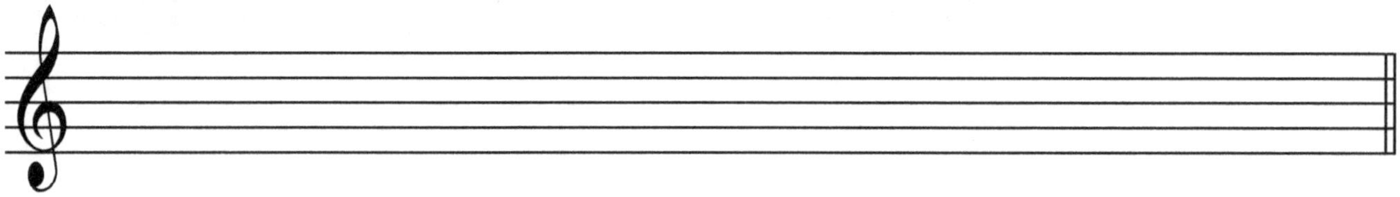

E harmonic minor

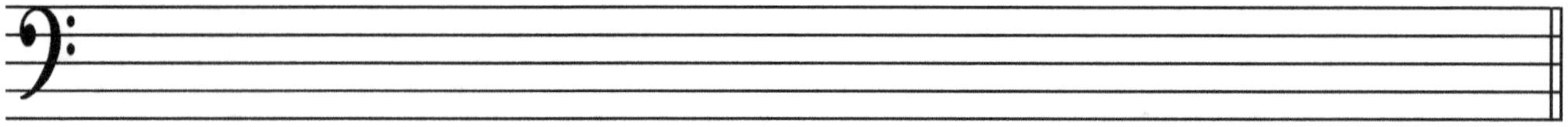

F# melodic minor

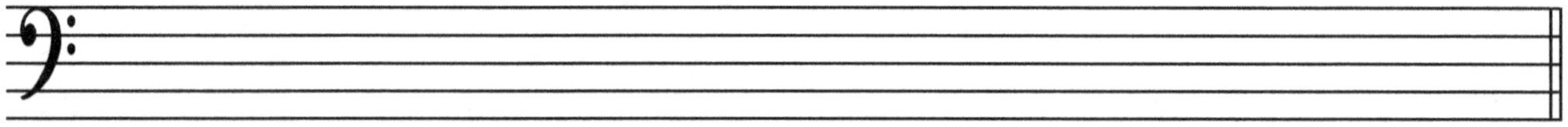

D natural minor

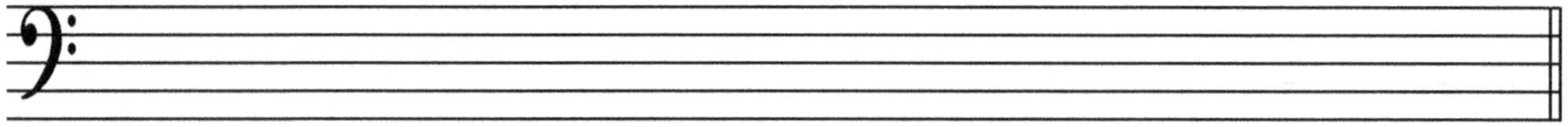

B harmonic minor

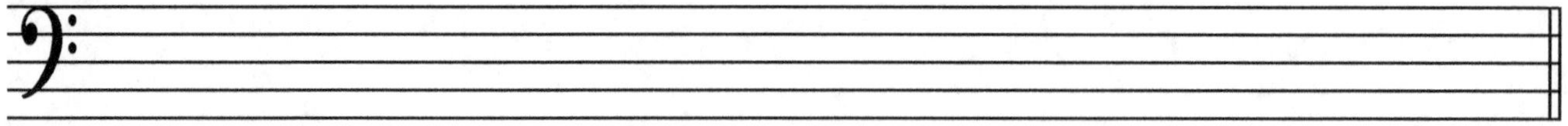

© San Marco Publications 2023

Minor Scales

Music Terms

Review the following musical terms from Levels 1 to 4 that are related to tempo.

accelerando, accel.	becoming quicker
adagio	a slow tempo between andante and largo
allegretto	fairly fast, a little slower than allegro
allegro	fast
lento	slow
moderato	at a moderate tempo
presto	very fast
prestissimo	as fast as possible
rallentando	slowing down
ritardando	slowing down gradually
tempo	speed at which music is performed
Tempo primo, Tempo I	return to the original tempo
vivace	lively, brisk

❺The table in Figure 4.4 shows the minor scales with key signatures up to four sharps and flats.
❻

Figure 4.4

Minor Key	Key Signature	Harmonic form Raise $\hat{7}$ in ascending and descending scales	Melodic form	
			Ascending raise $\hat{6}$ and $\hat{7}$	Descending lower $\hat{7}$ and $\hat{6}$
A	no sharps or flats	G♯	F♯, G♯	G♮, F♮
E	F♯	D♯	C♯, D♯	D♮, C♮
B	F♯, C♯	A♯	G♯, A♯	A♮, G♮
F♯	F♯, C♯, G♯	E♯	D♯, E♯	E♮, D♮
C♯	F♯, C♯, G♯, D♯	B♯	A♯, B♯	B♮, A♮
D	B♭	C♯	B♮, C♯	C♮, B♭
G	B♭, E♭	F♯	E♮, F♯	F♮, E♭
C	B♭, E♭, A♭	B♮	A♮, B♮	B♭, A♭
F	B♭, E♭, A♭, D♭	E♮	D♮, E♮	E♭, D♭

1. Name the key and following scales as natural, harmonic or melodic. e.g. *D harmonic minor.*

Scale:_____

Scale:_____

Scale:_____

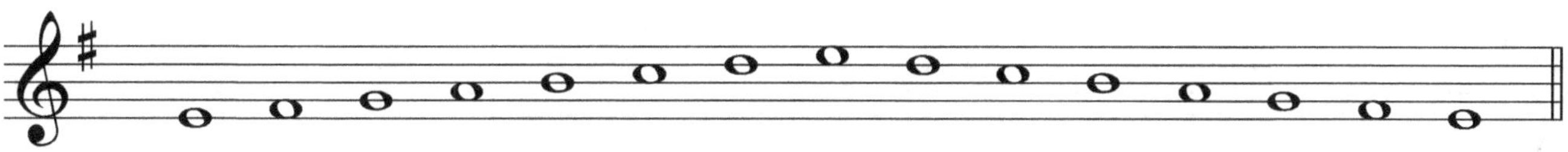

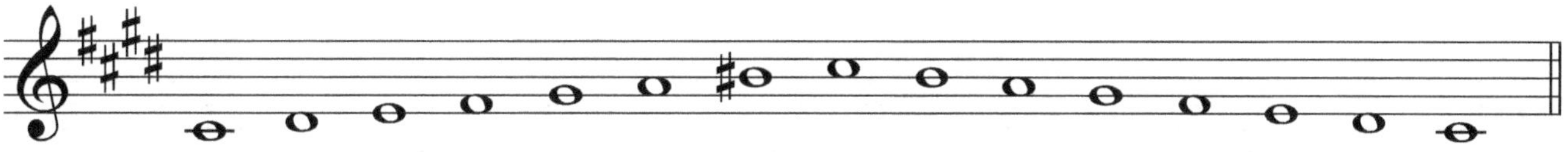

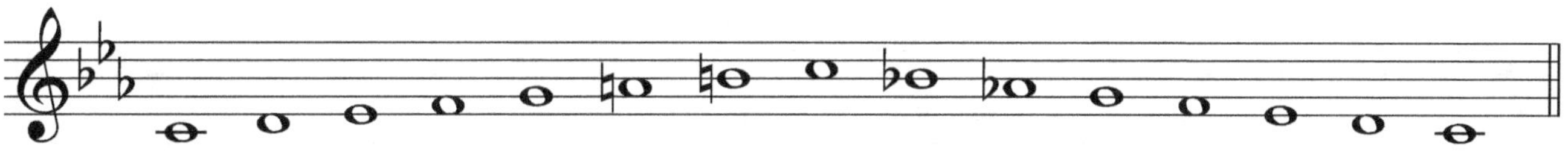

Scale:_____

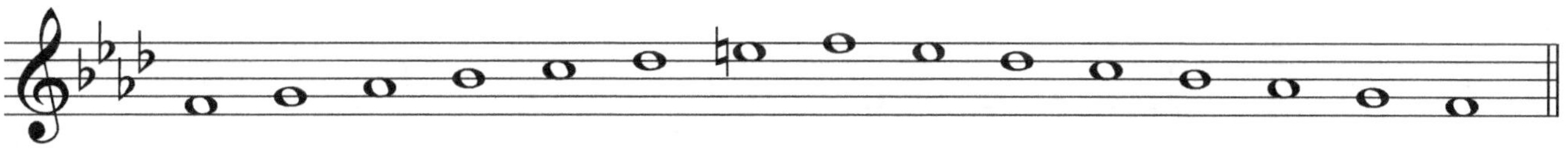

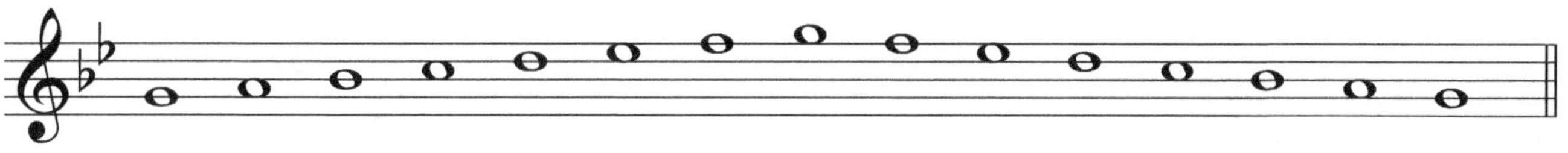

Scale:_____

Scale:_____

Scale:_____

Minor Scales

❺ 2. Write the following scales ascending and descending in quarter notes using a key signature.
❻   Label the leading tones (LT).

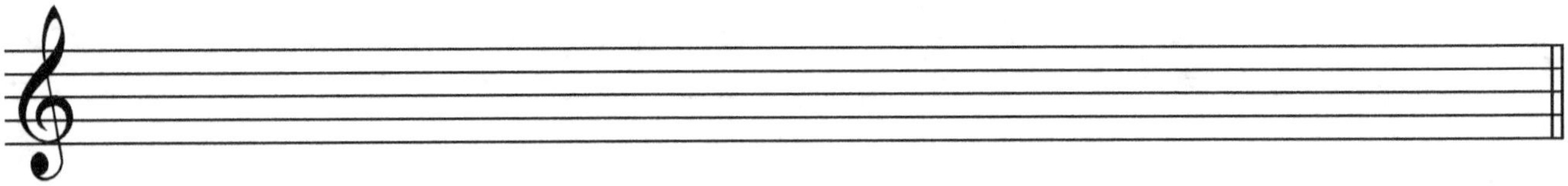

C# harmonic minor

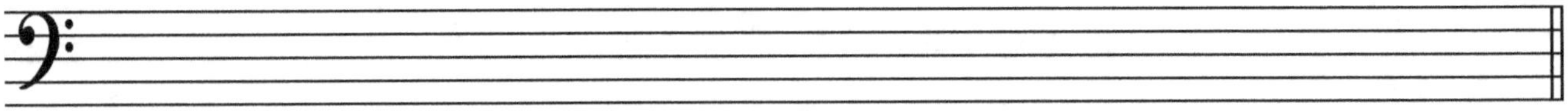

F melodic minor

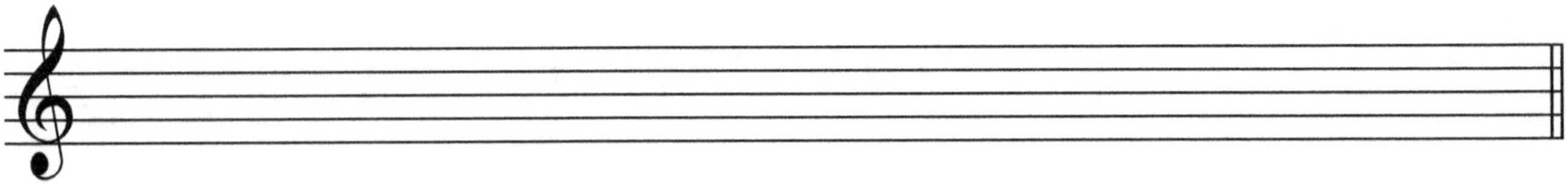

D natural minor

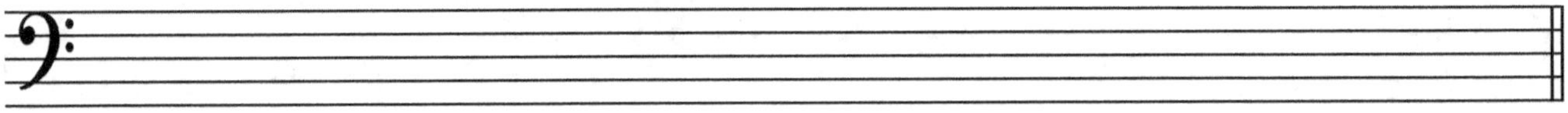

F# harmonic minor

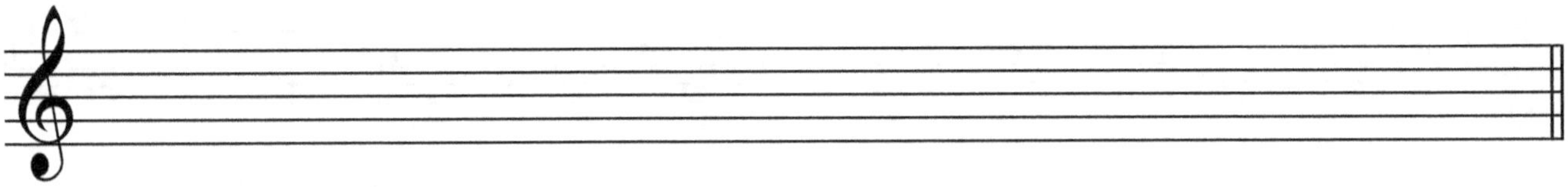

C melodic minor

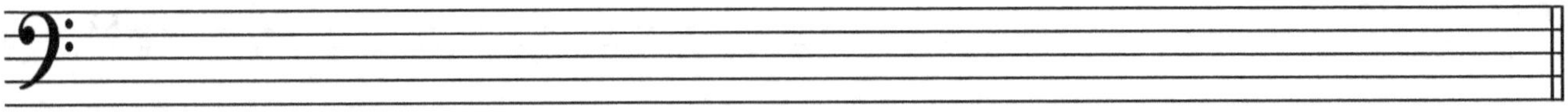

B natural minor

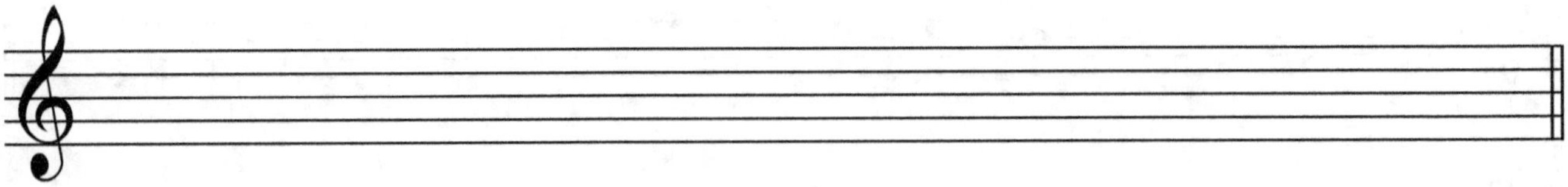

E harmonic minor

❺ 3. Write the following scales ascending and descending in half notes using a key signature.
❻ Label the subtonic notes (ST).

The harmonic minor scale with the key signature of 4 flats

The melodic minor scale with the key signature of 2 sharps

The natural minor scale with G as the subtonic

The harmonic minor scale with F♯ as the leading tone

The melodic minor scale with C♯ as the tonic

The natural minor with G as the dominant

The harmonic minor scale with A major as its relative major

Parallel Keys and Scales

The scales covered to this point may also be known as *modes*. Mode is just another name for the word scale.

Thus far you have learned about the major mode and the three minor modes – natural, harmonic and melodic. Composers often move back and forth between the major and minor modes within the same piece to make their compositions interesting.

Because of the common notes and key signatures, composers may also change keys, or modulate back and forth between relative major and minor keys. For example, a piece in G minor often moves to the key of B♭ major. G minor and B♭ major are relative minor and major keys and share the same key signature of B♭ and E♭. Because of this, many notes are the same between the two keys, and it is easy to move between them.

Composers may also keep the tonic the same but change the mode of the piece from major to minor, or vice-versa. For example a piece in C major might change keys to C minor. These two keys are related because they share the same tonic, C.

Major and minor keys that use the same tonic are known as *parallel* major and minor keys. For example, F major and F minor are parallel keys. They both have F as the tonic.

1. Write the following scales ascending and descending in whole notes using a key signature. Name each scale.

G major

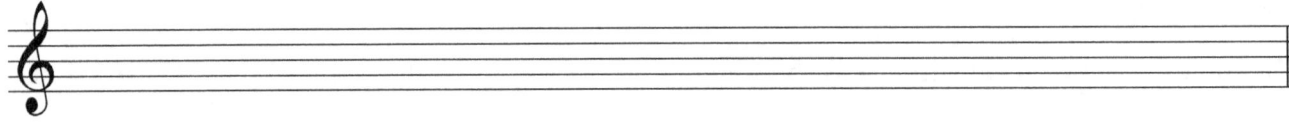

G major's parallel minor, harmonic form

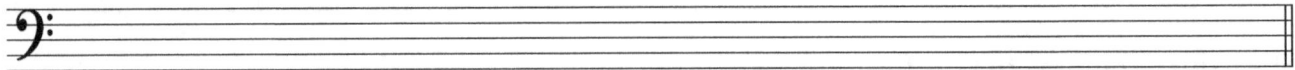

G major's relative minor, melodic form

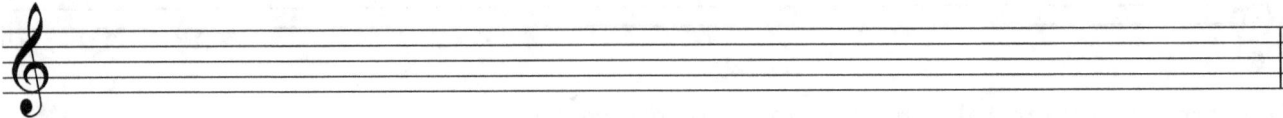

Minor Scales

5 D natural minor
6

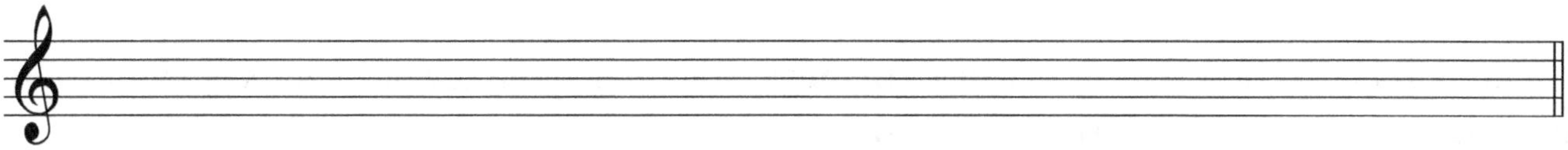

D minor's relative major

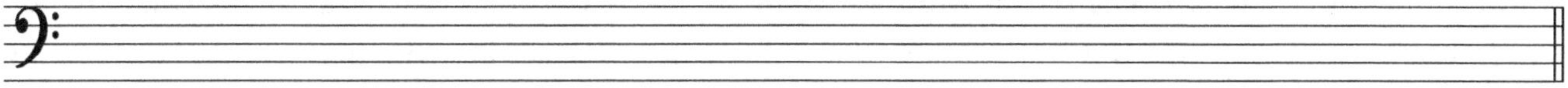

D minor's parallel major

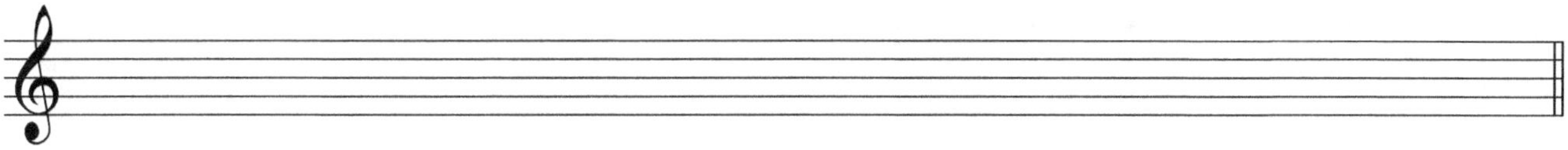

A major

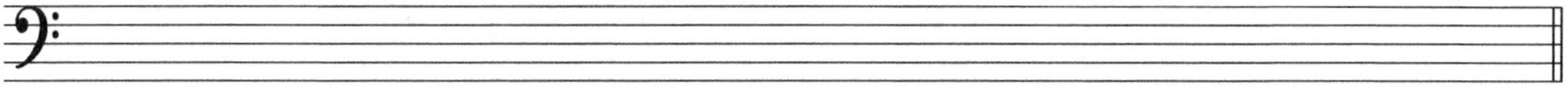

A major's parallel minor, melodic form

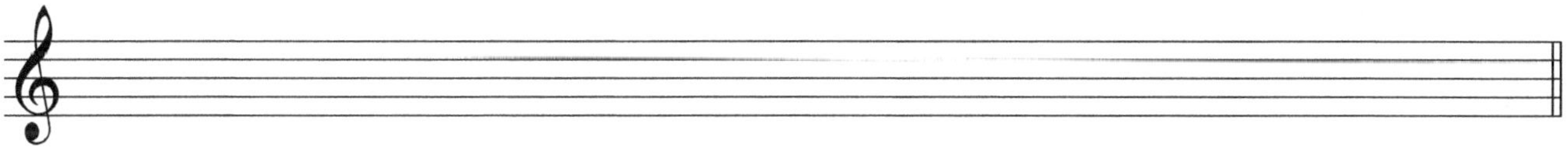

A major's relative minor, harmonic form

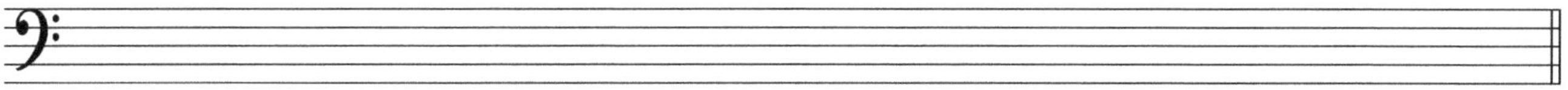

Identifying the Key of a Melody

It is important to know the key of a piece of music. Identifying the key of a composition helps us to understand, analyze, perform and memorize it.

Study the melody in Figure 4.5.

This melody has a key signature of one sharp. This key signature suggests G major or it's relative minor, E minor. This melody also has the accidental D sharp. Often, music in a minor key will have accidentals indicating raised $\hat{7}$. In the key of E minor raised $\hat{7}$ is D♯. This melody ends on E, approached by the leading tone D♯. There is an E minor arpeggio in m.4. All of these elements point to the key of E minor. This melody is in E minor.

Melodies in minor keys may contain raised $\hat{6}$ as well as raised $\hat{7}$ since the melodic minor scale includes these notes. In fact, a melody in a minor key could be based on any of the three forms of the minor scale: natural, harmonic, or melodic minor.

Figure 4.5

Felix Mendelssohn
Quartet No. 4

The melody is Figure 4.6 has a key signature of three sharps. This key signature suggests A major or it's relative minor, F♯ minor. The melody starts and ends on A. There are no E♯'s suggesting the raised $\hat{7}$ of F♯ minor. Therefore, it is in the key of A major.

Figure 4.6

Ludwig van Beethoven
Sonata no. 3 for Cello and Piano

Minor Scales

❺ 1. Name the keys of the following melodies.
❻

Joseph Haydn
Drum Roll Symphony, III

key: _____

Hector Berlioz
Symphonie Fantastique, IV

key: _____

J.S. Bach
English Suite No. 6, Courante

key: _____

Arcangelo Corelli
Concerto Grosso, I

key: _____

Frederic Chopin
Nocturne Op.72, No. 1

key: _____

Gustav Mahler
Resurrection Symphony

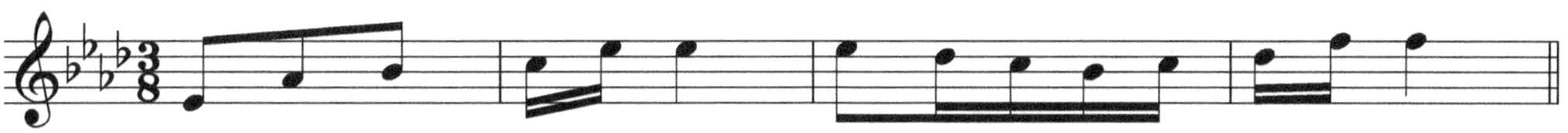

key: _____

Robert Schumann
Piano Sonata Op. 15

key: _____

Minor Scales

⁶The Circle of Fifths With Minor Keys

Figure 4.7 is the circle of 5ths with added minor keys. The circle of 5ths shows that some of the flat keys sound the same as some of the sharp keys. The key of six flats (E♭minor, G♭major) sounds the same as the key of six sharps (D♯minor, F♯major). Keys which contain the same pitches but are notated differently are called *enharmonic keys* or *enharmonic equivalents*.

Figure 4.7

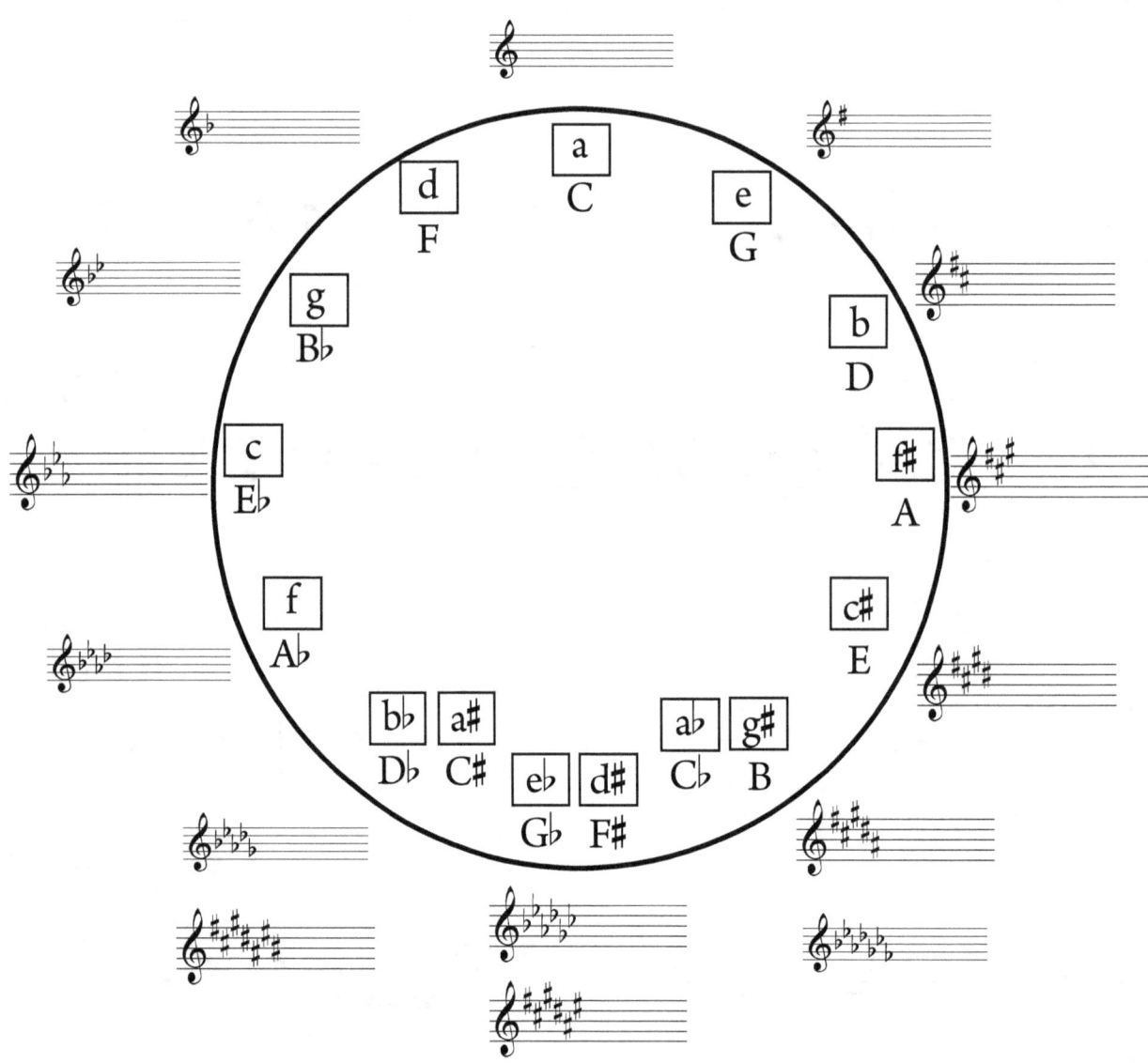

Minor keys are shown with lower case letters.

1. Name the key and following scales as natural, harmonic or melodic. e.g. *D harmonic minor.*

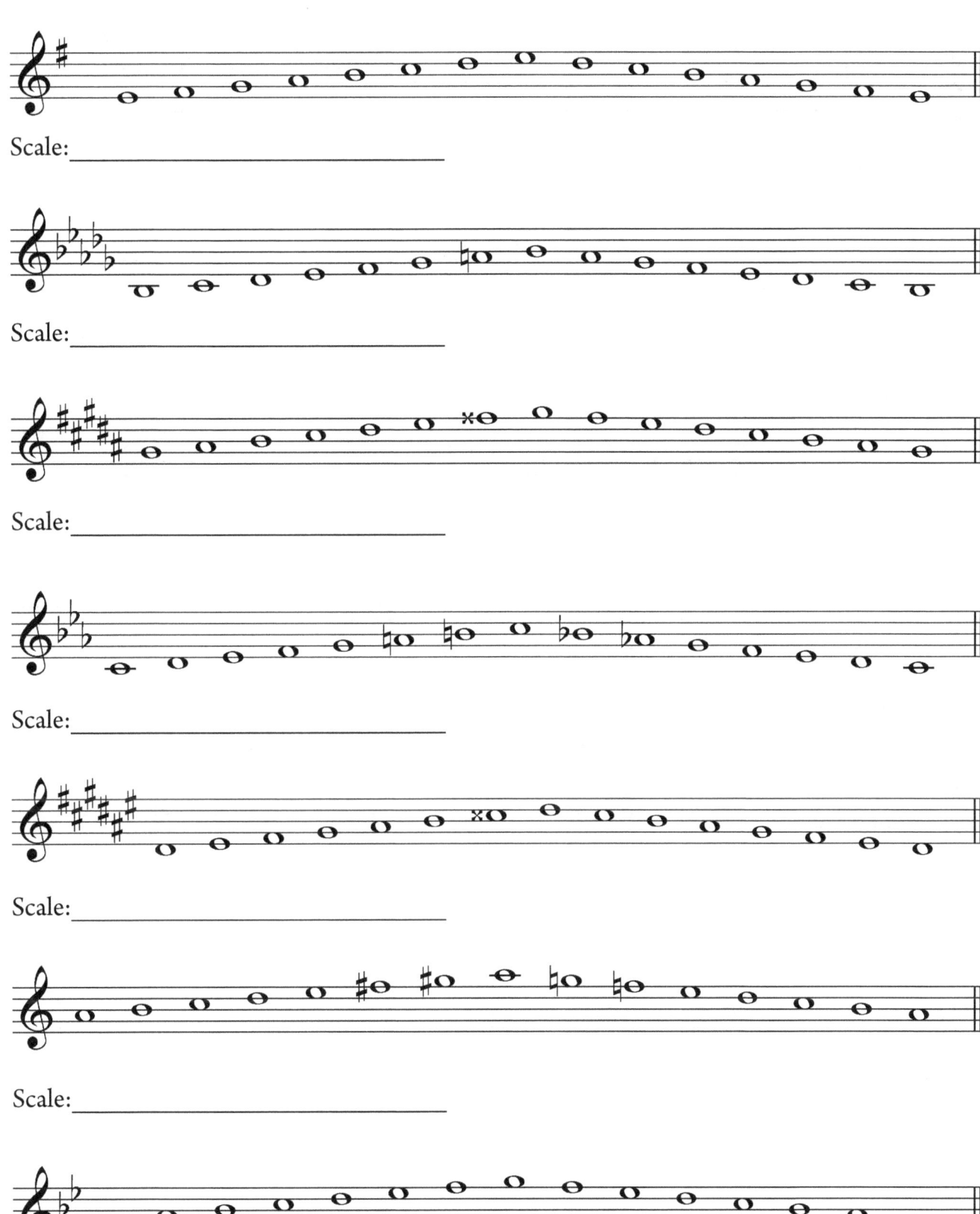

Scale:_____

Scale:_____

Scale:_____

Scale:_____

Scale:_____

Scale:_____

Scale:_____

2. Write the following scales ascending and descending in quarter notes using a key signature.

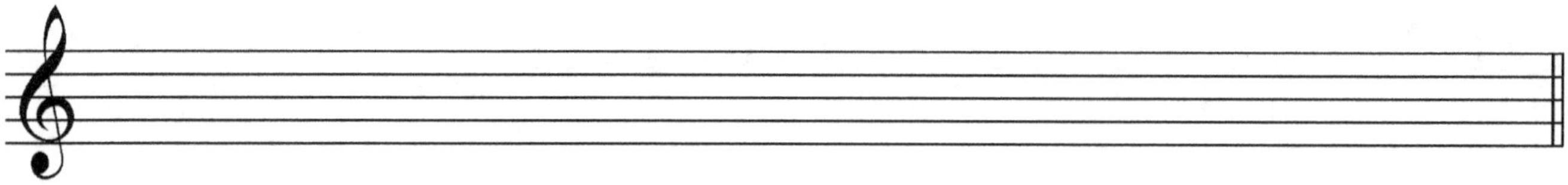

C# harmonic minor

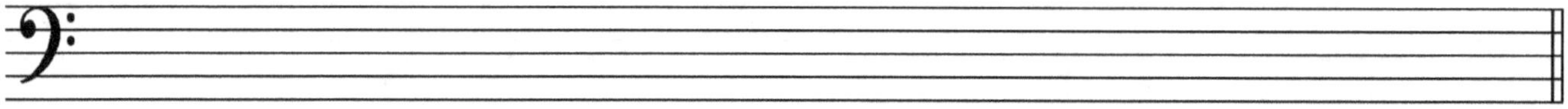

E♭ melodic minor

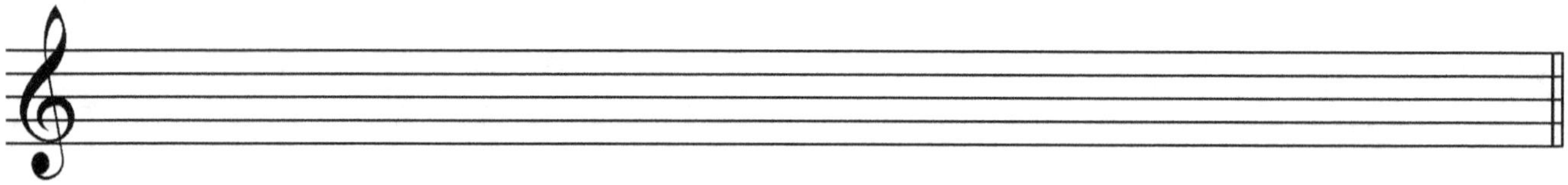

D natural minor

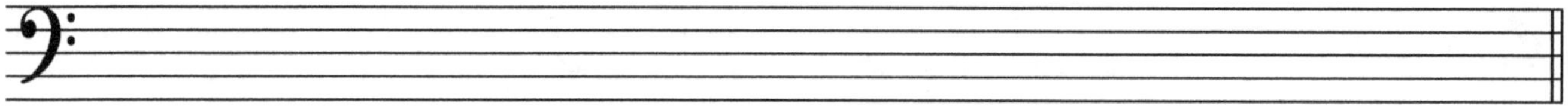

F# harmonic minor

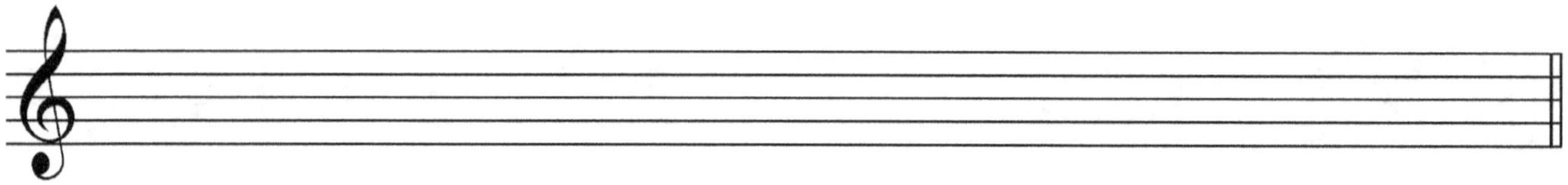

C melodic minor

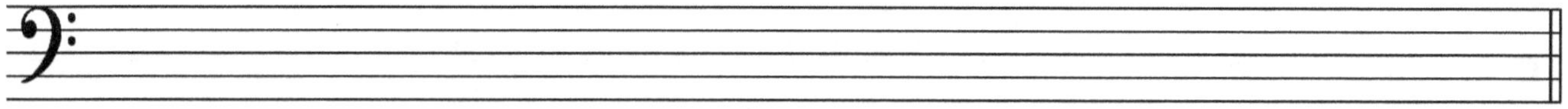

B♭ natural minor

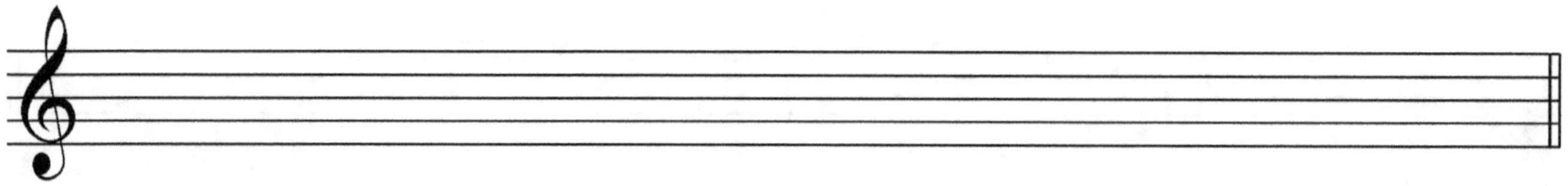

E harmonic minor

❻Parallel Major and Minor Keys Review

Major and minor keys that share the same root or tonic are considered *parallel major* and *minor keys*. Sometimes they are called *tonic major and minor*. C major and C minor are parallel major and minor or tonic major and minor. This means that they share the same tonic.

Enharmonic Tonic Major and Minor Keys

Enharmonic major or minor keys are keys with the same tonic that have a different name. For example, C♯ major and D♭ major are enharmonic tonic majors. They are major scales that share the same tonic, but have a different name. C♯ and D♭ are the same note.

The enharmonic tonic minor of G♭ minor is F♯ minor. The same tonic, named differently.

The tonic minor of G♭ major is G♭ minor.
The enharmonic tonic minor of G♭ major is F♯ minor. All this means is that it is the minor scale with the same tonic as G♭ major, but renamed. Its name has been changed enharmonically from G♭ to F♯.

❻1. Complete the following.

a. The enharmonic tonic major of C♯ major is _____

b. The enharmonic tonic minor of B♭ major is _____

c. The enharmonic tonic major of C♭ major is _____

d. The parallel minor of D major is _____

e. The tonic major of G minor is _____

f. The enharmonic tonic minor of E♭ major is _____

❻ 2. Write the following scales ascending and descending in half notes using a key signature.

The harmonic minor scale with the key signature of 4 flats

The melodic minor scale that is the parallel minor of D major

The natural minor scale with G as the subtonic

The harmonic minor scale with A as the leading tone

The melodic minor scale with E♭ as the tonic

The natural minor with G as the supertonic

The enharmonic tonic melodic minor, of D♭ major

5

Intervals

We use whole and half steps to understand the structure of scales. These are *intervals*. In music, the term interval refers to the distance between two notes. An interval consists of two elements: numeric size and quality or type. Understanding the interval is essential to understanding music theory.

Major Intervals

Major intervals only occur on the following numbers: 2, 3, 6, and 7. In order for an interval to be major it must be one of these numbers, and the top note must be a member of the bottom notes major scale.

Figure 5.1 illustrates major intervals on different notes.

a. C to D is a major 2nd because D is the second note of the C major scale.
b. D to F♯ is a major 3rd. F must be sharp since it is the third note of the D major scale. F♮ would not be a major 3rd here.
c. E♭ to C is a major 6th because C is the 6th note of the E♭ major scale.
d. G to B is major 3rd since B is scale degree $\hat{3}$ of the G major scale.
e. D to C♯ is a major 7th since the scale of D major has C♯ as its 7th note.

When you write and solve intervals, the key signature of the bottom notes major scale is crucial. Knowing the key signatures is essential when dealing with intervals.

Figure 5.1

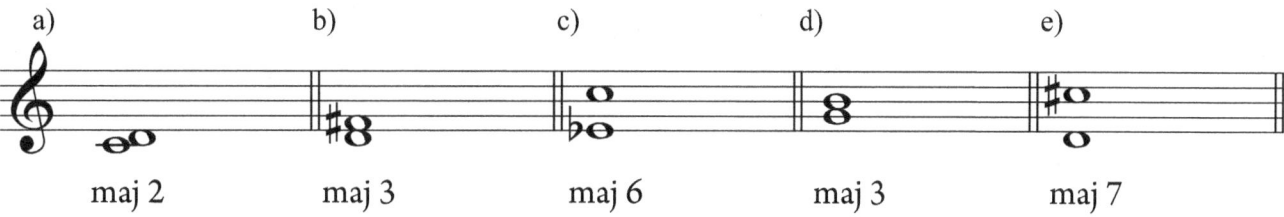

Perfect Intervals

The number of a perfect interval is always 1, 4, 5, or 8. Even though a unison (1) isn't really an interval, since there is no distance between its notes, it is still considered perfect. For an interval to be perfect the top note must be a member of the bottom notes major scale.

Figure 5.2 illustrates a number of perfect intervals. a) is a perfect unison. In b), A♭ is a perfect 4th above E♭ because A♭ is the fourth note of the E♭ major scale. A♮ would not be a perfect 4th here because it is not a member of E♭'s scale. When solving intervals always think of the major scale of the bottom note. Is the top note a member of the bottom notes major scale? If it is, the interval will be perfect, or major depending on the number.

Figure 5.2

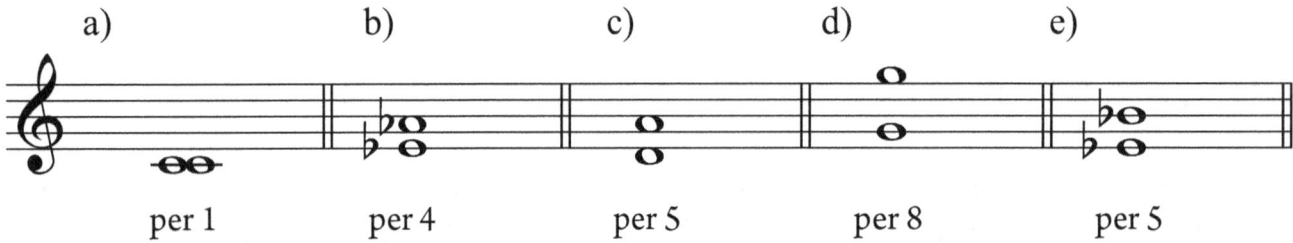

1. Name the following intervals.

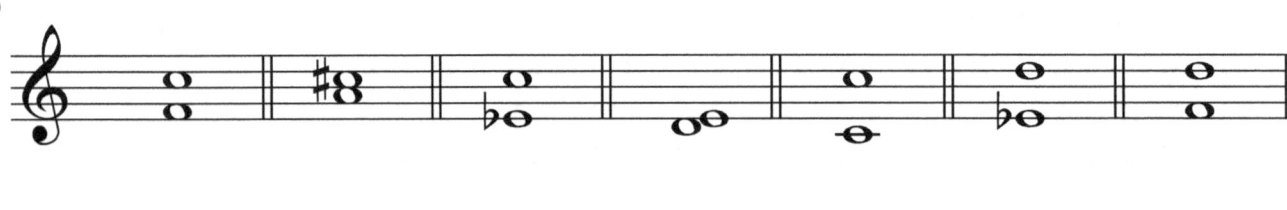

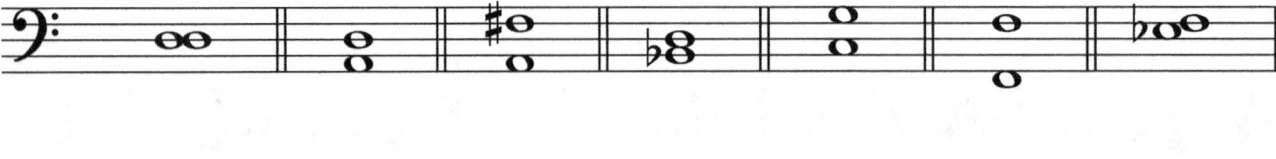

Intervals in a Major Scale

Figure 5.3 shows the C major scale with its intervals. The intervals are measured from the root C to the notes above it. The intervals that result are all major or perfect. 2nds, 3rds, 6ths and 7ths are major intervals. Unisons (1s), 4ths, 5th, and octaves (8ths) are perfect intervals.

Figure 5.3

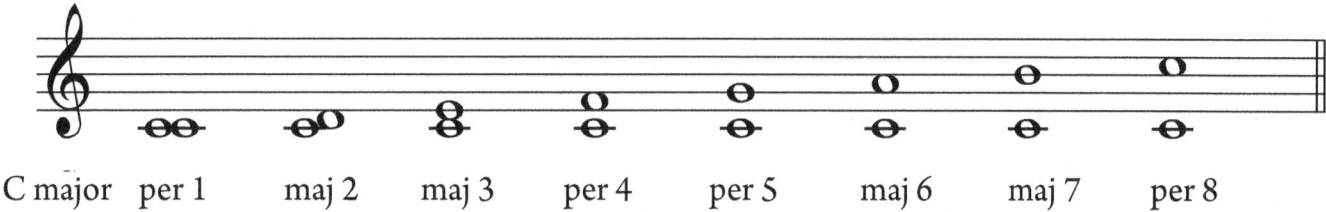

1. Using accidentals write the intervals that occur on the following major scales.

F major

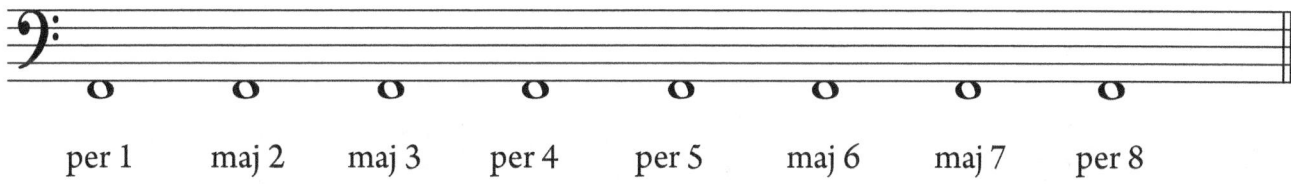

B♭ major

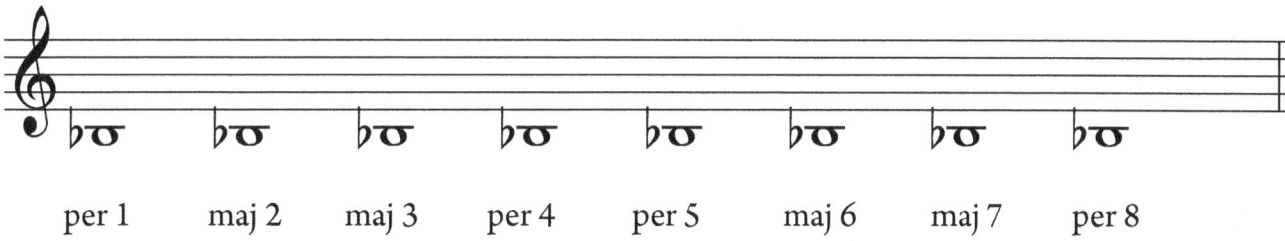

E♭ major

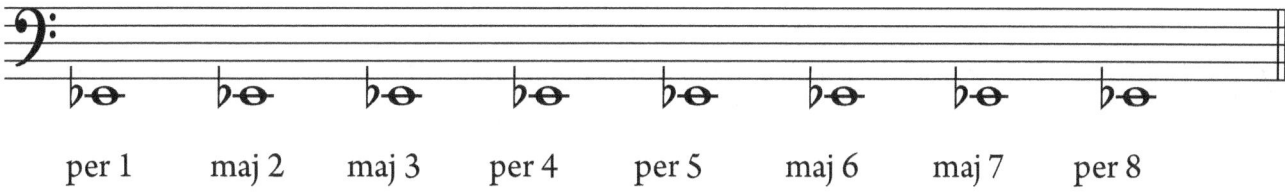

Minor Intervals

Only 2nds, 3rds, 6ths, and 7ths can be *minor intervals*. They are always a half step smaller or closer together than a major interval that has the same number. A minor 2nd is the smallest interval. The half step is a minor 2nd.

Figure 5.4 shows the differences between major and minor intervals.

a. C to D is a major 2nd, because D is a note of the C major scale. C to D♭ is one half step smaller or closer together and is a minor 2nd. D♭ is not a note of the C major scale.
b. D to F♯ is a major 3rd because F♯ is a note of the D major scale. D to F♮ is a minor 3rd because it is one half step closer together than the major interval D- F♯.
c. F to D is a major 6th because D is the sixth note of the F major scale. F to D♭ is a half step closer together and is a minor 6th.
d. D to C♯ is a major 7th. D to C♮ is a half step closer togeher so it is a minor 7th.

A minor interval is one half step smaller or closer together than a major interval. Only major intervals (2nds, 3rds, 6ths and 7ths) can become minor intervals. Perfect intervals (1, 4, 5, and 8) never become minor intervals.

Figure 5.4

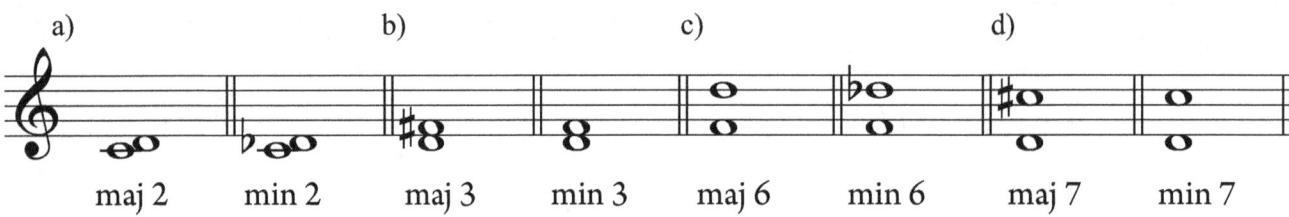

1. Name the following major intervals. Rewrite them making them minor intervals by lowering the top note one half step.

Intervals

❹
❺ Solving Intervals
❻

Use the following steps to solve an intervals number and quality:

1. Count the notes from the bottom up to determine the interval number. Always start by counting the bottom note as 1. In Figure 5.5 A to F is a 6th. A-B-C-D-E-F is 1-2-3-4-5-6.
2. Determine by the number if the interval should be major or perfect. A 6th would be a major interval.
3. Decide if the top note is a member of the bottom notes major scale. Here, F♮ is not a member of the A major scale since A major has an F♯. It has been lowered one half step making this interval a minor 6th.

Figure 5.5

min 6

❹
❺ 2. Name the following intervals.
❻

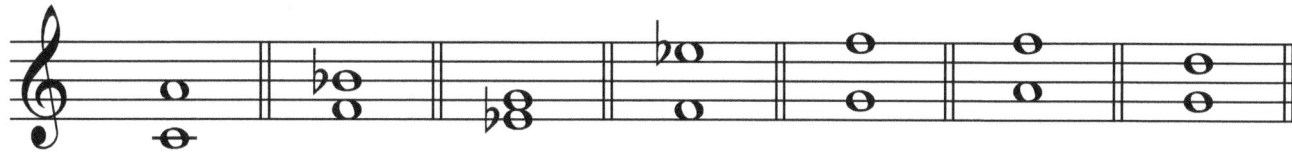

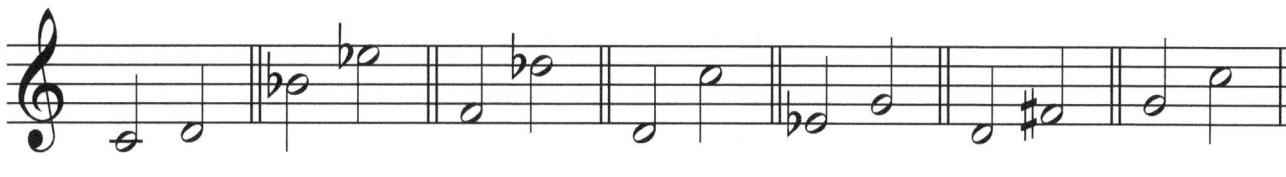

❹ 3. Write the following harmonic intervals.
❺
❻

    min 6   maj 3   per 5   min 7   min 3   per 1   min 3   per 4

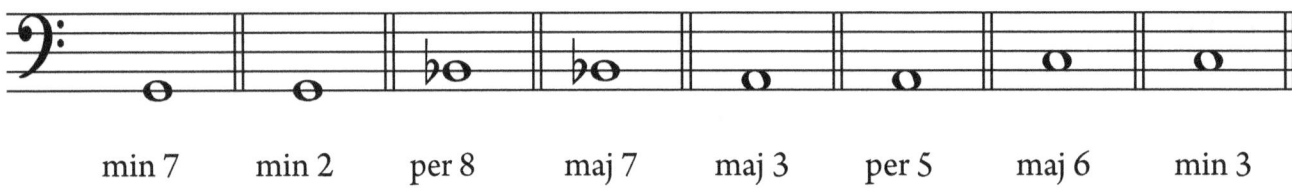

    min 7   min 2   per 8   maj 7   maj 3   per 5   maj 6   min 3

❹ 4. Write the following harmonic intervals.
❺
❻

    per 5   maj 3   min 7   maj 6   min 3   per 1   maj 6   min 6

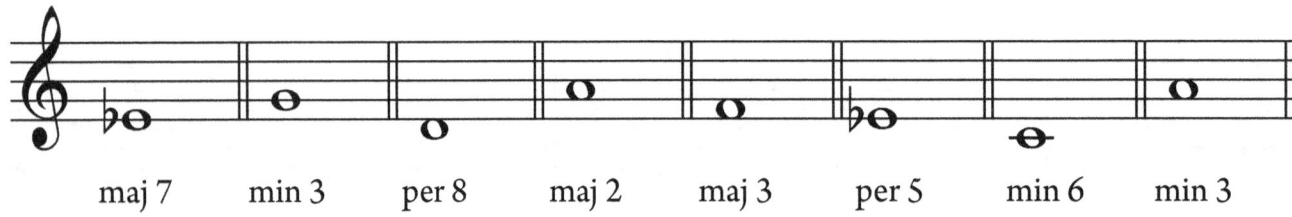

    maj 7   min 3   per 8   maj 2   maj 3   per 5   min 6   min 3

5. Write the following harmonic intervals.

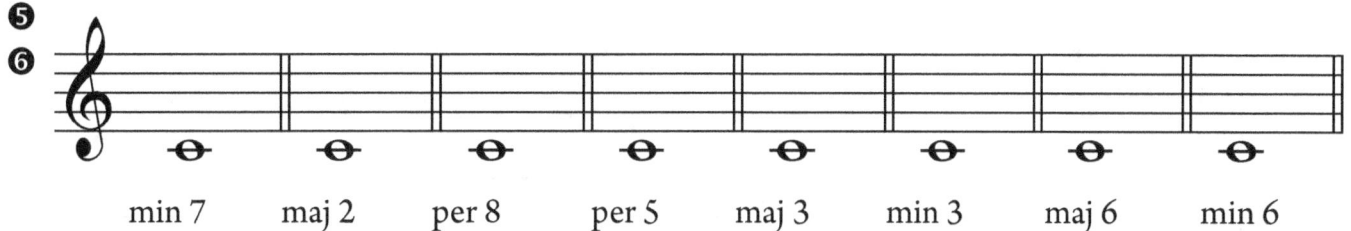

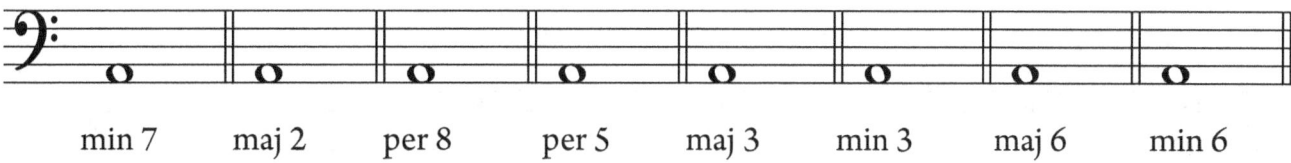

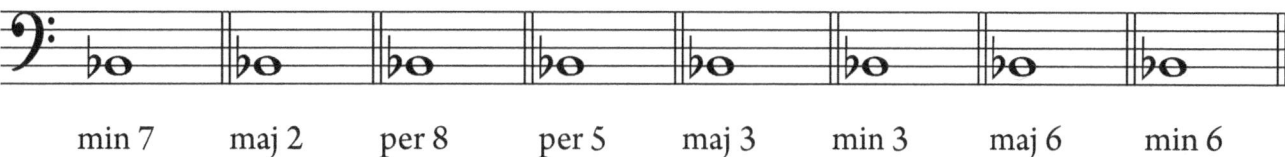

6. Name the melodic intervals under the brackets.

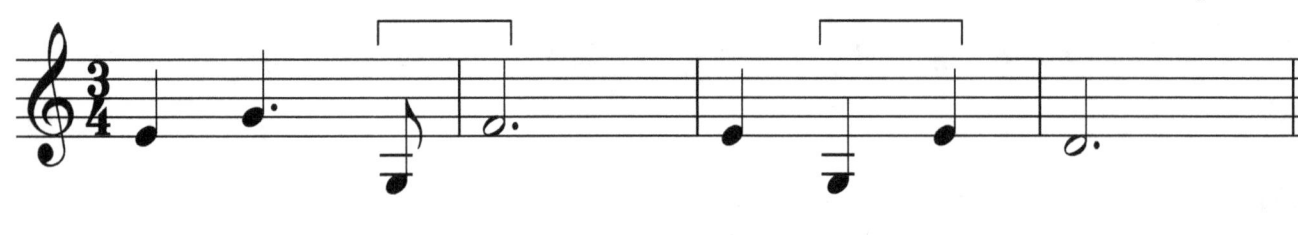

Johann Strauss
Emperor Waltz

Traditional
All Through the Night

Wofgang Amadeus Mozart
Minuet, K. 3

Johann Sebastian Bach
Passacaglia for Organ

Chromatic Half Steps

An *interval* can be defined as the distance from one note to the next. The smallest interval in the music we are studying is a half step.

Half steps may occur between two notes using the same letter name as shown in Figure 5.6. When a half step contains two notes with the same letter name, it is known as a ***chromatic half step***. For example, a chromatic half step above F is F♯. A chromatic half step below A is A♭. These half steps use the same letter name.

Study how sharps, flats, and naturals can raise or lower a note without changing its letter name.

Figure 5.6

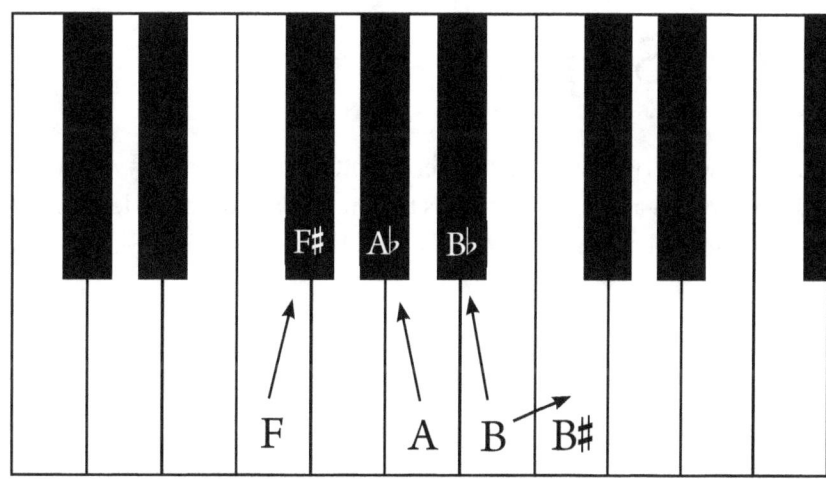

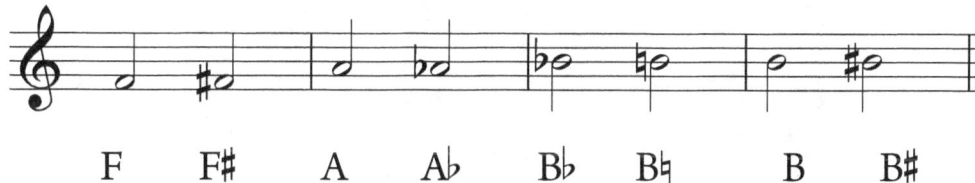

F   F♯   A   A♭   B♭   B♮   B   B♯

❺ 1. Write chromatic half steps above the following notes.
❻

2. Write chromatic half steps below the following notes.

❺❻ Diatonic Half Steps

Half steps may also occur between two notes with different letter names. Figure 5.7 shows half steps between notes using different letter names. When a half step contains two notes with different letter names it is known as a *diatonic half step*. The notes names occur in alphabetical order. For example, E♭ - F♭, F♯ - G, A - B♭, etc.

Figure 5.7

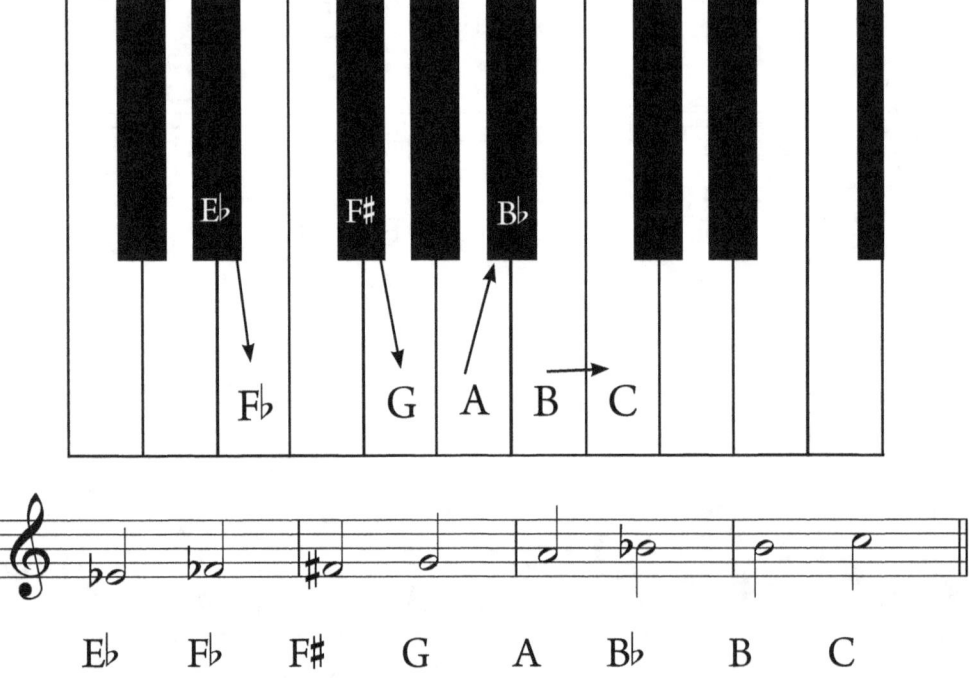

❺ 1. Write diatonic half steps above the following notes.
❻

2. Write diatonic half steps below the following notes.

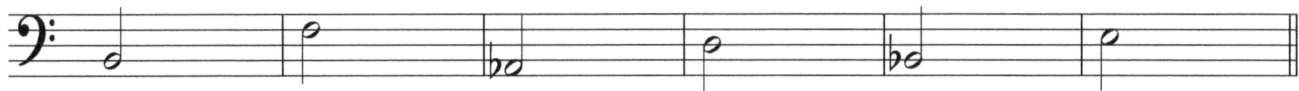

3. Name the following halfs steps as chromatic half steps (CHS) or diatonic half steps (DHS).

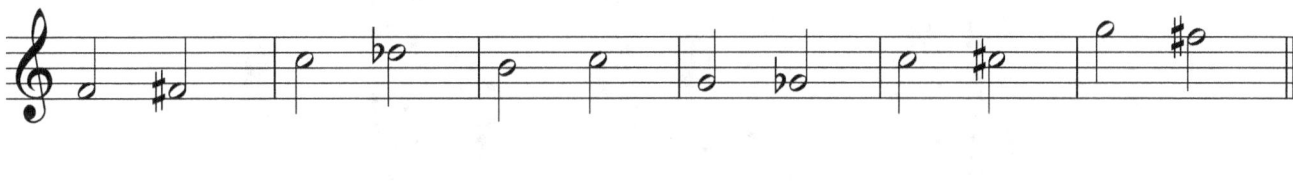

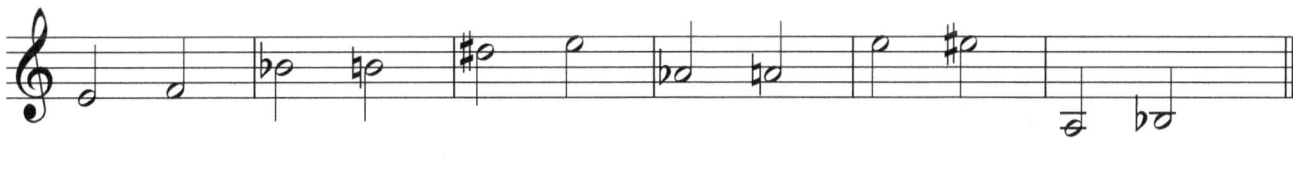

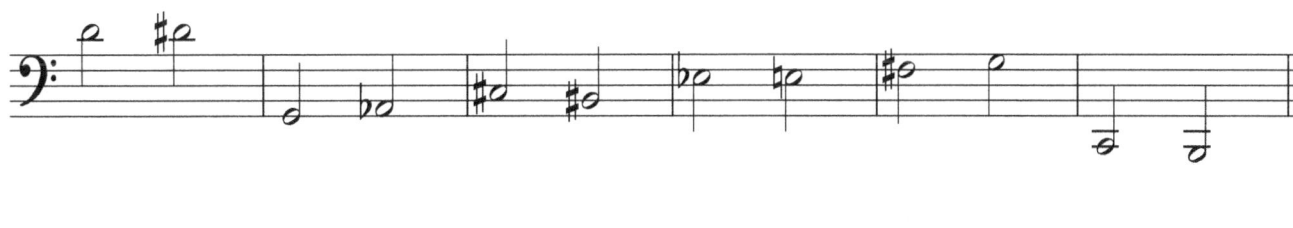

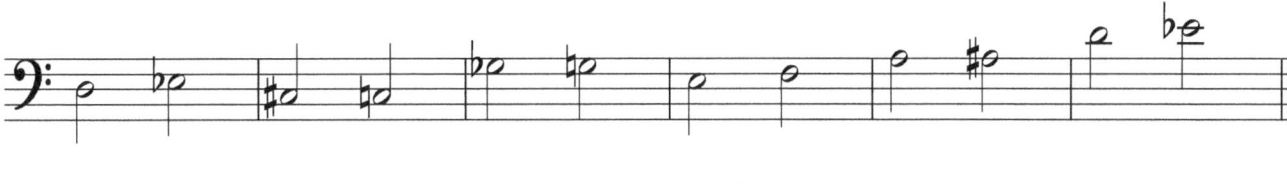

Intervals

Whole Steps

A ***whole step*** is made up of two half steps. On the keyboard, there is always one key in the middle of a whole step. Sometimes the key is black, and sometimes it is white.

Figure 5.8 shows whole steps written on the score in music notation and where they occur on the keyboard. A whole step always contains two different letter names in alphabetical order. For example, F - G, A♭ - B♭, C♯ - D♯, or if it's a whole step below, D - C, B♭ - A♭, etc.

Figure 5.8

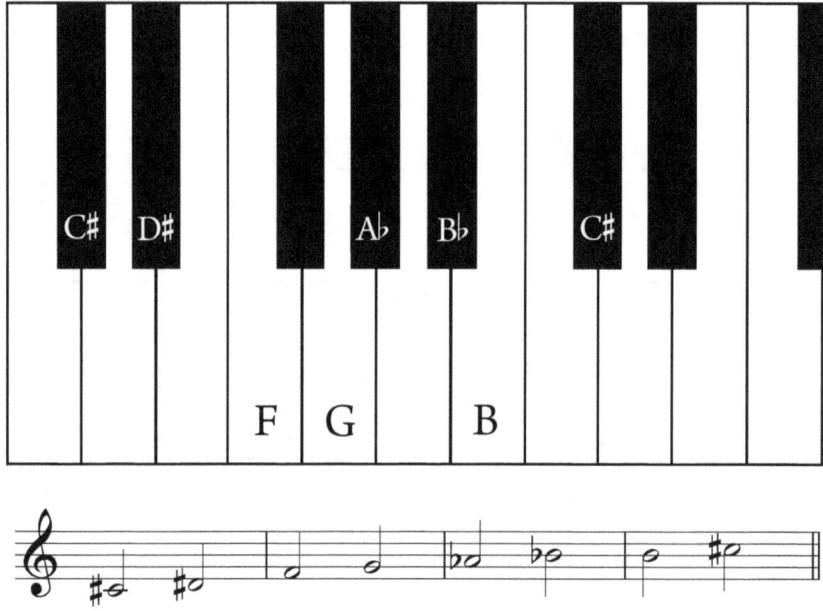

1. Write whole steps above the following notes.

2. Write whole steps below the following notes.

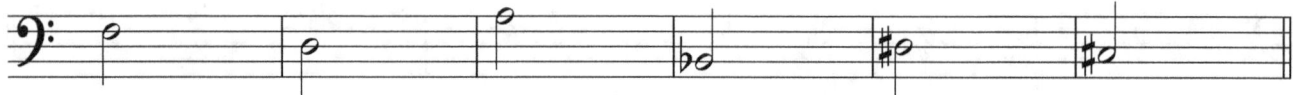

Intervals

1. Name the following major intervals. Rewrite them, making them minor, by lowering the top note one half step. Rename each interval. The first one is done for you.

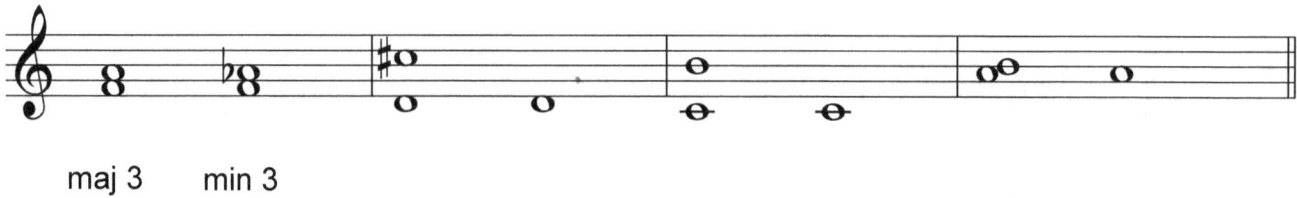

maj 3   min 3

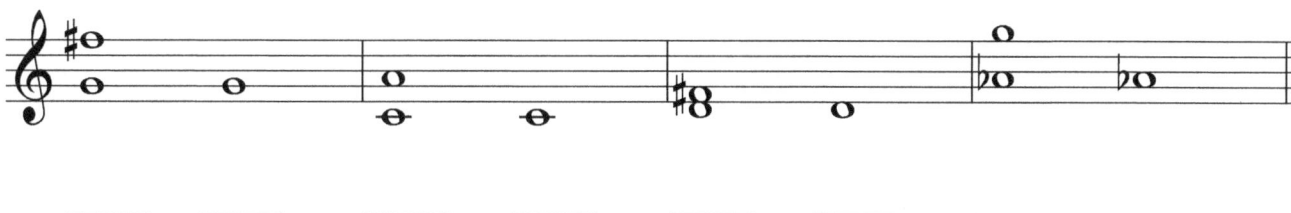

2. Name the intervals under the brackets.

Carl Maria von Weber
Der Freischutz

Ludwig van Beethoven
Sonata Op. 10 No. 2

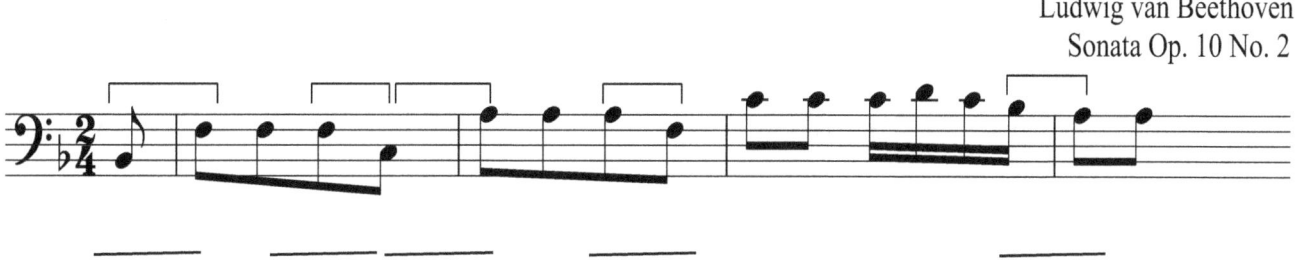

❺ 3. Name the following intervals.
❻

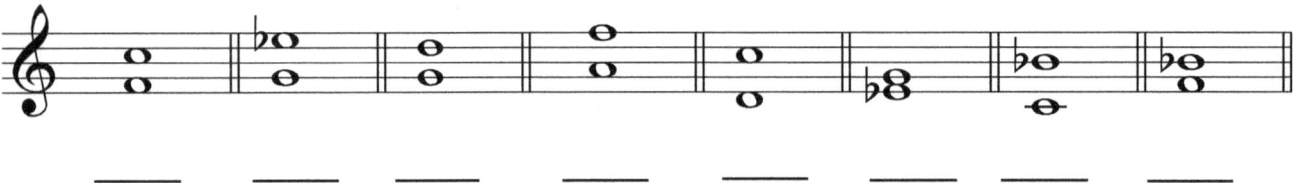

4. Write the following harmonic intervals above the given notes.

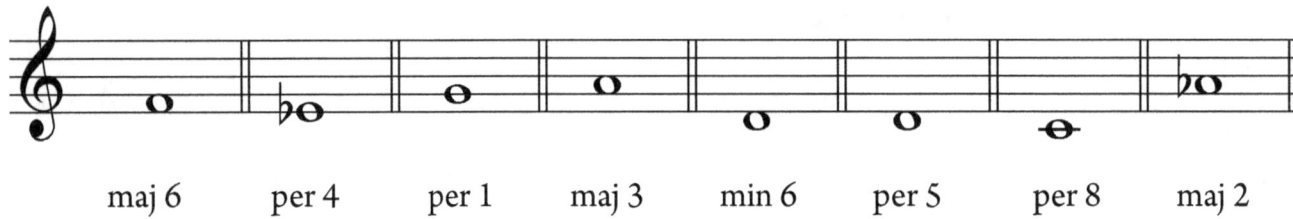

maj 6   per 4   per 1   maj 3   min 6   per 5   per 8   maj 2

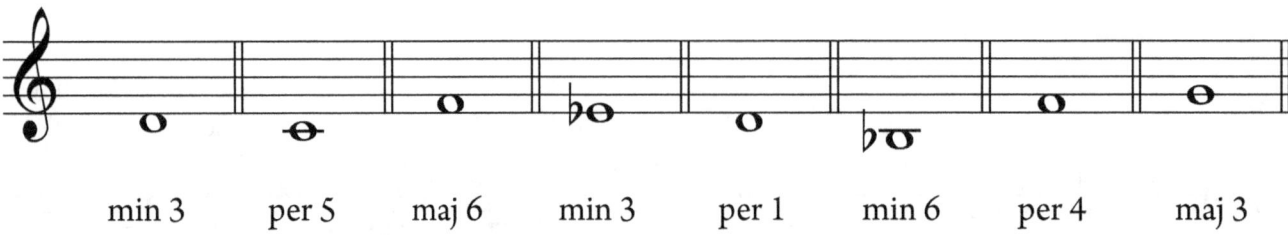

min 3   per 5   maj 6   min 3   per 1   min 6   per 4   maj 3

Accidental Placement

When placing accidentals in front of intervals:

a. For interval numbers from 2 to 6, place the upper accidental closest to the note and the lower accidental to the left.
b. If the two accidentals of a 6th don't collide, they can be aligned vertically.
c. For an interval greater than a 6th, the intervals can align vertically.

Figure 5.9

1. Name the following intervals.

2. Write the following melodic intervals above the given notes.

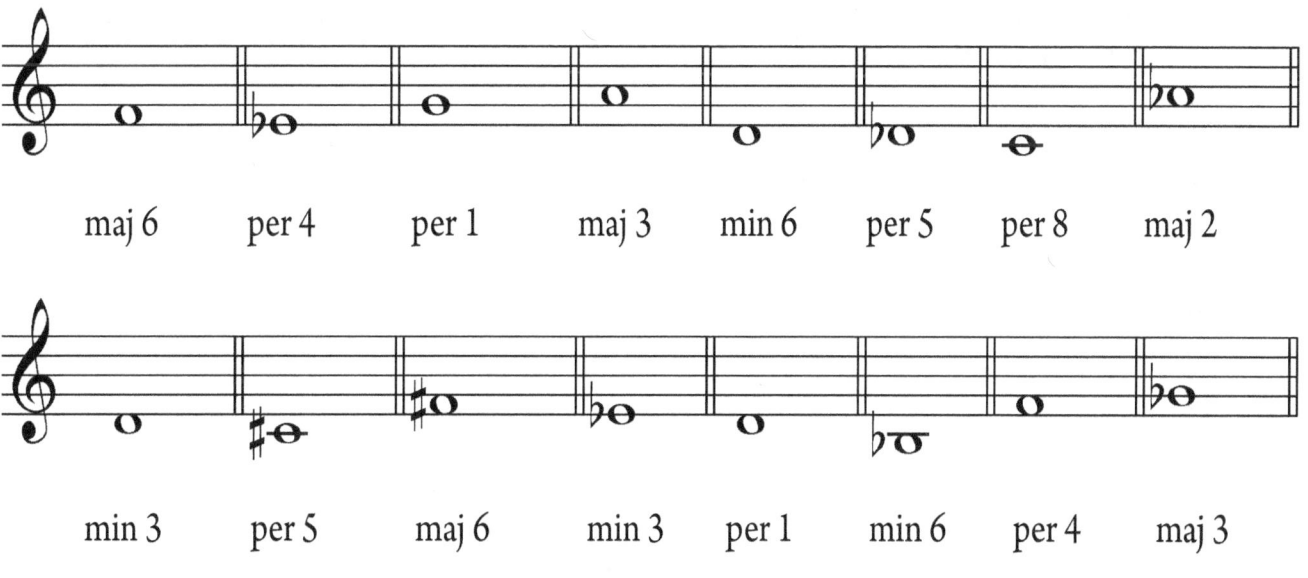

Augmented Intervals

An ***augmented interval*** is an interval that is a half step larger than a perfect or major interval. Another way to look at this is: the notes of the augmented interval are one half step further apart than the notes of a major or perfect interval.

Figure 5.10 shows that raising the top note of a major or perfect interval creates an augmented interval. Compare these intervals with those found in Figure 6.44.

Figure 5.10

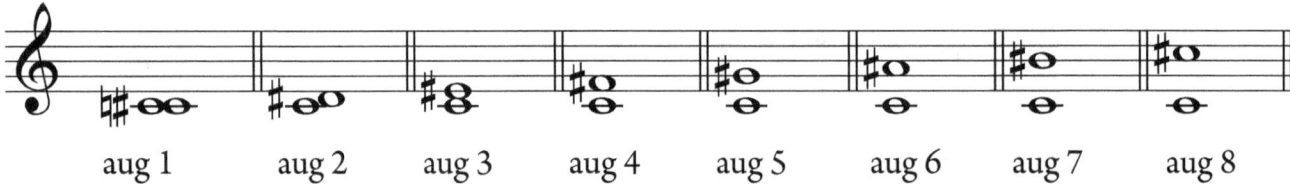

aug 1   aug 2   aug 3   aug 4   aug 5   aug 6   aug 7   aug 8

Another way to create an augmented interval is to lower the bottom note one half step. This makes the note one half step further apart and results in an augmented interval.

The intervals in Figure 5.11 are all augmented.

Figure 5.11

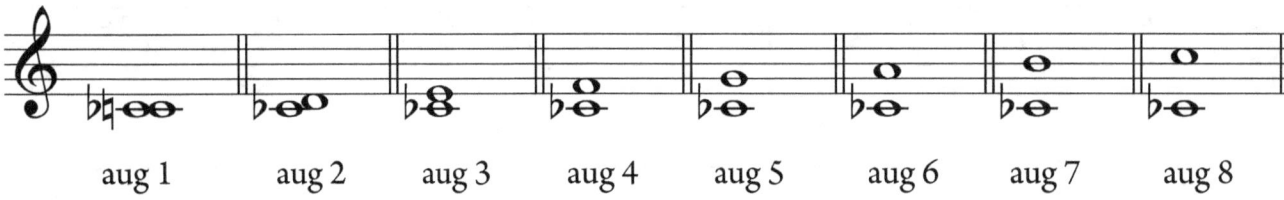

aug 1   aug 2   aug 3   aug 4   aug 5   aug 6   aug 7   aug 8

1. The following intervals are major or perfect. In the second measure, rewrite them and change the top note to make them augmented. Name each interval.

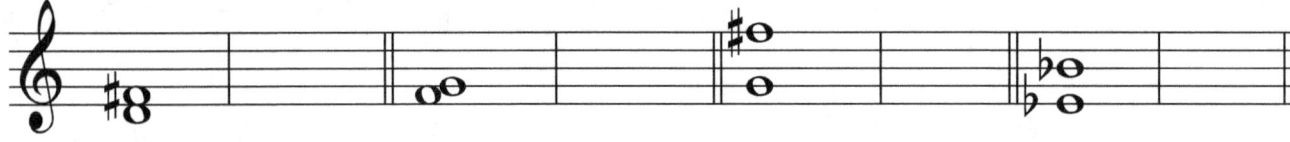

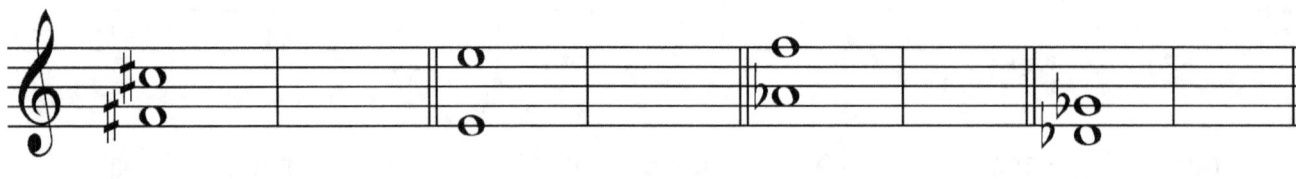

2. The following intervals are major or perfect. In the second measure, rewrite them and change the bottom note to make them augmented. Name each interval.

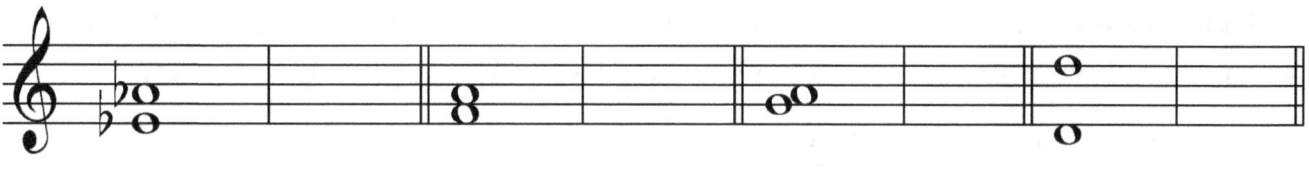

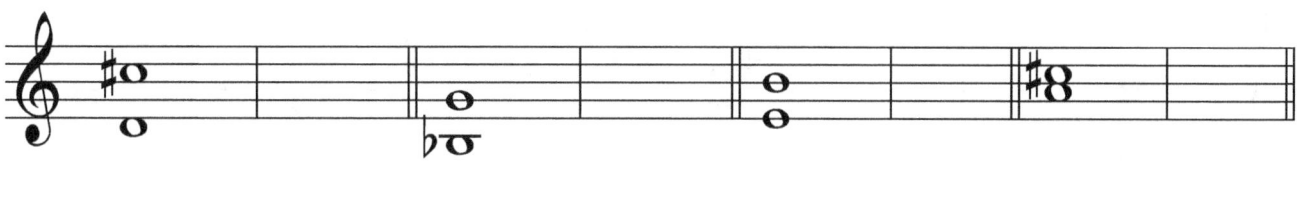

3. Write the following melodic intervals above the given notes.

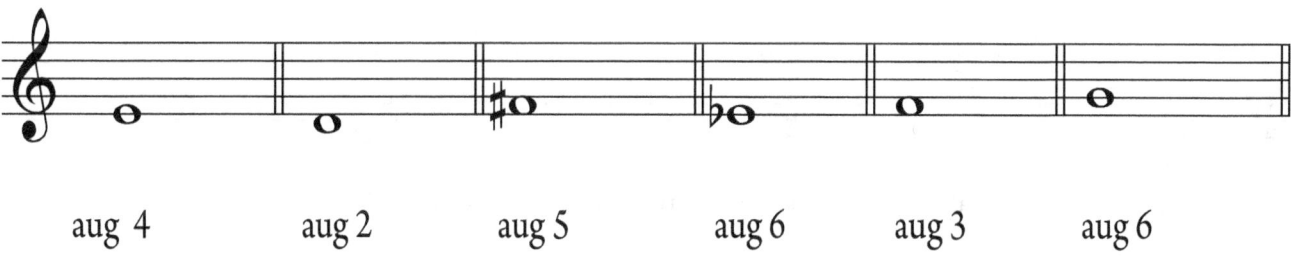

aug 4   aug 2   aug 5   aug 6   aug 3   aug 6

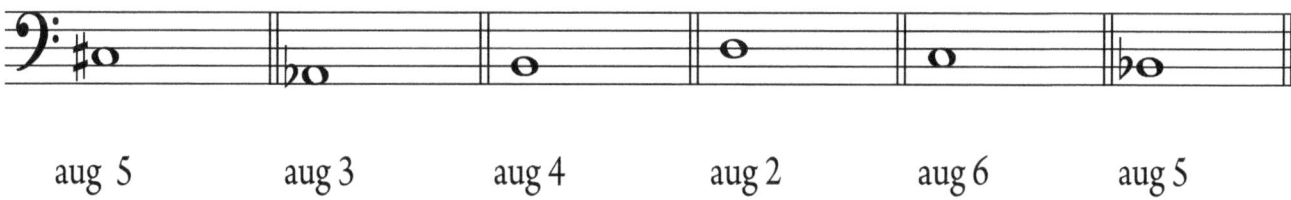

aug 5   aug 3   aug 4   aug 2   aug 6   aug 5

Diminished Intervals

A ***diminished interval*** is one half step smaller than a perfect interval. Lowering the top note or raising the bottom note of a perfect interval one half step results in a diminished interval.

Figure 5.12 contains diminished intervals.

Figure 5.12

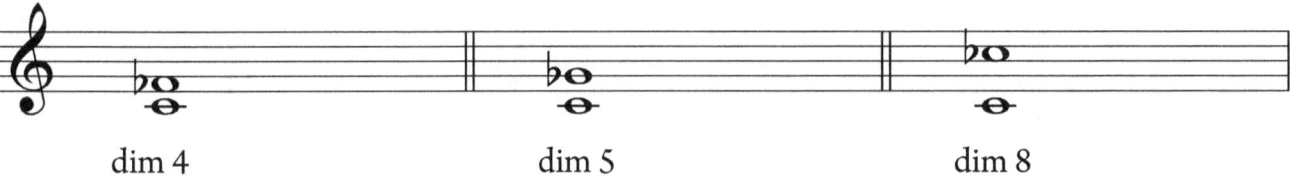

dim 4   dim 5   dim 8

When the top note of a major interval is lowered one half step it becomes minor. When it is lowered two half steps the interval becomes diminished.

Figure 5.13 shows these interval relationships.

Figure 5.13

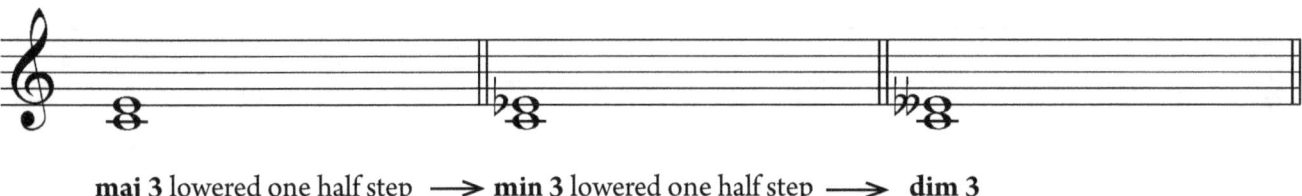

maj 3 lowered one half step ⟶ **min 3** lowered one half step ⟶ **dim 3**

A major interval can be made diminished by raising the bottom note two half steps. Raising the bottom note brings the notes closer together.

Figure 5.14 shows that raising the bottom note of a major 3rd one half step produces a minor 3rd. Raising it two half steps produces a diminished 3rd.

Figure 5.14

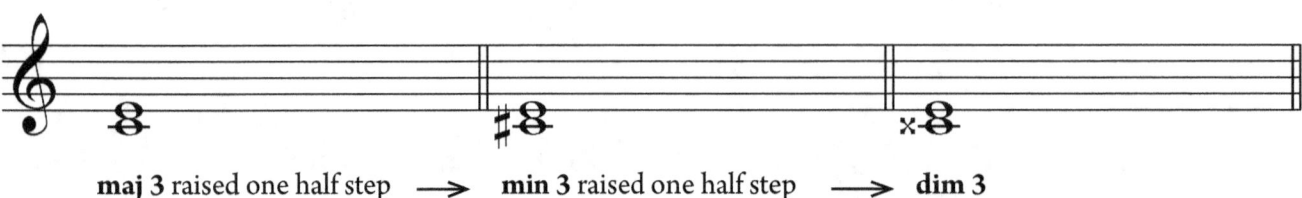

maj 3 raised one half step ⟶ **min 3** raised one half step ⟶ **dim 3**

❻ Intervals are always solved using the bottom note as the key note. This is true even if the bottom note comes after the top note in a melodic interval.

In Figure 5.15 both intervals are a minor 6th. The lowest note in the second interval comes after the highest note but the interval is still a minor 6th.

Figure 5.15

min 6   min 6

We consider the perfect unison the smallest interval, even though a unison is not really an interval. An interval is defined as the distance between two notes. There is no distance between the notes of a unison.

The unison requires special consideration. Since there is no distance between the notes of a unison, it cannot be made smaller. Unisons can never be diminished intervals. If any note of a unison is altered, the notes become further away from each other, and it becomes augmented.
Study Figure 5.16.

Figure 5.16

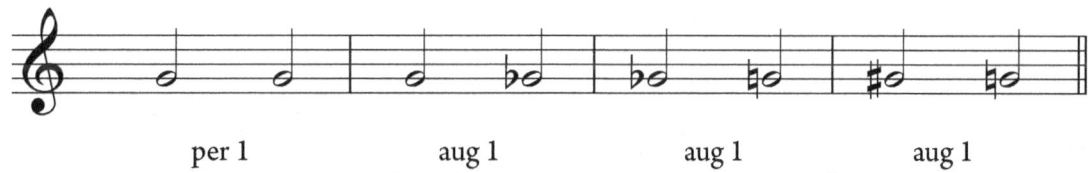

per 1   aug 1   aug 1   aug 1

This chart shows the relationship between intervals. The arrow indicates the movement of one half step.

diminished ← minor ← **major** → augmented

diminshed ← **perfect** → augmented

The intervals in each measure of Figure 5.17 sound exactly the same, but are named differently. The top note in example a) is changed enharmonically from B♭ to A♯, and the bottom note in example b) is changed enharmonically from A♭ to G♯. Even though the pitch does not change, the interval number and quality changes.

Figure 5.17

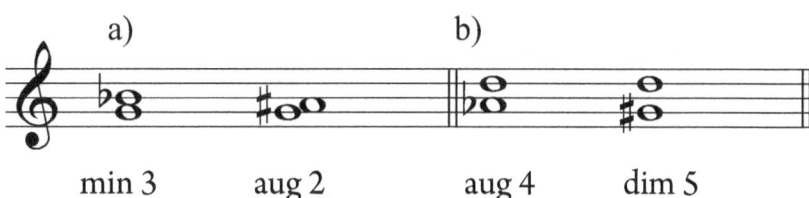

min 3   aug 2   aug 4   dim 5

1. The following intervals are major or perfect. In the second measure, rewrite them and change the top note to make them diminished. Name each interval.

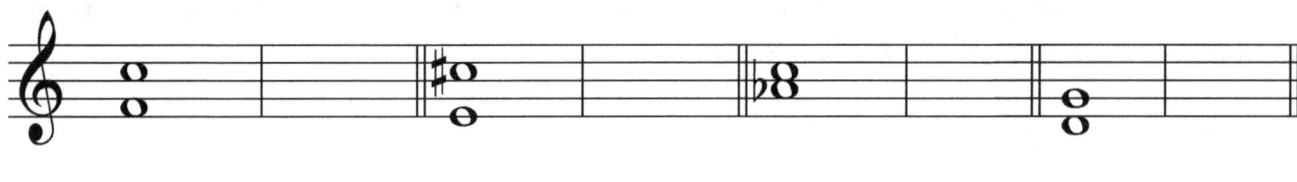

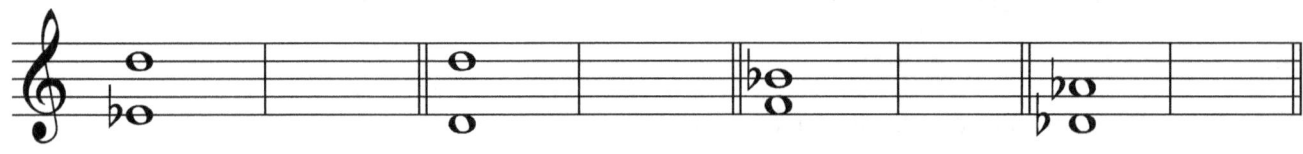

2. The following intervals are major or perfect. In the second measure, rewrite them and change the bottom note to make them diminished. Name each interval.

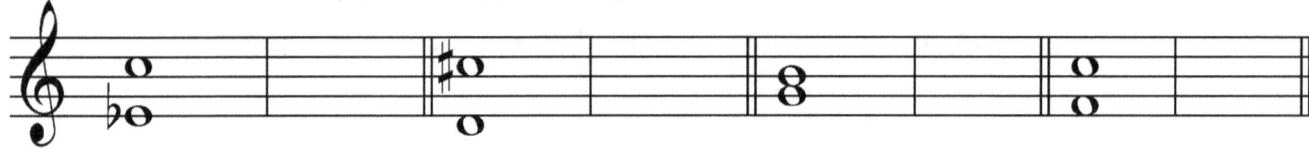

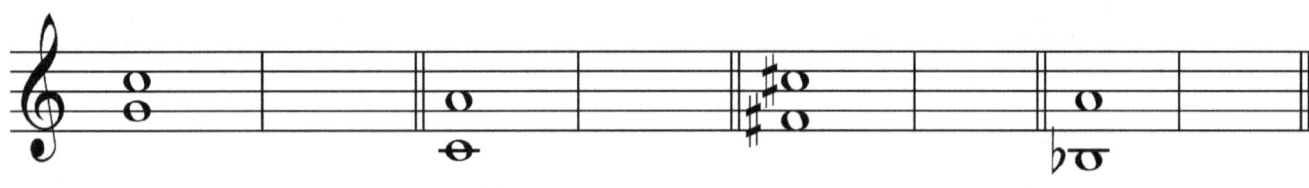

3. Write the following melodic intervals above the given notes.

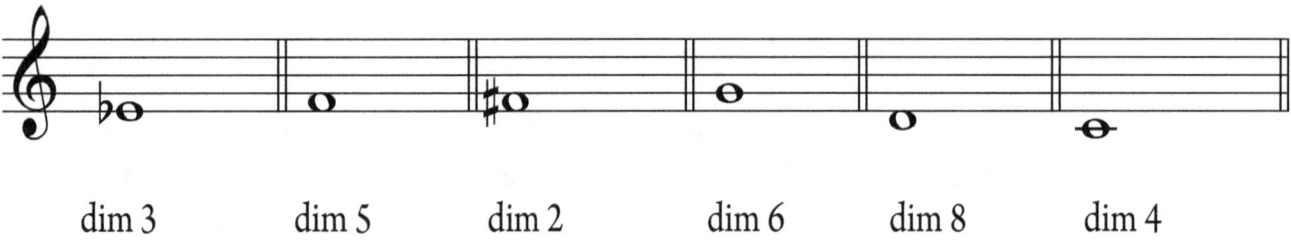

dim 3   dim 5   dim 2   dim 6   dim 8   dim 4

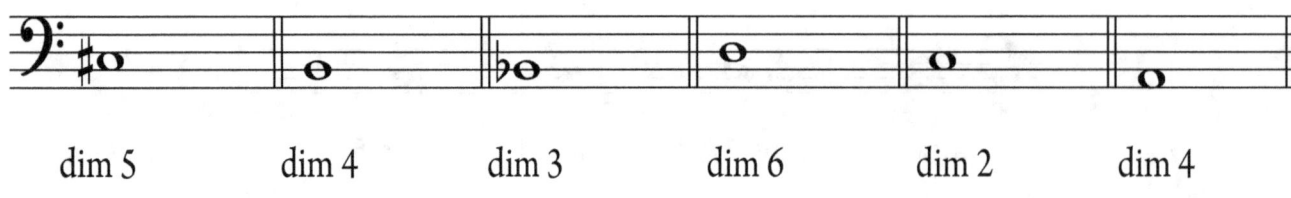

dim 5   dim 4   dim 3   dim 6   dim 2   dim 4

❻ 4. Name the following intervals.

5. Name the following melodic intervals.

Frederic Chopin
Ballade, Op 23, No. 1

6. Write the following melodic intervals.

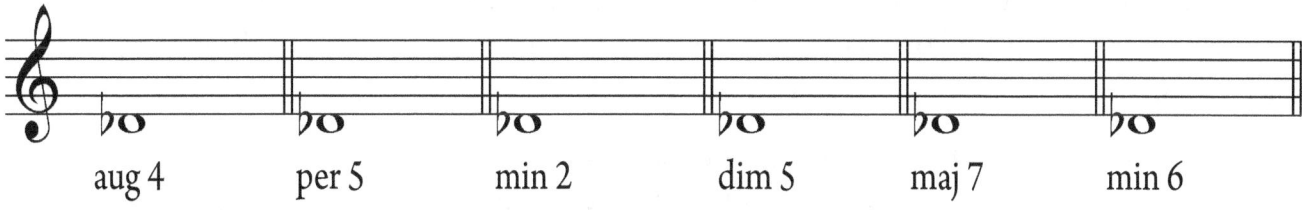

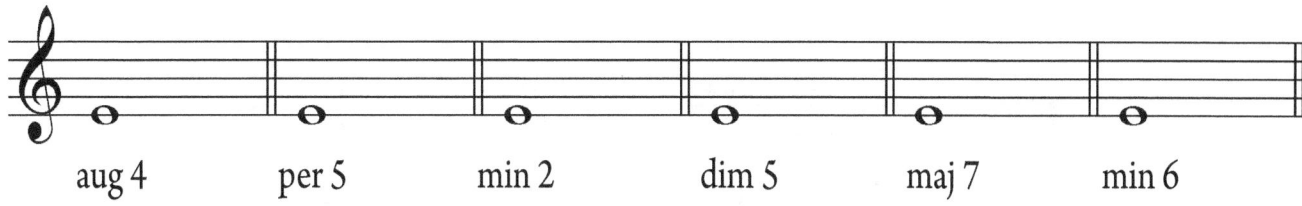

⁶Solving Unusual Intervals

Sometimes the bottom note of an interval is not the tonic of a logical major key.

The lowest note in the interval in Figure 5.18 is a D♯. D♯ is not the tonic of a major key.

Figure 5.18

? 3

To solve this interval:
1. Since both notes have the same accidental, a sharp, remove both sharps (Figure 5.19).
2. With the sharps removed the bottom note is now D, a logical key.
3. The interval D to F is a minor 3rd. Since D♯ to F♯ is the same distance a half step higher, it is also a minor 3rd. The interval number and quality is the same with the added sharps. D♭ to F♭ is also a minor 3rd, being a half step lower than D to F. The movement up or down by half step does not change the interval quality.

Figure 5.19

The interval in Figure 5.20a has an A♯ as its lowest note. We know this interval is a 4th since the letter names are A to D (A-B-C-D = 1-2-3-4). A♯ is not the tonic of a major key. By lowering it a half step to A♮, we have the tonic of logical key (A major). Since we lowered the bottom note one half step, we must lower the top note one half step. D becomes D♭. A to D♭ is a dim 4th. Therefore, A♯ to D is also a dim 4th.

Figure 5.20b contains F♭ as its lowest note. When we raise it one half step, we get a logical major key, F major. Since we raised the bottom note a half step, we must raise the top note a half step from D to D♯. F to D♯ is the interval of an aug 6th. Therefore, F♭ to D is also an aug 6th.

Figure 5.20

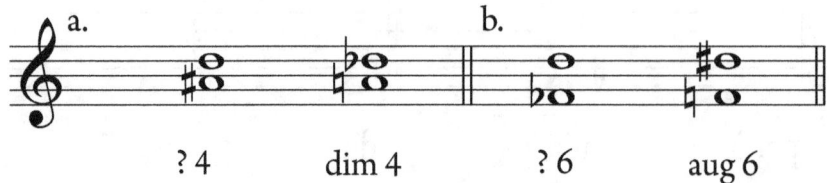

1. Name the following intervals.

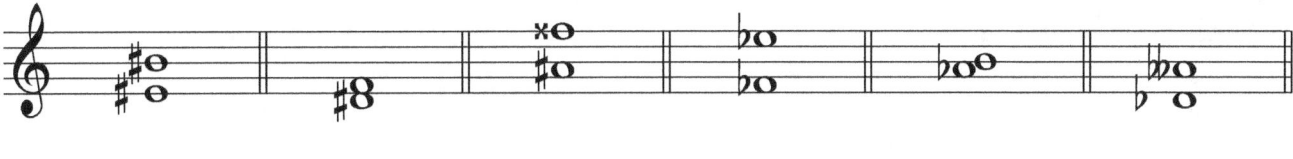

2. Name the following intervals.

3. Rewrite the above intervals changing the upper note enharmonically. Rename them.

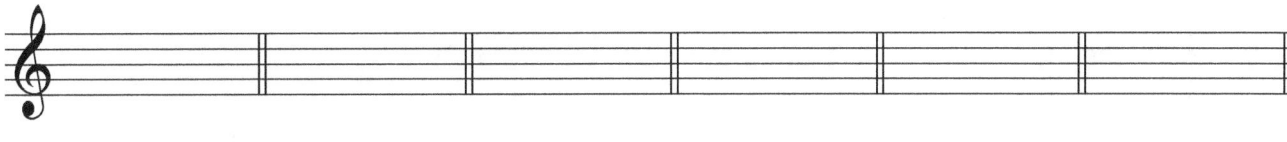

4. Name the intervals under the brackets.

Felix Mendelssohn
Trio in C minor

Antonin Dvorak
Trio in F minor, II

Ludwig van Beethoven
Symphony No. 9. III

Johann Sebastian Bach
Sonata No. 1 in B minor

Intervals

Music Terms

Study the following music terms

ad libitum, ad lib	at the liberty of the performer
alla, all'	in the manner of
animato	animated
loco	return to the normal register
ma	but
meno	less
meno mosso	less motion or movement
non	not
piu	more
piu mosso	more movement
poco a poco	little by little
primo, prima	first, the upper part of a duet
quasi	almost, as if

6
Chords

A chord consists of three or more notes that are sounded at the same time. Chords may be played by a solo instrument like a piano or a guitar. They may also be played by many instruments at once, like an orchestra or a string quartet. The instruments work together to create chords. Like intervals, there are different qualities of chords. The quality is determined by the intervals that make up the chord. In this level, we will study *major* and *minor triads*.

Major Triads

A triad is a three note chord consisting of a root, third and fifth. Major triads are considered "major" because they are made up of certain intervals.

A major triad consists of a major third and a perfect fifth above the root.

Figure 6.1 contains a major triad built on the root D. There is a major third between D and F♯ and a perfect fifth between D and A. All major triads contain these intervals between the root and third and the root and fifth.

Figure 6.1

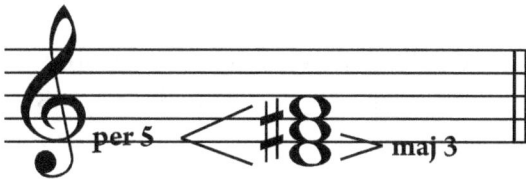

D - F♯ = major 3rd
D - A = perfect 5th

Triads in Major Keys

In a major key, there are three major triads. They occur when you build triads on $\hat{1}$, $\hat{4}$, and $\hat{5}$ of the major scale. They are considered the tonic, subdominant and dominant triads in a key. Figure 6.2 contains the triads built on these scale degrees in C major. All three are major triads because they consist of a major 3rd and perfect fifth above the root.

Figure 6.2

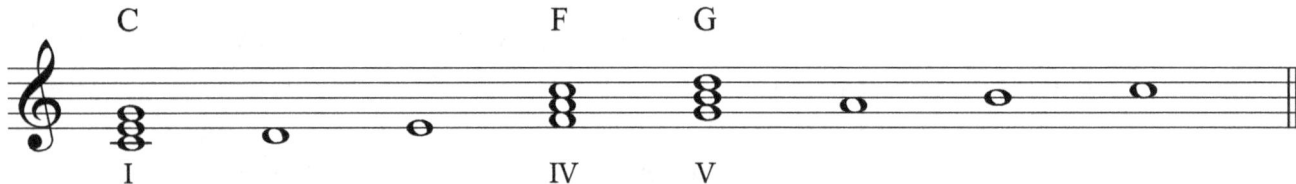

Chord Symbols

We label chords with symbols. A chord can have two symbols. A Roman numeral placed under the chord and a letter name placed above the chord. The Roman numeral is known as a ***functional chord symbol*** and the letter is known as a ***root/quality chord symbol***.

Each Roman numeral corresponds to the scale degree that the chord was built upon. Major triads always receive an uppercase Roman numeral as shown in Figure 6.2.

- The chord built on $\hat{1}$ is the *tonic triad* and it's Roman numeral is **I**.
- The chord built on $\hat{4}$ is the *subdominant triad* and it's Roman numeral is **IV**.
- The chord built on $\hat{5}$ is the *dominant triad* and it's Roman numeral is **V**.

Chords may also have a letter name called the root/quality chord symbol. This name comes from the root of the chord. The letter indicates the root of the chord. The letter written by itself as a capitol letter means that the chord is major.

In C major: The chord built on $\hat{1}$ (C), uses the root/quality chord symbol **C**.
The chord built on $\hat{4}$ (F), uses the root/quality chord symbol **F**.
The chord built on $\hat{5}$ (G), uses the root/quality chord symbol **G**.

❹ 1. Write triads on $\hat{1}$, $\hat{4}$, and $\hat{5}$ of the following major scales. Add the functional and the root/qual-
❺ ity chord symbols.
❻

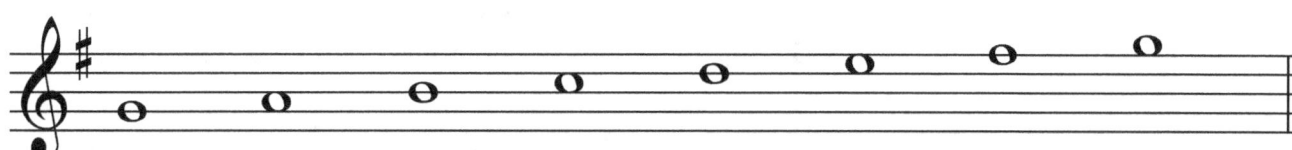

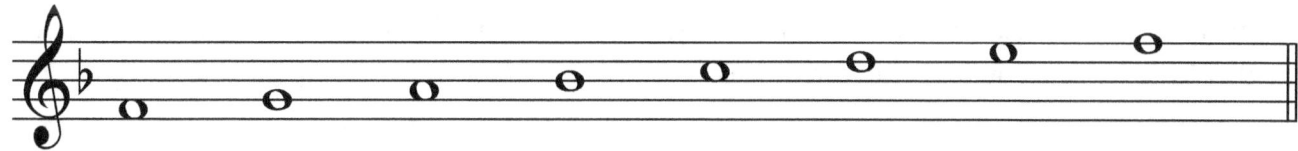

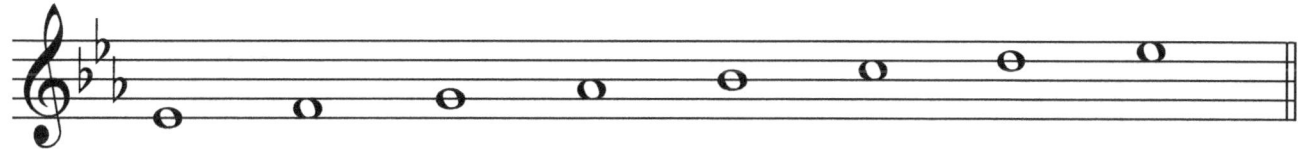

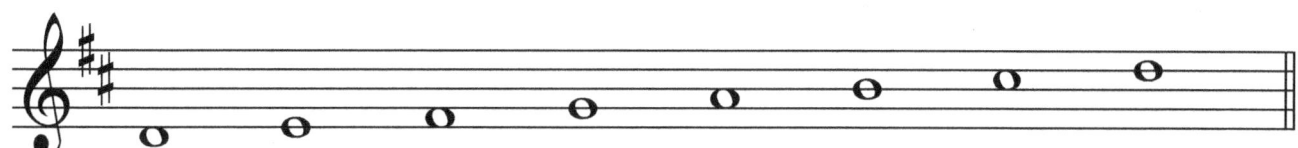

❹ 2. Write the following solid triads using key signatures. Add functional and root/quality chord
❺   symbols to each.
❻

| The tonic triad of C major | The dominant triad of E♭ major | The subdominant triad of D major | The tonic triad of F major |

| The dominant triad of A major | The tonic triad of B♭ major | The subdominant triad of C major | The dominant triad of G major |

| The tonic triad of G major | The dominant triad of B♭ major | The subdominant triad of F major | The tonic triad of A major |

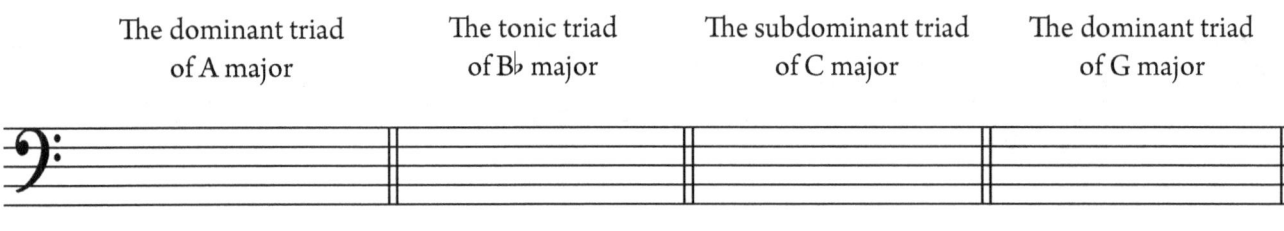

3. For the following triads: Name the major key. Identify the triad as tonic, subdominant, or dominant. Write the root/quality chord symbols for each.

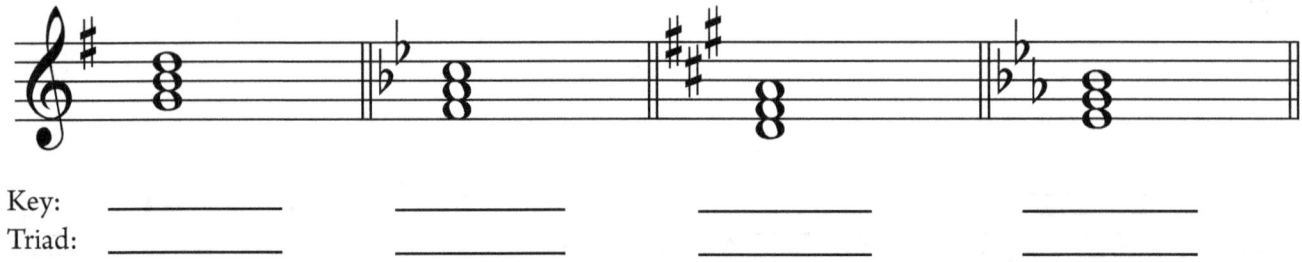

Key: _____   _____   _____   _____
Triad: _____   _____   _____   _____

Chords

Minor Triads

Minor triads are considered "minor" because they are made up of specific intervals.

A minor triad consists of a minor third and a perfect fifth above the root.

Figure 6.3 contains a minor triad built on the root D. There is a minor third between D and F and a perfect fifth between D and A. All minor triads contain these intervals between the root and third and the root and fifth.

Figure 6.3

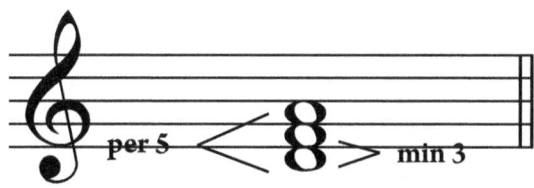

D - F = minor 3rd
D - A = perfect 5th

Triads in Minor Keys

Triads built on $\hat{1}$, $\hat{4}$, and $\hat{5}$ of the harmonic minor scale result in two minor triads (tonic and subdominant) and one major triad (dominant). The dominant triad contains raised $\hat{7}$ and is a major triad. For now, we will always use the harmonic form of the minor scale with raised $\hat{7}$ when building the dominant triad in the minor key.

Figure 6.4 contains the triads built on $\hat{1}$, $\hat{4}$, and $\hat{5}$ in D minor. Functional chord symbols for minor chords use lower case Roman numerals (i, iv). Root/quality symbols for minor chords use the letter name of the root with an "m" beside it to indicate minor (Dm, Gm). Some books use 'min' for minor chords (Dmin, Gmin)

Figure 6.4

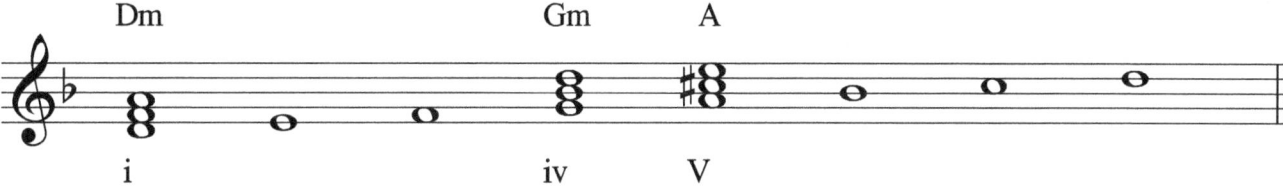

1. Write triads on $\hat{1}$, $\hat{4}$, and $\hat{5}$ of the following harmonic minor scales. Add the functional and the root/quality chord symbols.

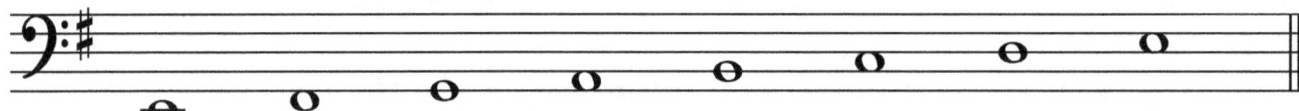

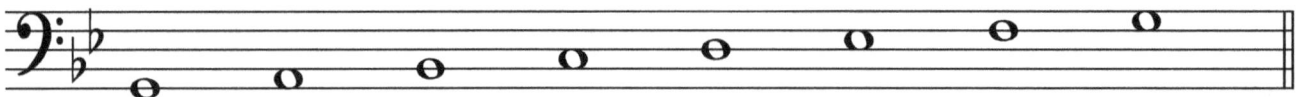

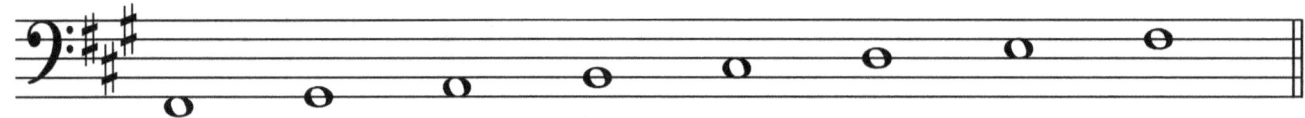

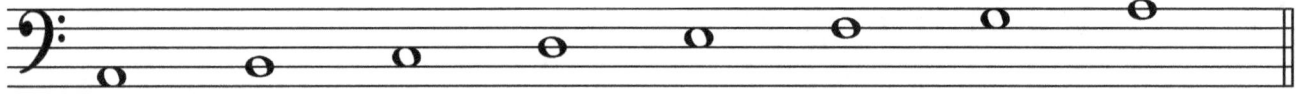

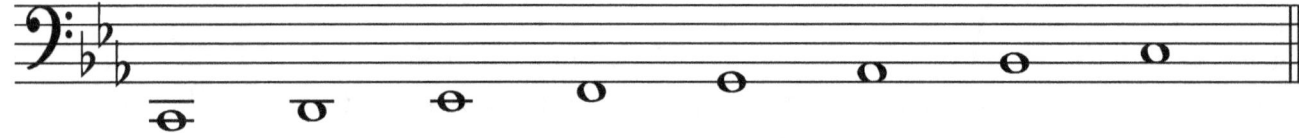

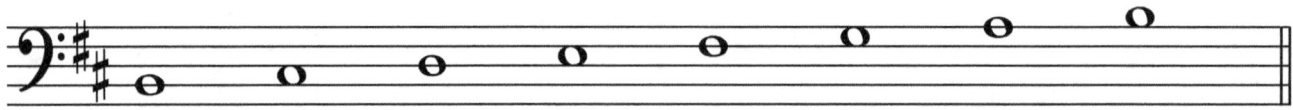

❹2. Write the following solid triads using key signatures. Add functional and root/quality chord
❺ symbols to each.
❻

| The tonic triad of D minor | The dominant triad of G minor | The subdominant triad of C minor | The tonic triad of A minor |

| The dominant triad of B minor | The tonic triad of F# minor | The subdominant triad of E minor | The dominant triad of E minor |

| The tonic triad of C minor | The dominant triad of F# minor | The subdominant triad of D minor | The tonic triad of E minor |

3. For the following triads: Name the minor key. Identify the triad as tonic, subdominant, or dominant. Write the functional chord symbols for each.

Key: _____ _____ _____ _____
Triad: _____ _____ _____ _____

⁵⁄₆ Triad Inversions

Root Position

The three notes of a triad can be placed in a different order within the chord. The lowest note of a triad is very important because it determines its position. If the lowest note is the root, the triad is in *root position*. This is the most common triad. The triads that we have studied so far have been in root position.

First Inversion

Whenever another note of the triad is the lowest note, the triad is in **inversion**. A *first inversion triad* has the third as the lowest note. The order of the notes of the rest of the chord makes no difference. The bottom note determines the position.

Figure 6.5 contains the E♭ major triad in root positon and first inversion. When the 3rd of the triad (G) is the lowest note, the triad in in first inversion.

The chords have been named in two ways. The root/quality symbol for first inversion is **E♭/G**. This means that it is the E♭ major triad with G on the bottom. This method of naming chords is typical in popular music. The formula for this is triad/bass note.

The functional chord symbol is **I⁶**. "I" indicates that it is a major triad built on $\hat{1}$ in E♭ major and the "6" indicates that it is in first inversion. The origin of the 6 comes from the interval of a 6th between the lowest note G and the highest note E♭ in the triad.

Figure 6.5

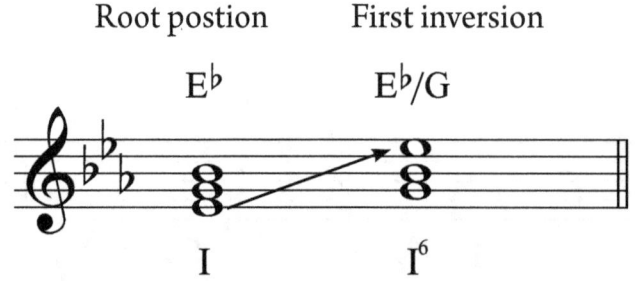

Second Inversion

When the fifth is the lowest note of a triad, it is in *second inversion*. Figure 6.6 contains the E♭ major triad in second inversion. The order of the remaining notes does not matter. The lowest note determines the position. Here, B♭, the fifth of the E♭ major triad is the bottom note making this triad second inversion.

The root/quality chord symbol is **E♭/B♭** indicating the E♭ major triad with B♭ as the lowest note. The functional chord symbol is **I$^6_4$** because the intervals above the lowest note are a 6th and a 4th.

Figure 6.6

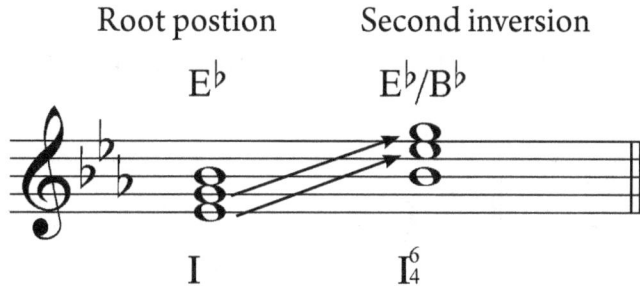

Minor Chord Symbols

The chord symbols for minor triads function in the same way as those for major triads with a few small differences. Figure 6.7 shows the chord symbols for minor triads. In root/quality chord symbols, minor triads are indicated with an "m" beside the uppercase letter. In functional chord symbols, minor triads are shown with a lower case Roman numeral.

Figure 6.7

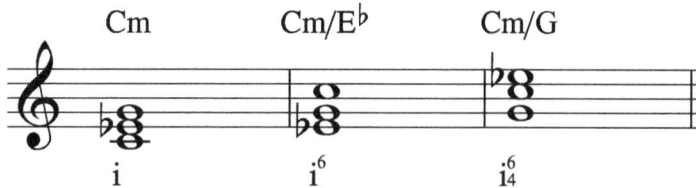

⑤⑥ Accidental Placement

When placing accidentals in front of a triad, if there are two accidentals, the upper accidental goes closest to the note and the lower accidental is placed to the left.

If there are three accidentals, the upper accidental is placed closest to the note, the lower accidental is placed slightly to the left, and the middle accidental is placed even farther left.

Figure 6.8

⑤⑥ 1. Identify the following triads as major or minor. Write the root/quality chord symbols for each.

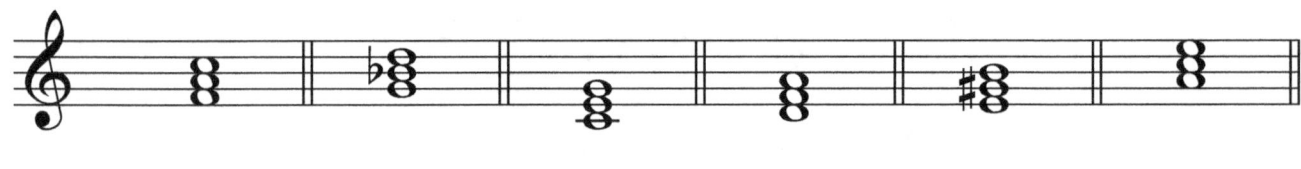

_____   _____   _____   _____   _____   _____

_____   _____   _____   _____   _____   _____

2. Write a major triad and its inversions using the following notes as the root. Write the root/quality chord symbols for each.

Chords

❺ 3. Write a minor triad and its inversions using the following notes as the root.
❻ Write the root/quality chord symbols for each.

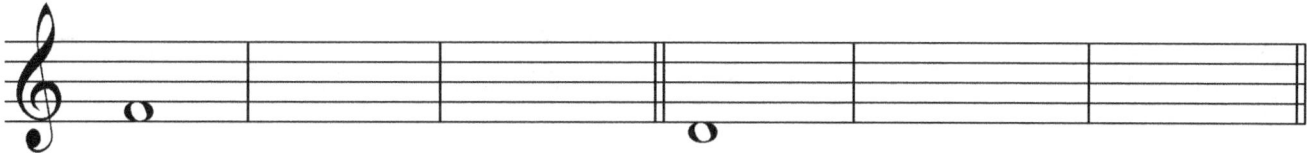

❺❻ Solving Triads

Solving a triad involves stating its root, quality and position. To solve a triad:

1. If it is not in root position, put it into root position. For Figure 6.9 the root is: **E♭**.

Figure 6.9

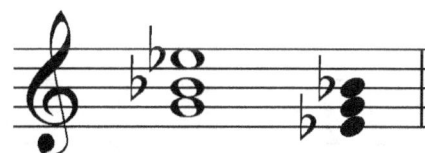

2. Determine the intervals between the root and 3rd and the root and 5th. In Figure 6.10 E♭ to G is a major 3rd and E♭ to B♭ is a perfect 5th making its quality **major**.

Figure 6.10

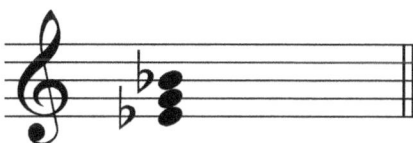

E♭ - G = maj 3   E♭ - B♭ = per 5

3. Examine the lowest note of the given triad. In Figure 6.9 it is the 3rd, G. When the 3rd is the lowest note, the position of the triad is **first inversion**. This triad is solved as follows:

Root: E♭
Quality: major
Position: 1st inversion

❺ 1. Name the root of the following triads.
❻

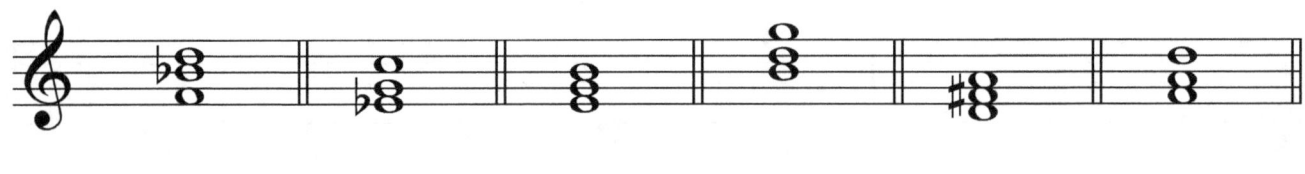

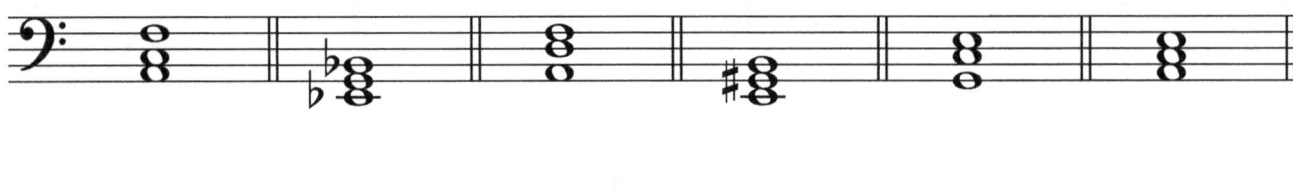

2. Solve the following triads by stating the root, quality, and position.

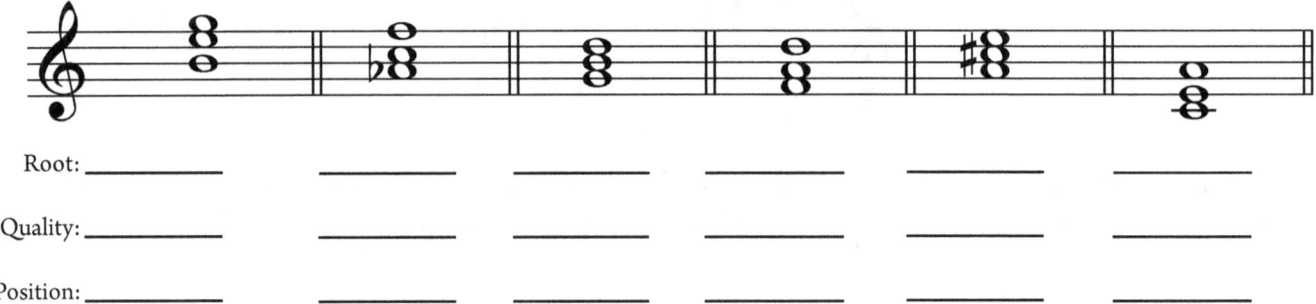

Root: _____   _____   _____   _____   _____   _____

Quality: _____   _____   _____   _____   _____   _____

Position: _____   _____   _____   _____   _____   _____

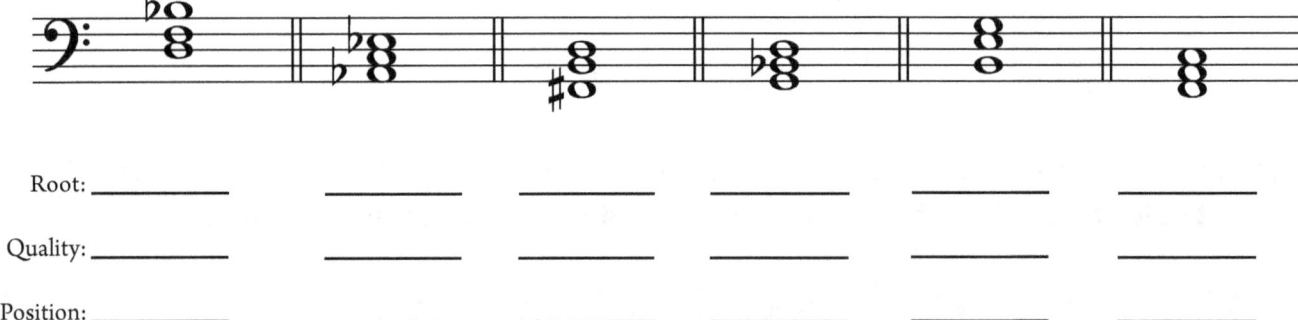

Root: _____   _____   _____   _____   _____   _____

Quality: _____   _____   _____   _____   _____   _____

Position: _____   _____   _____   _____   _____   _____

Primary Triads Built on Major and Minor Scales

The ***primary triads,*** which are the three central triads in any key, are built on scale degrees $\hat{1}$, $\hat{4}$, and $\hat{5}$ of the major and minor scale. Figure 6.11 shows the triads that occur on $\hat{1}$, $\hat{4}$, and $\hat{5}$ of the C major scale.

Each triad is named for the scale degree it is built upon. The triad built on $\hat{1}$, the tonic, is considered the ***tonic triad***. The triad built on $\hat{4}$, the subdominant, is considered the ***subdominant triad***. The triad built on $\hat{5}$ is the ***dominant triad***.

In major keys the triads built on $\hat{1}$, $\hat{4}$ and $\hat{5}$ are major triads.

Figure 6.11

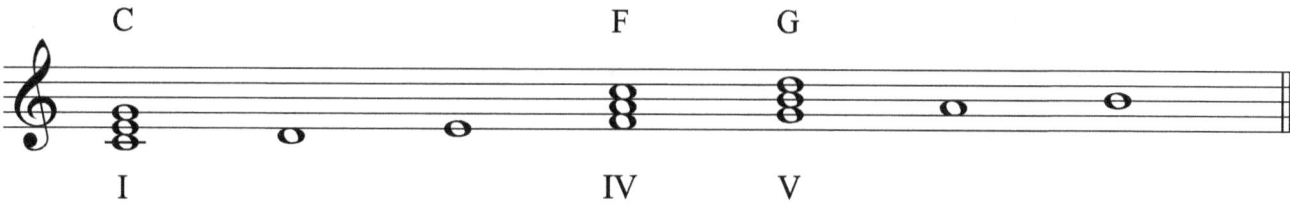

Figure 6.12 shows the triads built on $\hat{1}$, $\hat{4}$, and $\hat{5}$ of the A harmonic minor scale.

Minor triads occur on the tonic ($\hat{1}$) and subdominant ($\hat{4}$). A major triad occurs on the dominant ($\hat{5}$). The dominant triad contains raised $\hat{7}$.

Figure 6.12

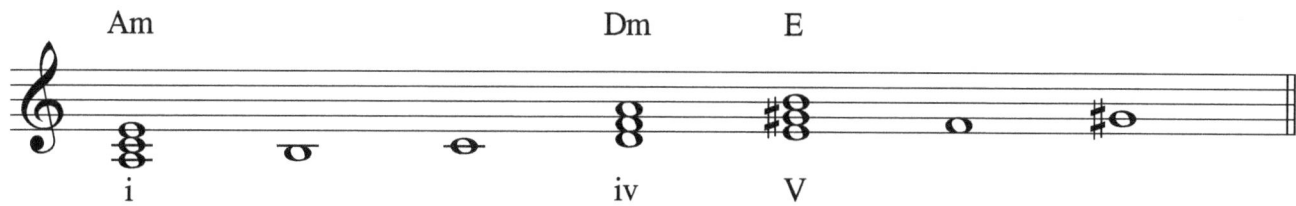

❺ 1. Build triads in the places indicated by Roman numerals on the following scales. Add the root/
❻   quality chord symbols above each triad.

D major

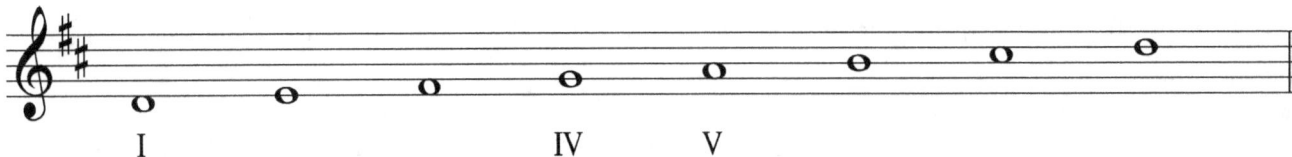

B♭ major

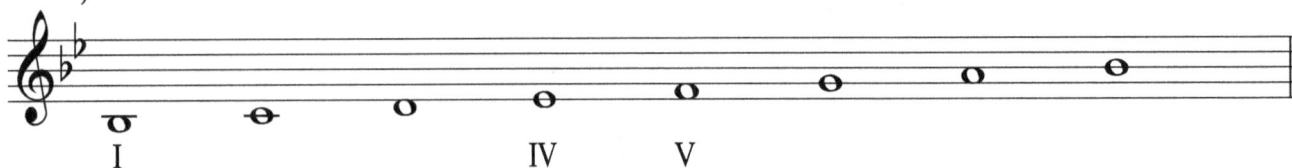

E minor

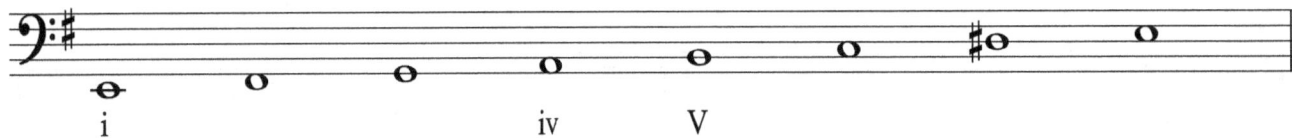

D minor

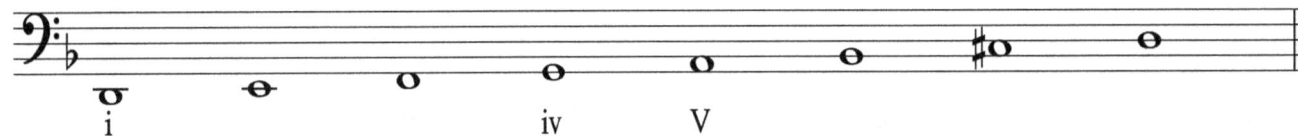

2. Write the following triads as indicated using a key signature for each. Add the root/quality chord symbol to each.

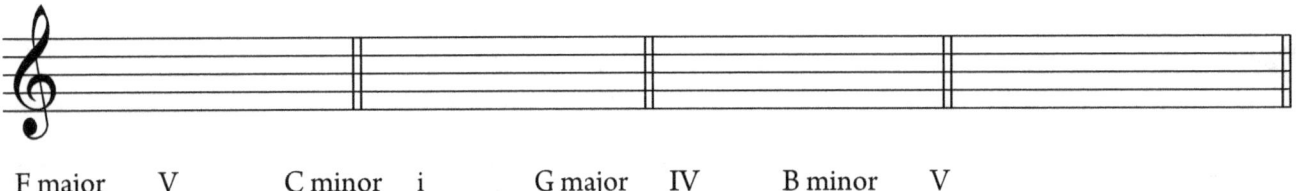

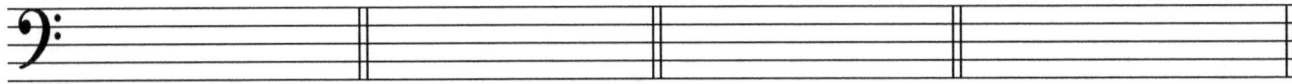

3. Write the following triads using a key signature for each. Write the functional chord symbol.

| The tonic triad in F major | The dominant triad in C minor | The subdominant triad in B♭ major | The dominant triad in D minor |

| The subdominant triad in F minor | The tonic triad in E major | The dominant triad in B minor | The subdominant triad in A♭ major |

4. Write the following triads using accidentals instead of a key signature.

    a) the tonic triad of G minor in second inversion
    b) the dominant triad of D major in root position
    c) the subdominant triad of E minor in first inversion
    d) the dominant triad of C♯ minor in root position
    e) the tonic triad of E♭ major in first inversion
    f) the subdominant triad of F♯ minor in second inversion

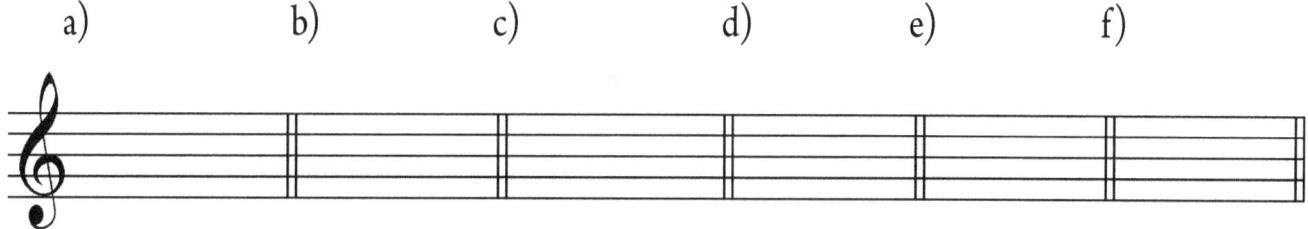

The Dominant Seventh Chord

Seventh chords are very common in Western music and we hear them all the time.

One of the most common seventh chords is the **dominant seventh.** The functional chord symbol for the dominant seventh is V^7. This means that the chord is built on scale degree $\hat{5}$ (the dominant) and there is the interval of a seventh above the root of the chord. It contains four notes: the root, the 3rd, the 5th and the 7th. V^7 is a major triad with a minor 7th above the root. In other words, the intervals above the root are a major 3rd, perfect 5th and a minor 7th.

Figure 6.13 contains the dominant triad and the dominant seventh chord in C major. The root/quality chord symbol for V^7 is G^7.

Figure 6.13

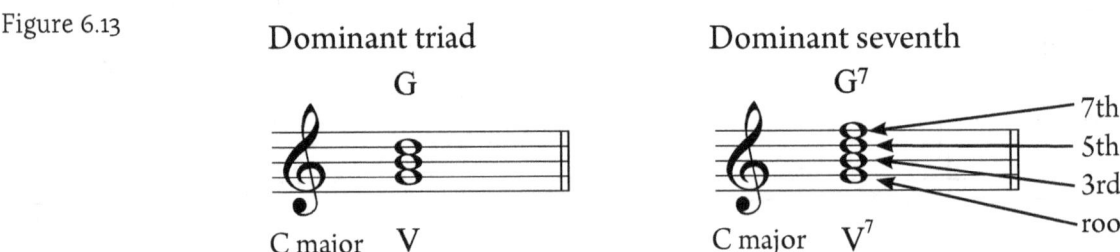

V^7 contains certain notes, like the leading tone, which pull our ear toward the tonic chord.

Figure 6.14 shows V^7 chords in C and G major and D and E minor. When we use a key signature for these chords, the seventh of V^7 is automatically a minor seventh. In minor keys V^7, like V needs a raised $\hat{7}$.

Figure 6.14

The dominant seventh sounds the same in tonic major and minor keys.

Figure 6.15 show the dominant seventh chords in F major and F minor. Even though the notation is different they sound the same and are made up of the same notes.

Figure 6.15

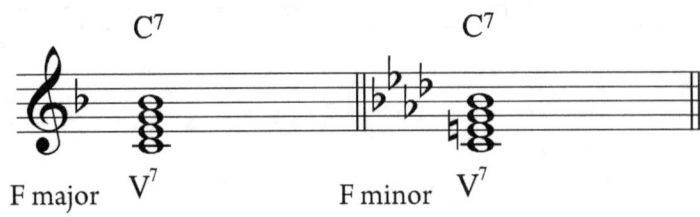

© San Marco Publications 2023

Chords

A Note About Terminology

The leading tone is the seventh degree of the scale. It may also be referred to as scale degree 7 ($\hat{7}$). We don't call the leading tone the "seventh." It is considered the *leading tone* or *scale degree seven* ($\hat{7}$). The word "seventh" is the term reserved to indicate the seventh of a seventh chord. In this case the word seventh may also be abbreviated to "7th."

The dominant 7th chord in C major is GBDF. F is the 7th of this chord. B, the 3rd of this chord, is the leading tone or scale degree $\hat{7}$ in C major. B is not called the *7th of C major*. The word "*seventh*" is reserved to indicate the 7th of a 7th chord.

1. Name the major key of the following dominant 7th chords.

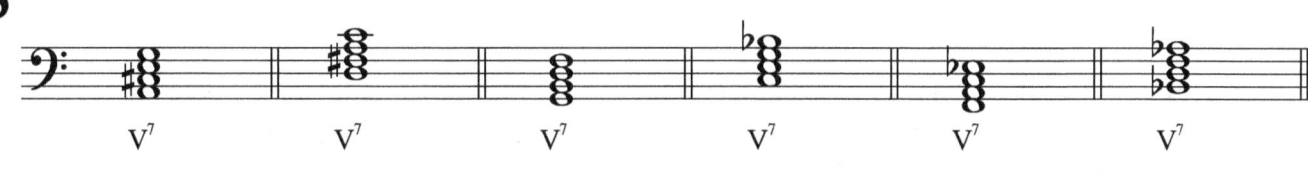

2. Each note below is the root of a dominant 7th chord. Build a dominant 7th chord above each by writing a major 3rd, perfect 5th and minor 7th above the root. Add the root/quality chord symbols above each chord.

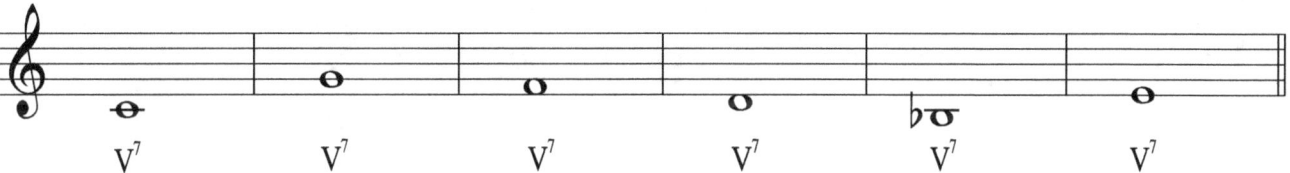

3. Write dominant 7th chords for the following keys. Use a key signature for each.

D minor   G major   A♭ major   C minor   E major   E minor

4. Write dominant 7th chords using a key signature according to the root/quality chord symbols. Name the **major key** for each.

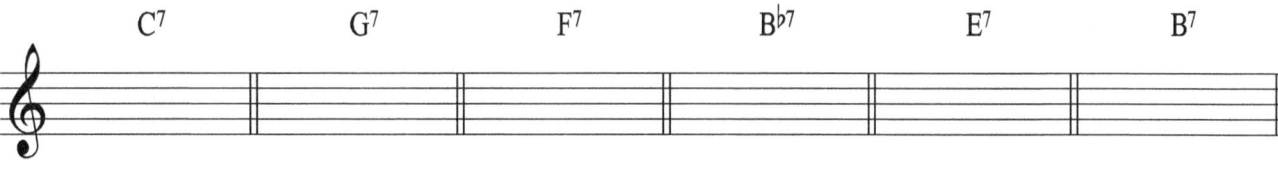

❻Triads Built on the Major and Minor Scale

Figure 6.16 illustrates the major and minor triads that occur on notes in the scale of C major. Each triad can be named for the scale degree it is built upon. The triad built on $\hat{1}$, the tonic, is considered the **tonic triad** in C major. The triad built on $\hat{2}$, the supertonic, is considered the **supertonic triad** in C major. The triad built on $\hat{3}$ is the **mediant triad**, etc.

Figure 6.16

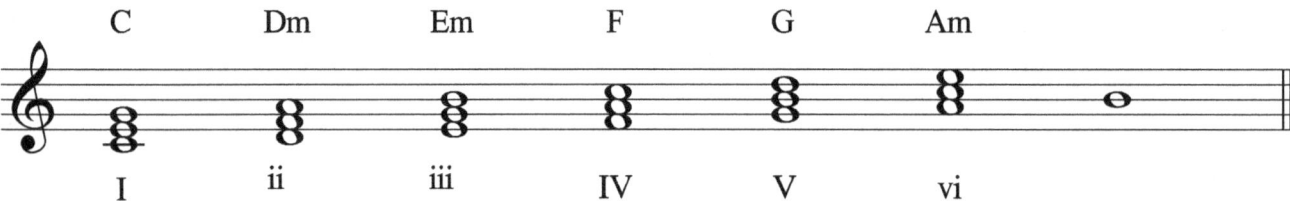

Both major and minor triads occur in the harmonic minor scale. Figure 6.17 shows the triads on the A harmonic minor scale. Major triads occur on the dominant ($\hat{5}$) and the submediant ($\hat{6}$). Minor triads occur on the tonic ($\hat{1}$) and subdominant ($\hat{4}$).
Any triads not shown have qualities other than major and minor and will be studied later.

Figure 6.17

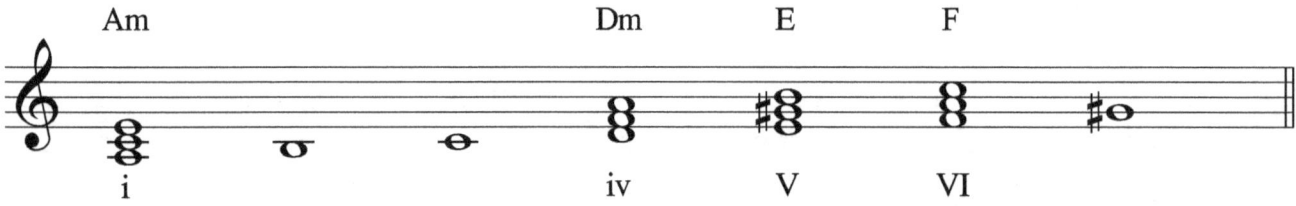

❻1. Write triads on the scale degrees indicated. Add root/quality and functional chord symbols.

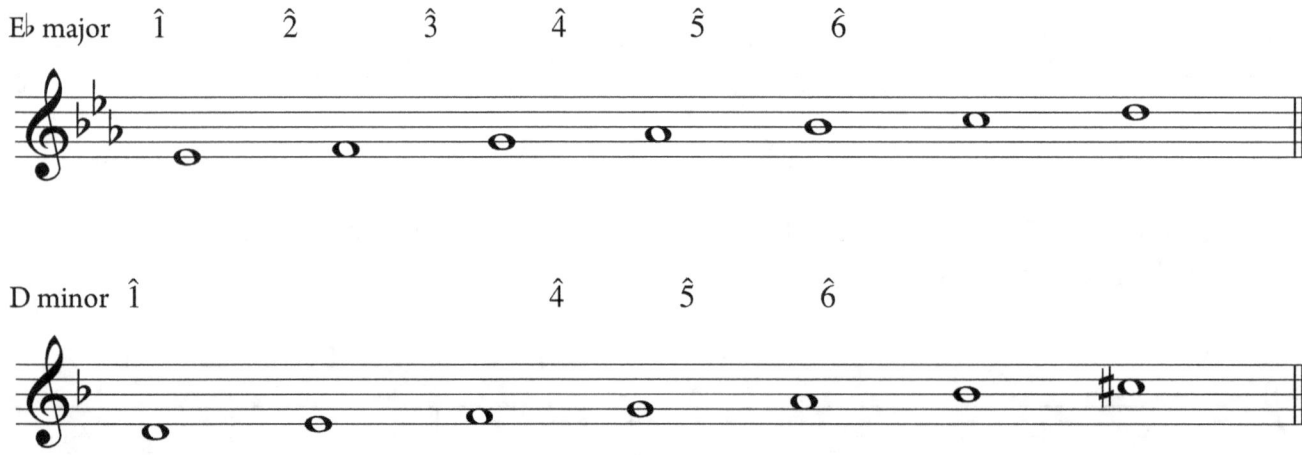

2. Write the following triads using a key signature for each. Write the functional chord symbol.

| The mediant triad in F major | The dominant triad in C minor | The supertonic triad in B♭ major | The submediant triad in D minor |

| The subdominant triad in F minor | The tonic triad in F♯ major | The dominant triad in B minor | The supertonic triad in A♭ major |

3. Write the following triads using accidentals instead of a key signature. Write the root/quality chord symbol.

   a) the tonic triad of G minor in second inversion
   b) the supertonic triad of D major in root position
   c) the submediant triad of E minor in first inversion
   d) the dominant triad of C♯ minor in root position
   e) the mediant triad of E♭ major in first inversion
   f) the subdominant triad of F♯ minor in second inversion

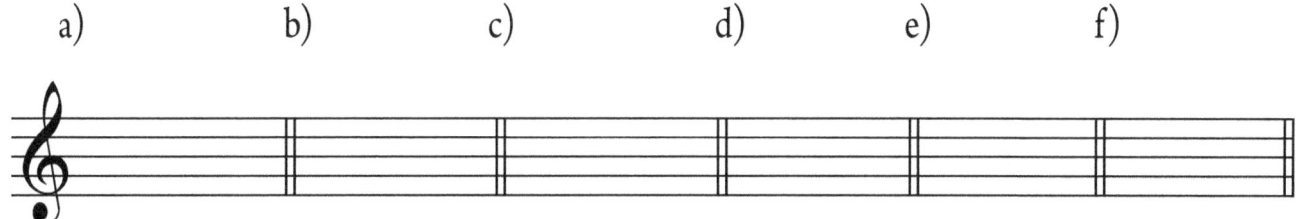

❻ Triads in Open Position

So far, we have studied triads in **close position**. Close position occurs when the notes of the triad are as close together as possible. Triads may also be written in **open position**. In open position, the notes of the triad are spaced out over more than one octave. Often one of the notes of the triad is written more than once or **doubled**. The most common note to double is the root. The lowest note of the triad determines the position of the triad no matter in what order the other notes appear. Figure 6.18 shows different positions of the D minor triad in open position.

Figure 6.18

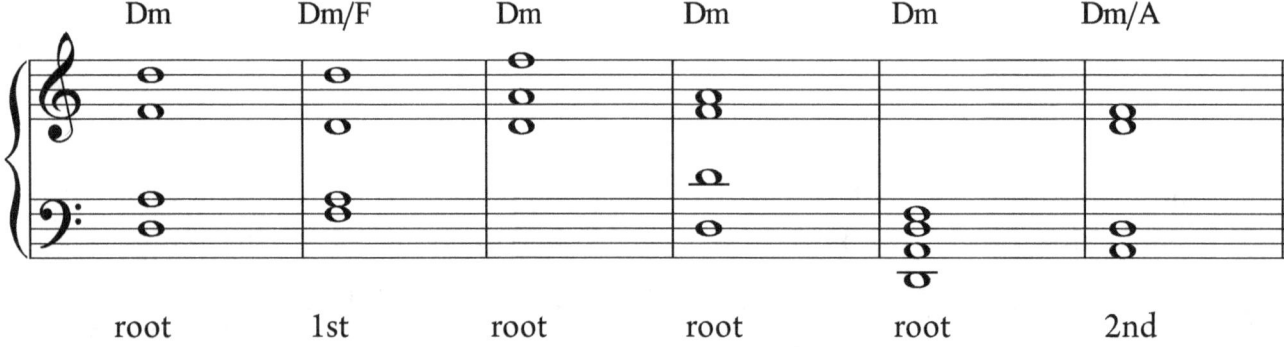

❻ 1. State the root, quality and position of the following triads.

root: _____ _____ _____ _____ _____ _____
quality: _____ _____ _____ _____ _____ _____
position: _____ _____ _____ _____ _____ _____

root: _____ _____ _____ _____ _____ _____
quality: _____ _____ _____ _____ _____ _____
position: _____ _____ _____ _____ _____ _____

2. The following dominant 7ths are written in open position without key signatures. Name the two keys where each one may be found.

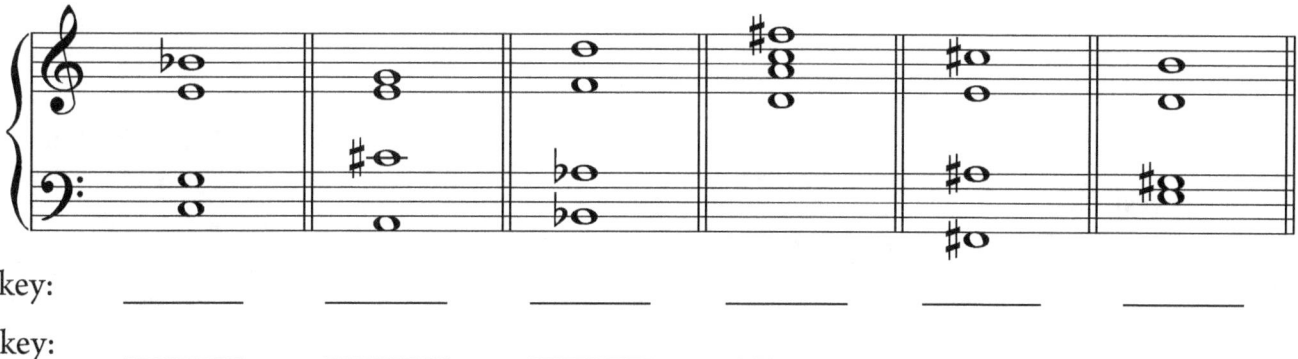

key: _____ _____ _____ _____ _____ _____

key: _____ _____ _____ _____ _____ _____

Chordal Texture in a Musical Score

Composers use chords in many different textures when writing a musical score. This depends on the style, type of composition, instruments, or performers needed to bring the score to life.

Figure 6.19 is the opening of "Hallelujah Chorus" from Handel's Messiah covered in Level 5. This work is written for a 4 voice choir. The four voices work together and create chords as they sing. The staff under the score is added here to show the chords that are formed when the choir sings together. On this staff, the chords are reduced to their simplest form. The bass voice, which is the lowest note, determines the inversion of the chord.

Figure 6.19

© San Marco Publications 2023

❻ Figure 6.20 contains a left hand accompaniment of broken triads. The first 2 measures contain the tonic triad in G major in root position. Measure 3 is the subdominant triad in 2nd inversion.

Figure 6.20

In Figure 6.21 the left hand is made up of extended broken D♭ major chords.

Figure 6.21

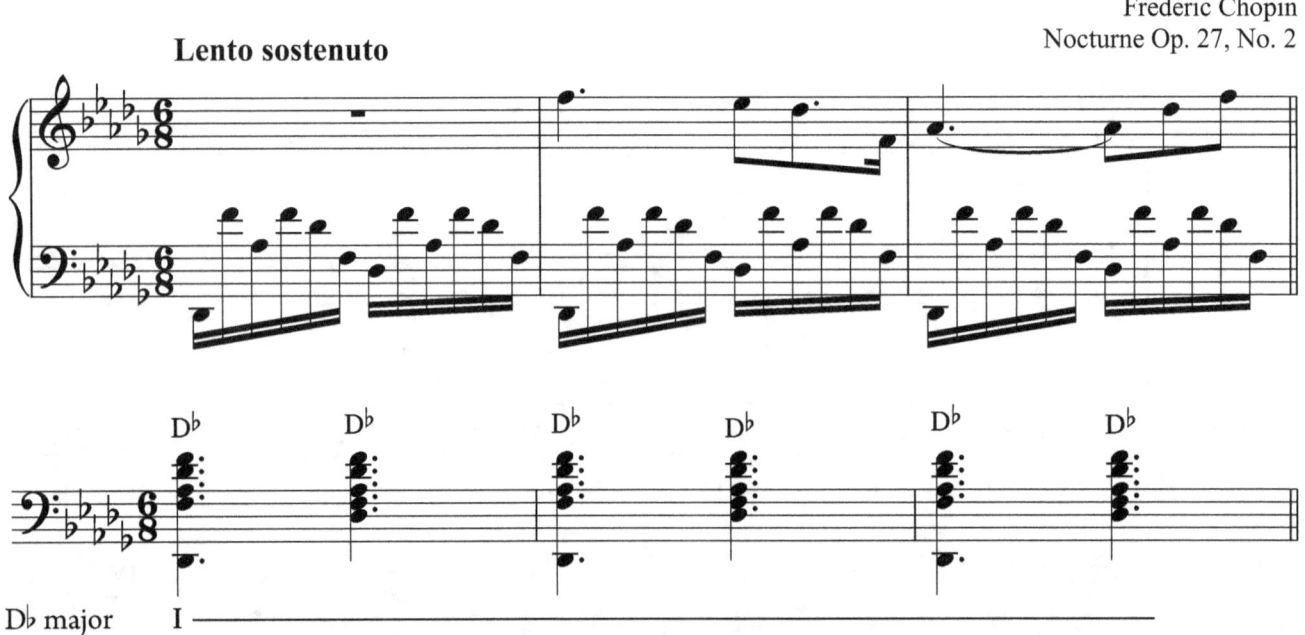

1. For the following musical examples: Name the key. For each outlined chord, state the root, type, position and scale degree on which the chord is built.

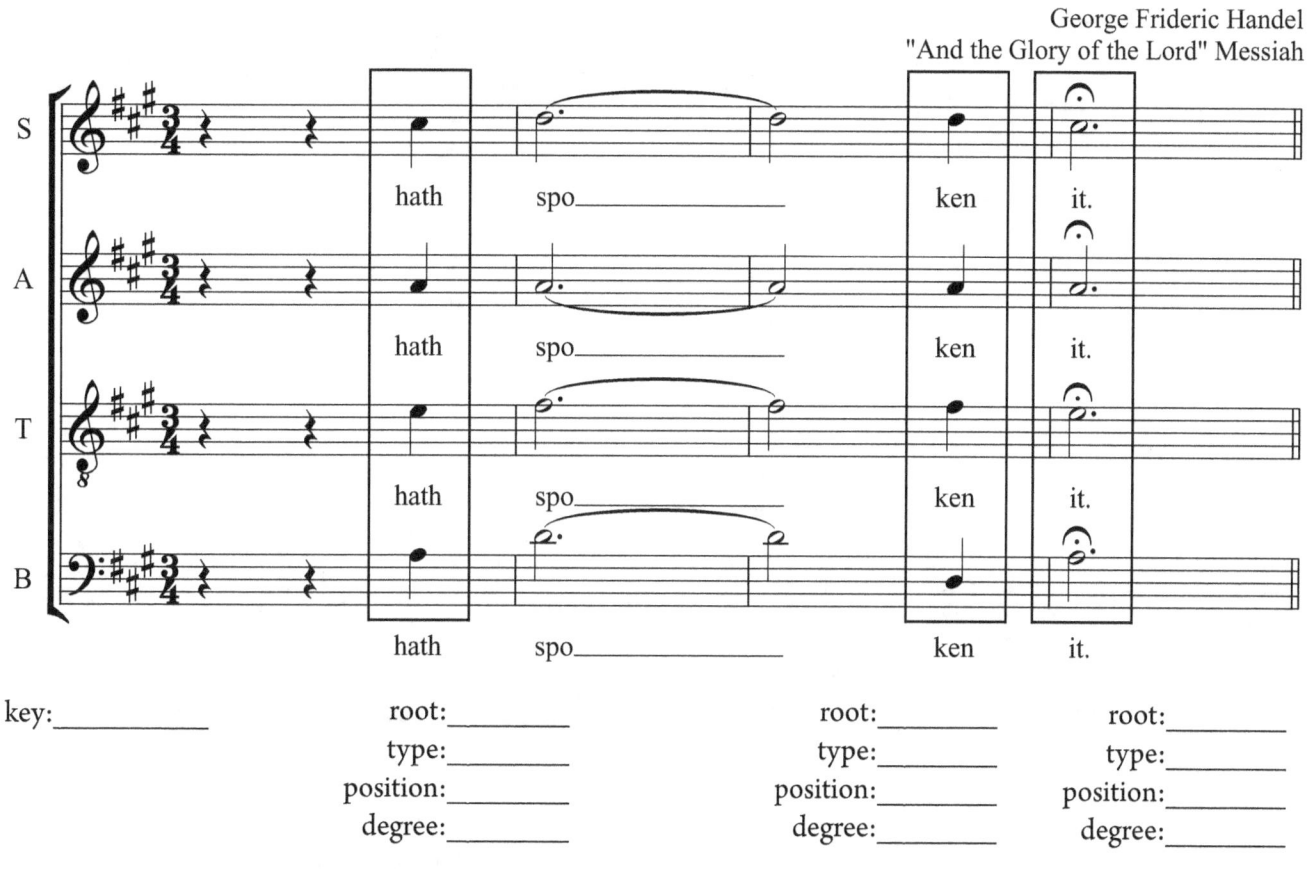

key:_____   root:_____   root:_____   root:_____
                  type:_____   type:_____   type:_____
                  position:_____ position:_____ position:_____
                  degree:_____   degree:_____   degree:_____

key:_____   root:_____   root:_____   root:_____   root:_____
                type:_____   type:_____   type:_____   type:_____
                position:_____ position:_____ position:_____ position:_____
                degree:_____   degree:_____ degree:_____ degree:_____

Chords

❻

Jiri Benda
Sonatina

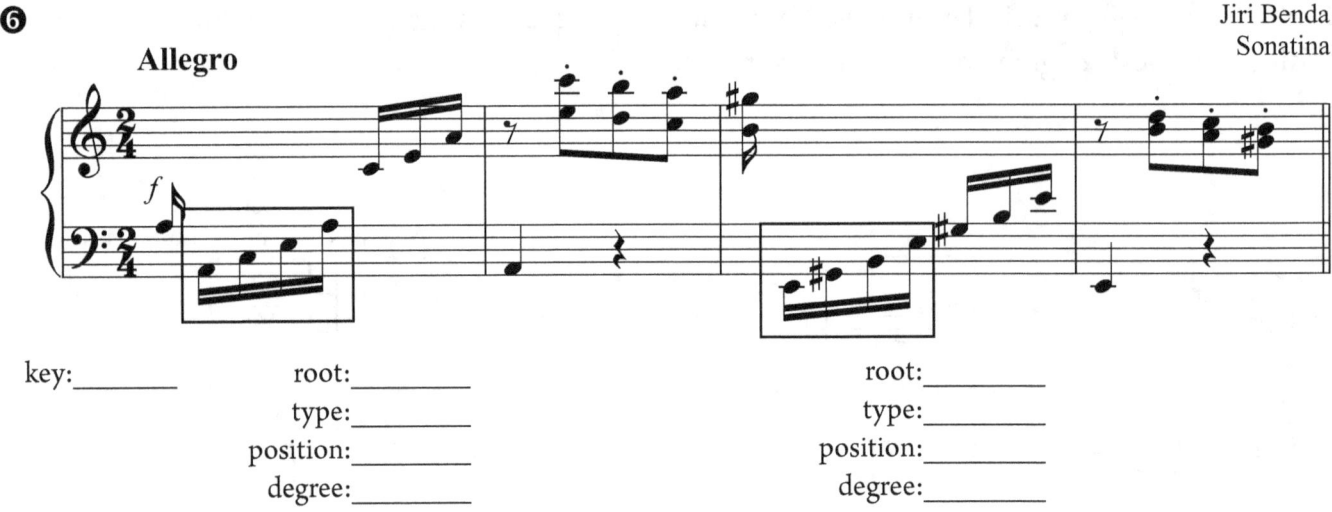

key:_____   root:_____   root:_____
               type:_____   type:_____
               position:_____   position:_____
               degree:_____   degree:_____

Muzio Clementi
Sonatina Op. 36, No. 2

key:_____   root:_____   root:_____
               type:_____   type:_____
               position:_____   position:_____
               degree:_____   degree:_____

Johann Sebastian Bach
Little Prelude VI

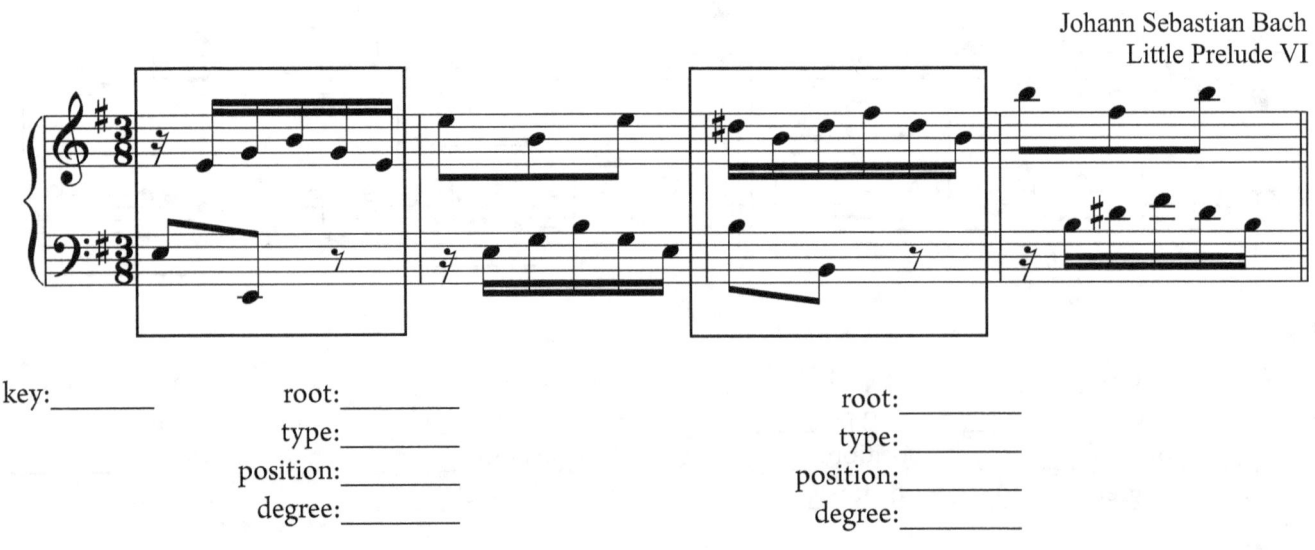

key:_____   root:_____   root:_____
               type:_____   type:_____
               position:_____   position:_____
               degree:_____   degree:_____

Chords

Music Terms

Study the following music terms

secondo, seconda	second, lower part of a duet
sempre	always
senza	without
sforzando, sf, sfz	sudden strong accent on a single note or chord
simile	continue in the same manner as has been indicated
subito	suddenly
tre corde	three strings, release the left pedal on the piano
troppo	too much
una corda	one string, depress the left pedal on the piano

7
Cadences

Music is divided into sections or units of various lengths called ***phrases***. A phrase is a musical idea, like a sentence in a story. Most phrases in traditional music are four measures long. A phrase ends with a ***cadence***, which is a place of rest in music. A cadence is like the period at the end of a sentence. Cadences consist of two chords which bring a phrase to a close.

There are two types of cadences: ***final*** and ***non-final***. Final cadences bring a phrase to a complete ending. Non-final cadences look forward, and do not complete a musical idea. Another phrase is required to complete their non-final character.

Study Figure 7.1. Each line presents a pair of phrases. The phrases move in continuous quarter notes until they pause on a half-note. Harmonically, the most important chord in a phrase is the last one. This is the target or goal of the phrase. It acts in the same way that a comma, question mark or period acts in a sentence. This harmonic event at the end of a phrase is called a cadence.

Figure 7.1

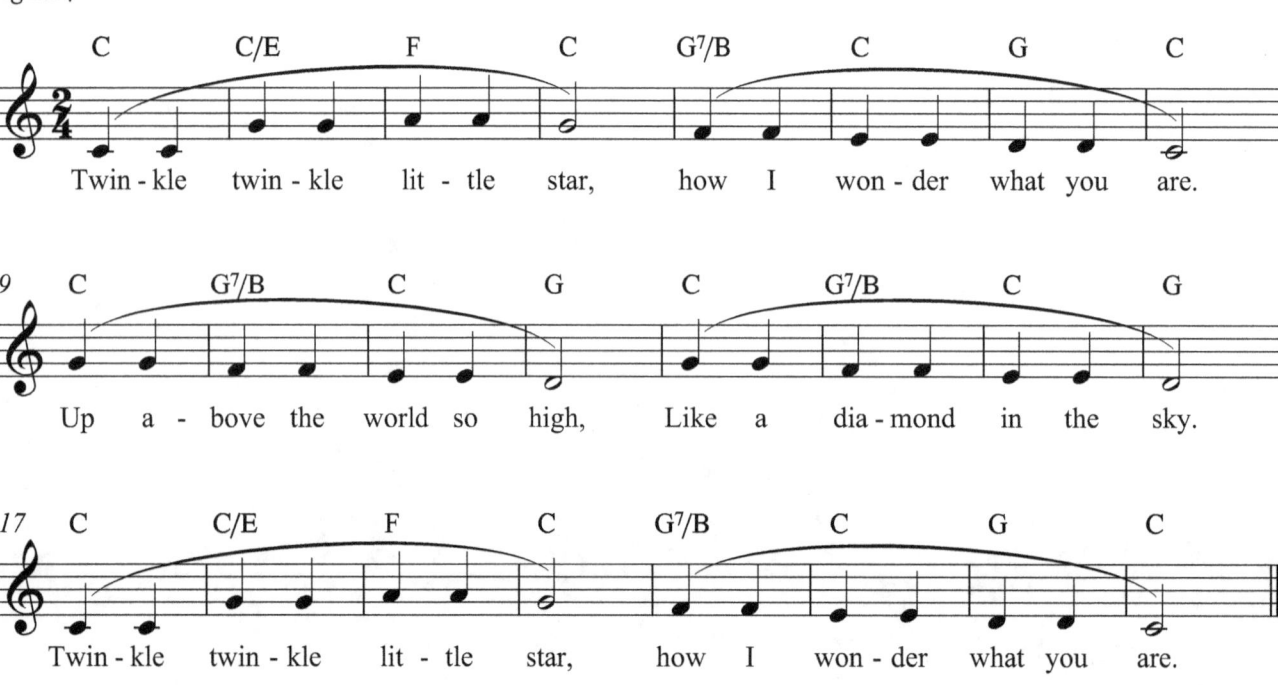

The Authentic Cadence

The most frequently used final cadence is the *authentic cadence*. It is the strongest and most conclusive cadence. It consists of the chords V - I or V - i (in minor keys). Figure 7.2 contains two authentic cadences in keyboard style. Notice the following common features of these cadences.

- They occur on the last two notes of the phrase.
- The first chord is on a weaker beat than the second chord.
- The V chord in a minor key contains raised $\hat{7}$.
- In keyboard style, three notes of the chord are placed in the treble staff, and the bass staff has the root of each chord.
- These cadences are considered *perfect authentic cadences* because they end with the tonic as the top note of the I chord. In the D major cadence, D is the final and top note. In the E minor cadence, E is the final and top note. Ending on the tonic confirms the key and gives the cadence a strong final sound.

Figure 7.2

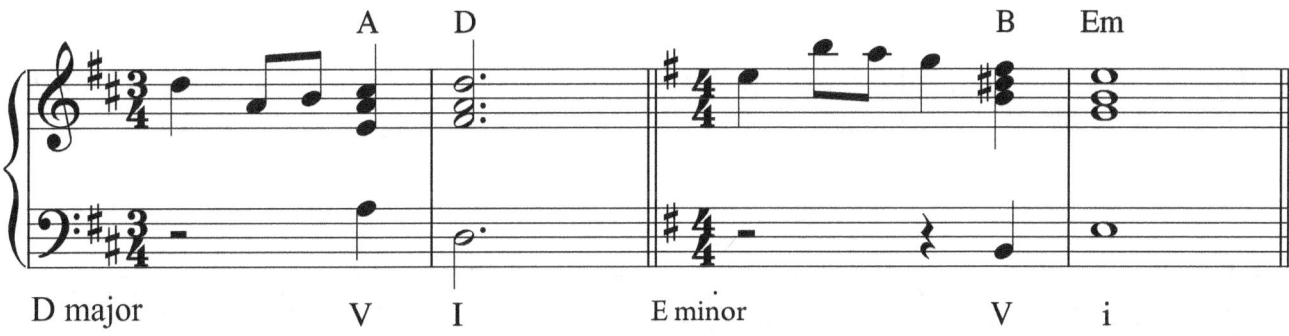

The cadences in Figure 7.3 are considered *imperfect authentic cadences* because they end on a note other than the tonic in the upper part. The D major cadence ends with the 5th (A) as the final and top note. The E minor cadence ends with the 3rd (G) as the final and top note. These are still final cadences but do not sound as strong and final as a perfect authentic cadence which ends with the tonic as the top note.

Figure 7.3

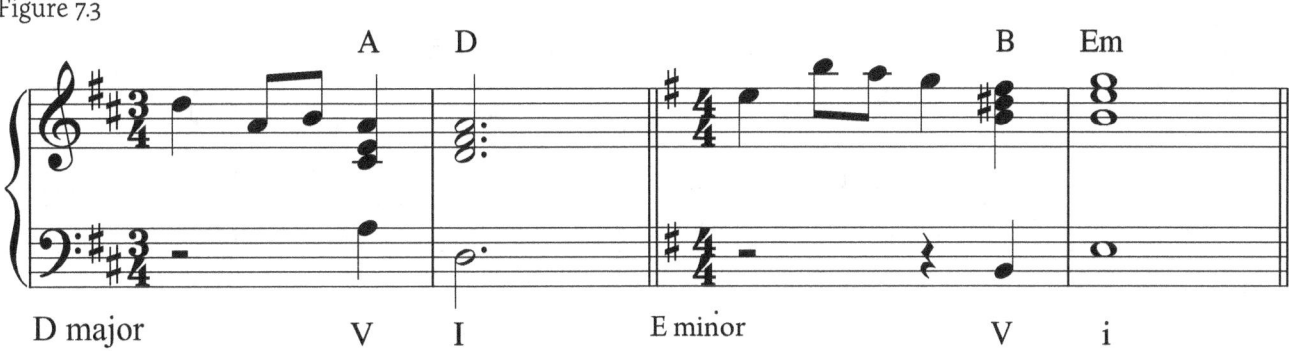

❻ **V⁷ - I is also an authentic cadence.** Figure 9.4 shows two authentic cadences using V⁷. In the first example in G major, the V⁷ chord is complete using all four notes, D F♯ A C. In the D minor example the V⁷ chord is considered incomplete. Here, the root is doubled, and the 5th of the chord is left out, A C♯ G A. Both of these examples are correct. The root of each chord must be in the bass. The cadence in G major is a *perfect authentic cadence* and the cadence in D minor in an *imperfect authentic cadence*.

Figure 7.4

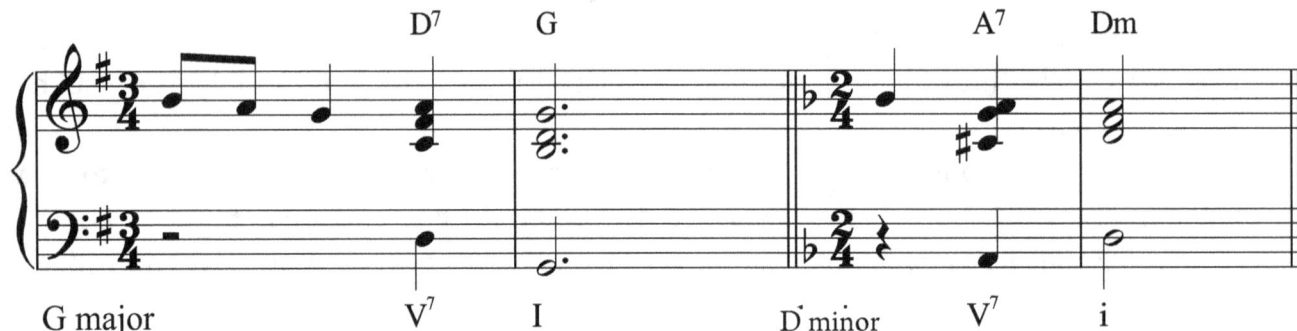

❻ 1. For the following authentic cadences: Name the key, write the functional and root/quality chord symbols and name them as perfect authentic or imperfect authentic.

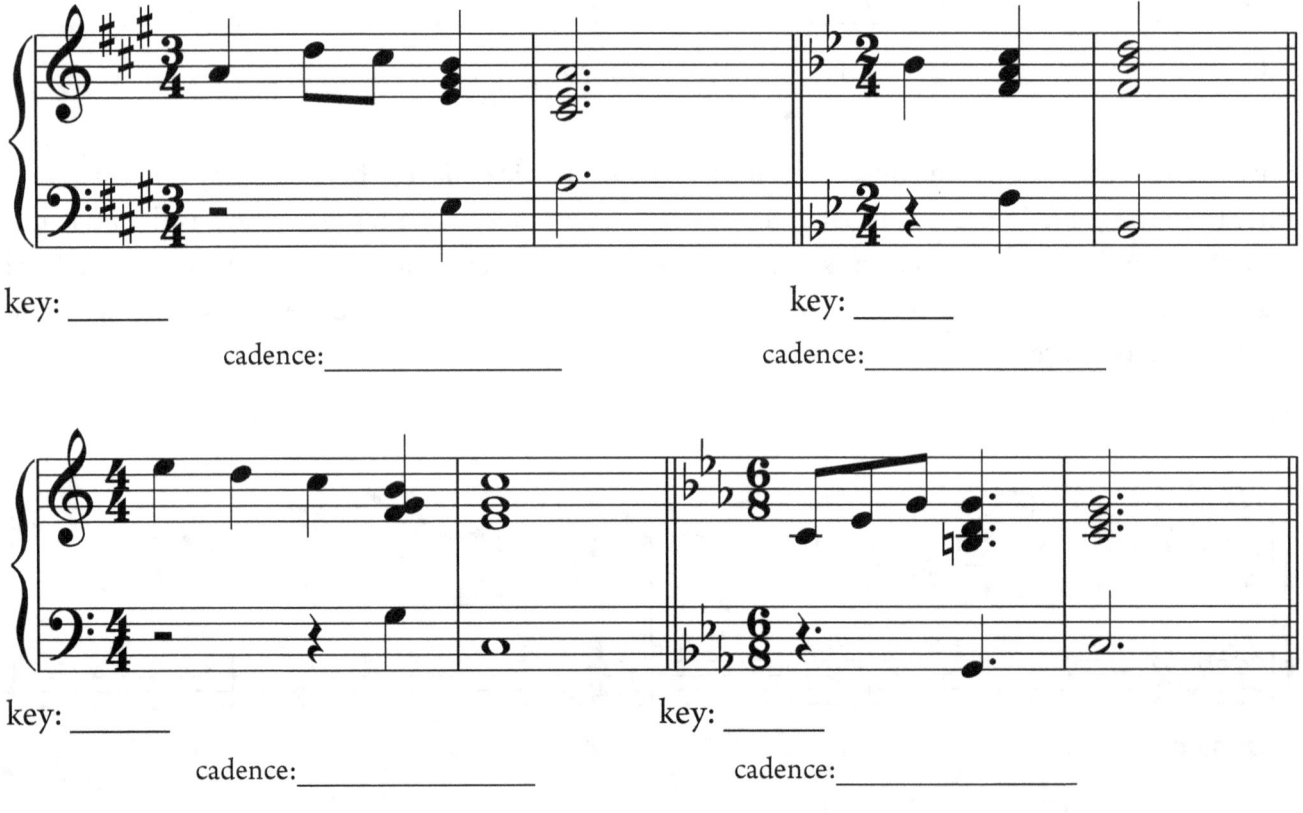

key: _____
    cadence:_____

key: _____
    cadence:_____

key: _____
    cadence:_____

key: _____
    cadence:_____

key: _____
    cadence:_____

key: _____
    cadence:_____

key: _____
    cadence:_____

key: _____
    cadence:_____

⁶The Half Cadence

The **half cadence** is a non-final cadence. It ends on the V chord. Ending a phrase on the V chord leaves the music with an open or unfinished sound. For this reason, a piece of music does not end with a half cadence. Half cadences never end on the dominant seventh (V^7). V^7 contains too many strong tones that do not allow a feeling of rest. We will study two half cadences, I - V and IV - V.

Study the half cadences in keyboard style in Figure 7.5.

Figure 7.5

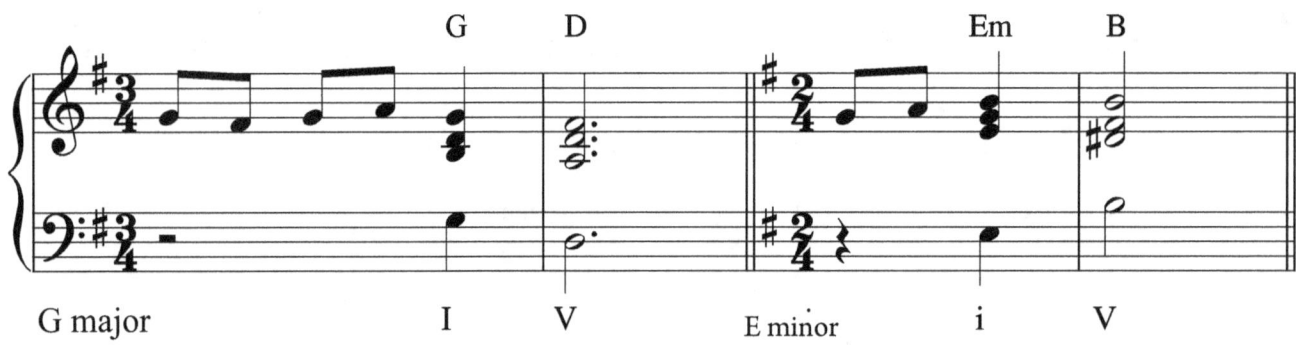

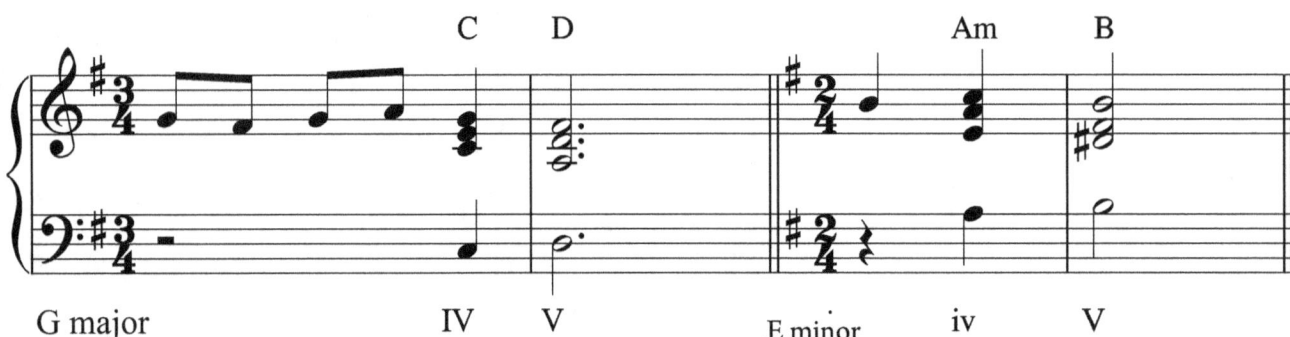

❻ 1. For the following cadences: Name the key, write the functional and root/quality chord symbols and name them as half, perfect authentic, or imperfect authentic.

key: _____

cadence:_____

key: _____

cadence:_____

key: _____

cadence:_____

key: _____

cadence:_____

key: _____

cadence:_____

key: _____

cadence:_____

key: _____

cadence:_____

key: _____

cadence:_____

Cadences

8
Transposition

❹
❺
❻

The Octave

An octopus has 8 legs. An octagon has 8 sides. We know from studying intervals than an *octave* is the interval that spans 8 notes.

An octave is from one letter name to the **same** letter name, up or down.

1. Write octaves on the grand staff below.

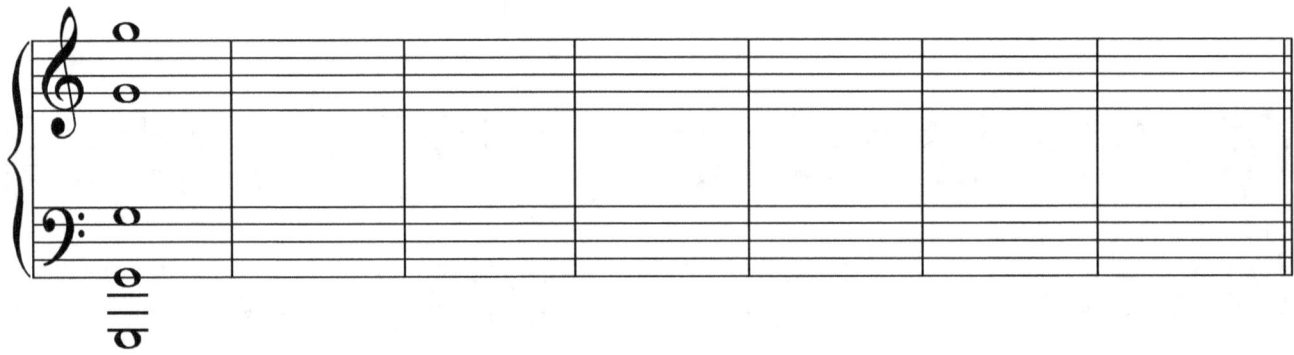

| 5 different | 5 different | 5 different | 5 different | 5 different | 5 different | 5 different |
| Gs | As | Bs | Cs | Ds | Es | Fs |

2. Circle all the octaves found in the example below.

Octave Transposition

Transposition takes place when a group of notes is moved up or down.

In this level we are going to transpose by writing melodies at a different octave.

Figure 8.1 shows a short melody transposed up one octave from the bass staff onto the treble staff.

Figure 8.1

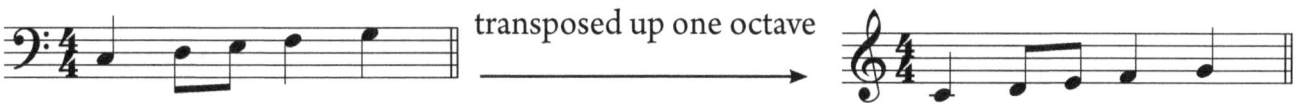

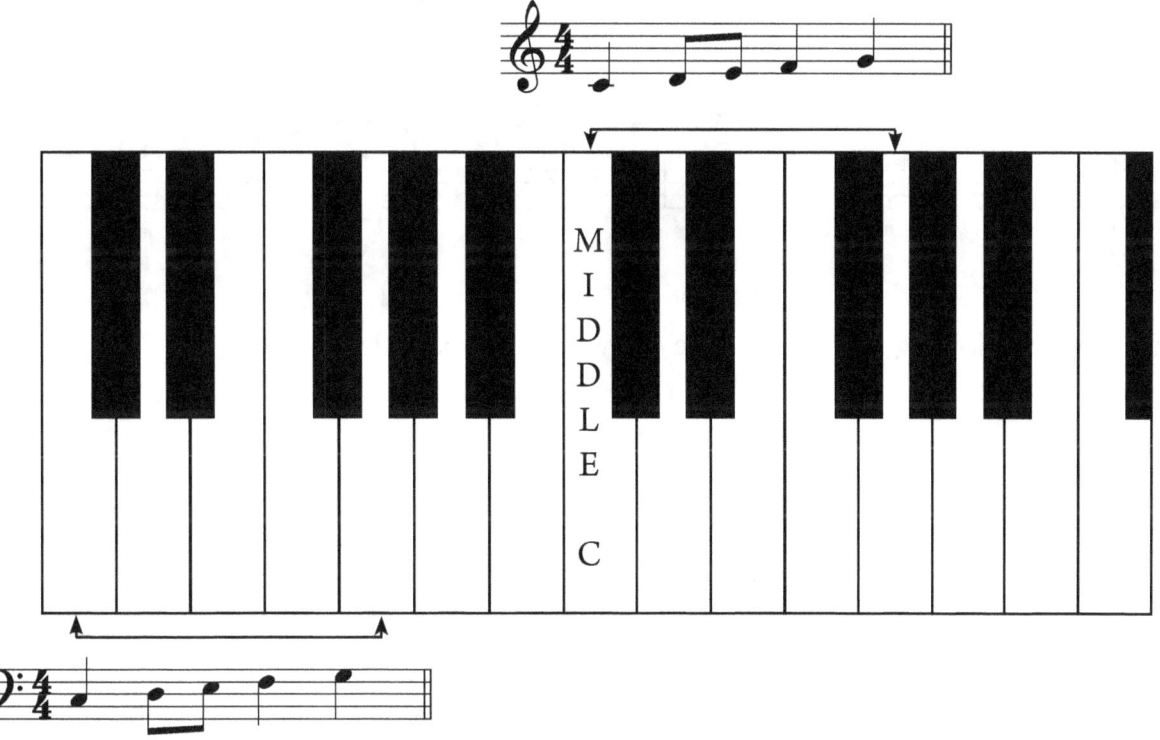

This is not the only way to transpose. Notes on the treble staff may be transposed down into the bass staff.

❹ The melody in Figure 8.2 is transposed down one octave from the treble staff to the bass staff.
❺
❻ When you transpose by an octave:

1. The key remains the same. The clef changes, and the same key signature is used but it is written correctly for the new clef.
2. The time signature remains the same.
3. Every note moves the interval of a perfect octave.
4. The normal rules of stem direction are followed.

The melody in Figure 8.2 requires quite a few ledger line notes on the bass staff to obtain the correct pitch.

Figure 8.2

Francois Couperin
Concerto No. 8

Francois Couperin
Concerto No. 8

❹ 1. Transpose the following notes down one octave into the bass clef.
❺
❻

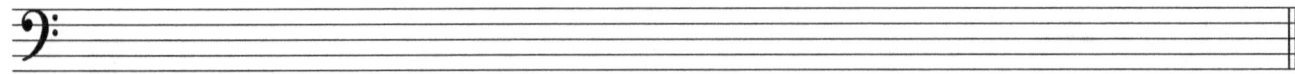

Transposition

2. Transpose the following notes up one octave into the treble clef.

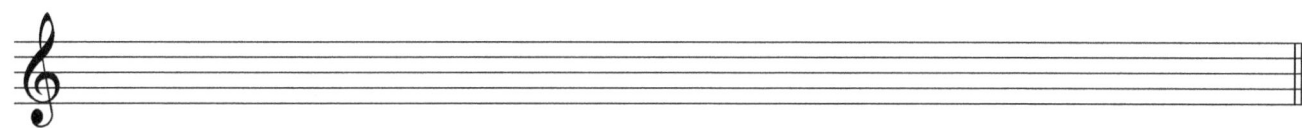

3. Transpose the following melodies up one octave into the treble clef.

Ludwig van Beethoven
Leonore, No. 2

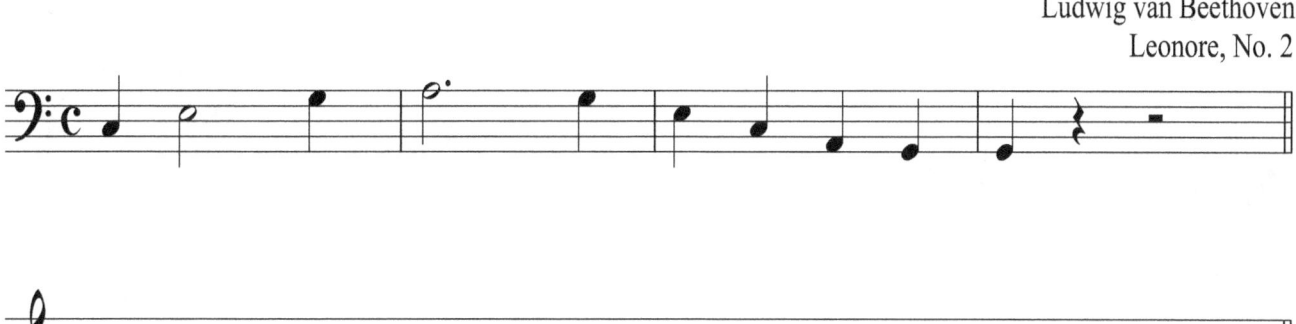

Enrique Granados
Spanish Dance, No. 6

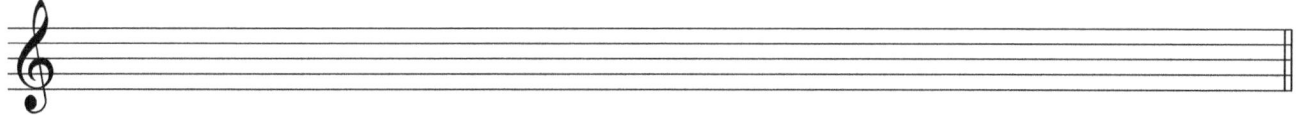

4. Transpose the following melodies down one octave into the bass clef.

Johannes Brahms
Seranade in D, V

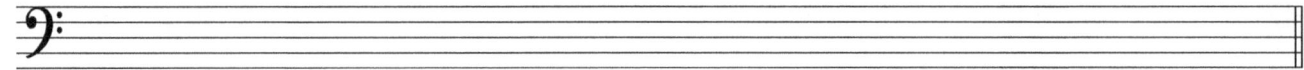

Frederic Chopin
Nocturne Op. 72, No. 1

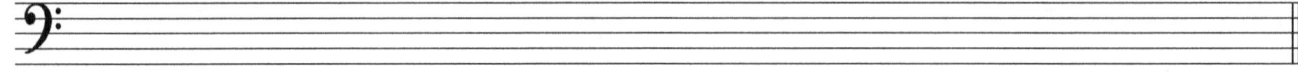

Giuseppe Verdi
March from Aida

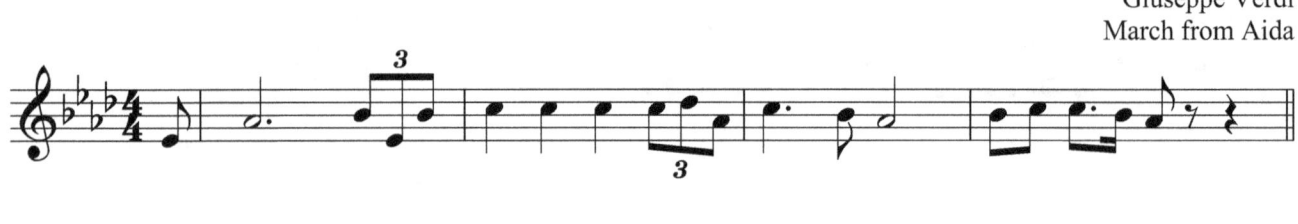

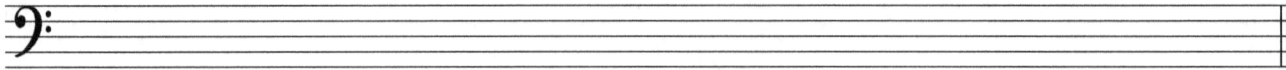

5. Rewrite the following melodies at the same pitch in the bass clef.

6. Rewrite the following melodies at the same pitch in the treble clef.

⑥ Transposition to Another Key

Music may be transposed from one key to another. Major key melodies can only be transposed to other major keys and minor keys to other minor keys.

Transposition Up By Interval

A melody can be transposed up by a specific interval. For example, you can transpose a melody up a perfect 5th, or a minor 3rd, or a major 2nd, or any other interval. Here are the steps for transposing a melody up by the interval of a major 3rd:

1. Determine the key of the original melody. You have to know what key you are starting in before you can determine the key to which you are going. The melody in Figure 8.3 is in F major.

Figure 8.3

Traditional
Early One Morning

F major

2. Determine the interval of a major 3rd above F. Figure 8.4 shows that a major 3rd above F is A. The new key will be A major. The key signature of A major is three sharps. A major key can only be transposed to another major key.

Figure 8.4

The interval of a major 3rd above F is A

© San Marco Publications 2023   159   Transposition

❻ 3. Write the new key signature. In this case, three sharps for A major. Rewrite the melody moving every note up a 3rd. The key signature takes care of the quality of the intervals in the transposition. Copy everything from the original including the time signature, composer, dynamics, etc. Be sure to follow the normal rules of stem direction. Figure 8.5 contains the original melody transposed into the key of A major.

Figure 8.5

Traditional
Early One Morning

A major

You can only transpose from one major key to another major key. Even if you transpose by a minor interval, the melody still remains major. Figure 8.6 is in F major and contains two accidentals. Let's transpose it up a minor 3rd.

Figure 8.6

F major

A minor 3rd above F is A♭. The new key will be A♭ major. Write the key signature of A♭ major (4 flats), add the time signature, and move every note up a 3rd. There are 2 accidentals that will be part of the transposition. Beat 1 of m.2 is lowered one half step in the original and must be lowered in the transposed version. Beat 2 of m.3 is raised one half step in the original and must be raised in the transposed version.

Figure 8.7

A♭ major

Figure 8.8 is the original F major melody transposed up a minor 2nd to the key of G♭ major.

Figure 8.8

G♭ major

1. In the following examples you are given the original key. Transpose the tonic of these keys by the following intervals. Write the new key signature, the new tonic, and name the key.

2. Name the key of the following melody. Transpose it according to the given intervals. Name the new keys.

Traditional
Drink to Me Only

Key: _____

Transpose up a maj 3rd

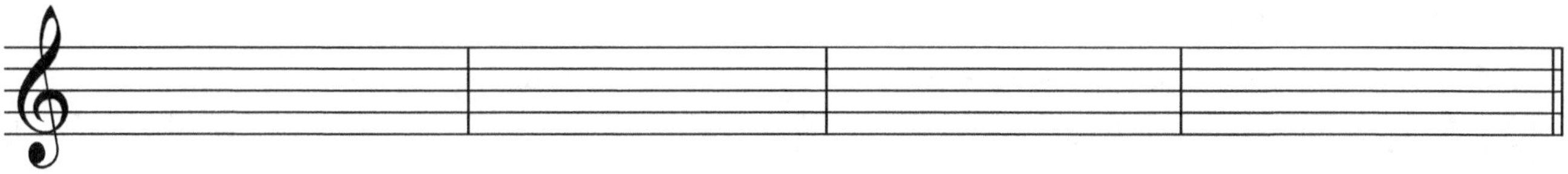

Key: _____

Transpose up a per 5th

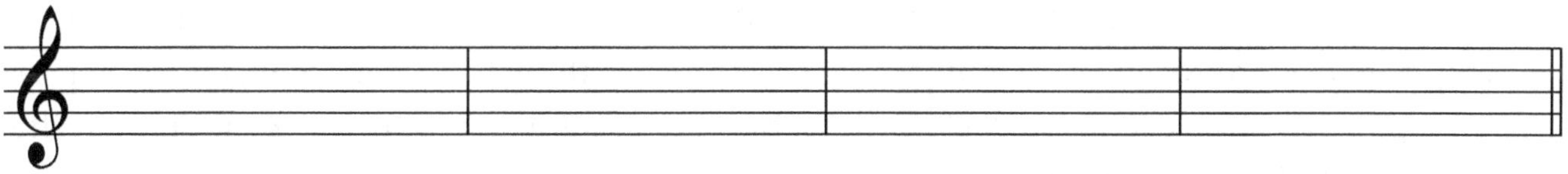

Key: _____

Transpose up a maj 6th

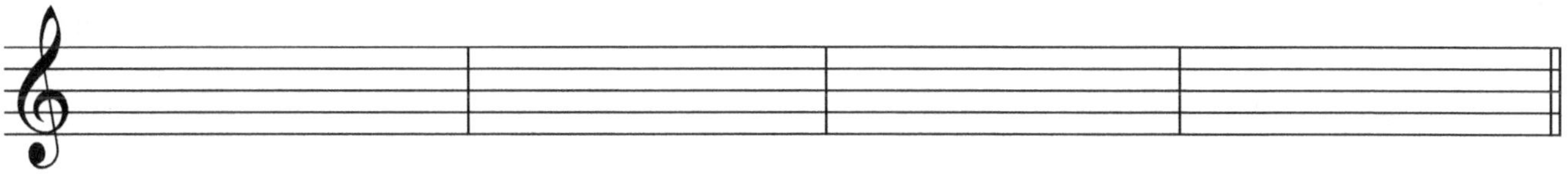

Key: _____

Transpose up a min 7th

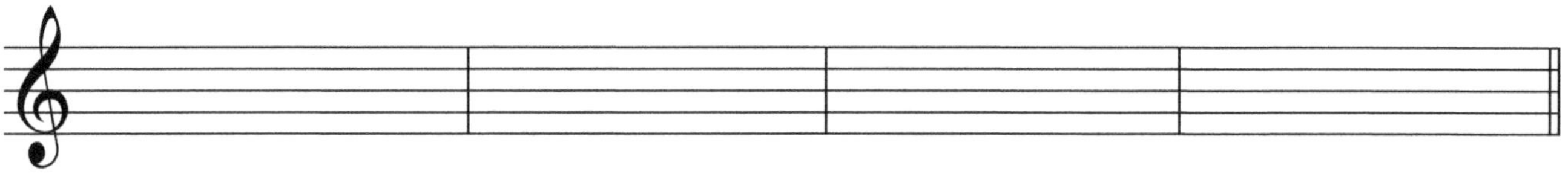

Key: _____

⁶Transpostion By Key

You may be asked to transpose to a specific key. The steps for this are similar to transposing by interval. To transpose a melody into the key of B♭ major:

1. Determine the key of the original melody. The melody in Figure 8.9 is in G major.

Figure 8.9

Franz Schubert
Unfinished Symphony, I

Allegro moderato

G major

2. The distance from G to B♭ is up a minor 3rd. Write the key signature of B♭ major and move every note from the original melody up a 3rd. Copy everything from the original including the time signature, composer, tempo, etc. follow the rules of stem direction. Figure 8.10 contains the original melody transposed into the key of B♭ major.

Figure 8.10

Franz Schubert
Unfinished Symphony, I

Allegro moderato

B♭ major

1. Name the key of the following melody. Transpose it **up** to the indicated keys.

key: _____

D major

E♭ major

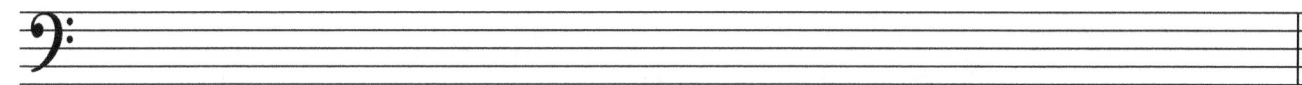

B major

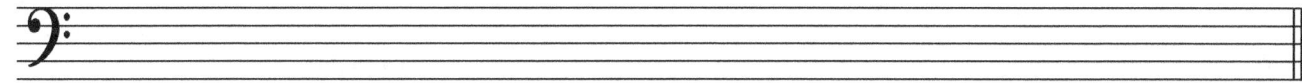

A major

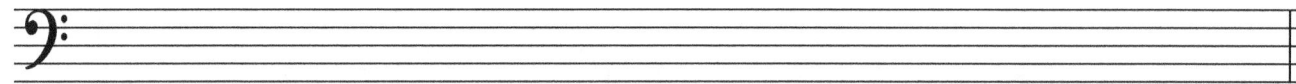

9
Melody

❹❺❻ Review - The Motive

A *motive* is a short melodic idea that may be repeated higher or lower. This repetition of a musical idea at a higher or lower pitch is called a ***sequence***. In Figure 9.1 the melodic motive is repeated three times, descending by the interval of a third each time.

Figure 9.1

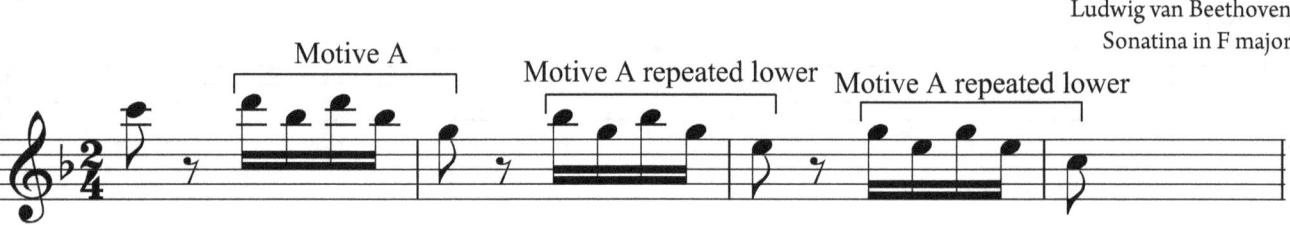

1. Identify the motives and sequences in the following melodies.

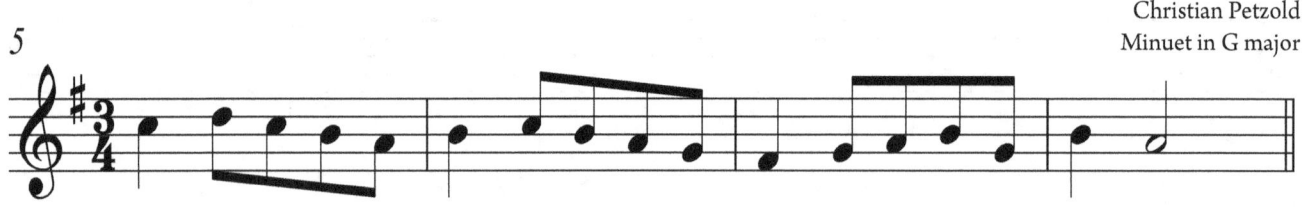

Melodic Movement

Most melodies contain three different types of motion (Figure 9.2):

1. **Conjunct motion** which is stepwise movement.
2. **Disjunct motion** which is movement by leap. A leap is the interval of a 3rd or larger.
3. **Repetition**.

Most good melodies are a combination of some or all of these types of movement. A melody should have a sense of shape or direction. A melody often rises to a high point, or climax, and then moves down again. Motion by step is most common.

Study the motion in Figure 9.2. The movement is indicated with brackets. 1. for conjunct, 2. for disjunct, and 3. for repetition.

Figure 9.2

2. Identify and bracket the movement in the following melodies as: 1. Conjunct, 2. Disjunct, or 3. Repetition.

Melodic Leaps

Leaps are an important part of melody writing. A leap is considered the interval of a 3rd or larger. Leaps within a melody have to be treated carefully. They add interest and contrast, but too many leaps may cause a melody to lose its shape. Instrumental melodies are often different than vocal melodies since the range and abilities of certain instruments are greater than those of the human voice. The treatment of leaps is an important element in good melody writing.

Figure 9.3 shows the treatment of some basic leaps. a) A leap of a 3rd is the smallest leap. After a leap of a 3rd a melody can proceed in any direction. For now, leaps larger than a 3rd like a 4th, 5th, 6th and octave should be followed by step or skip in the opposite direction. The leaps in b), c), and d) are approached and left by step in the opposite direction. **Don't leap the interval of a 7th.**

Figure 9.3

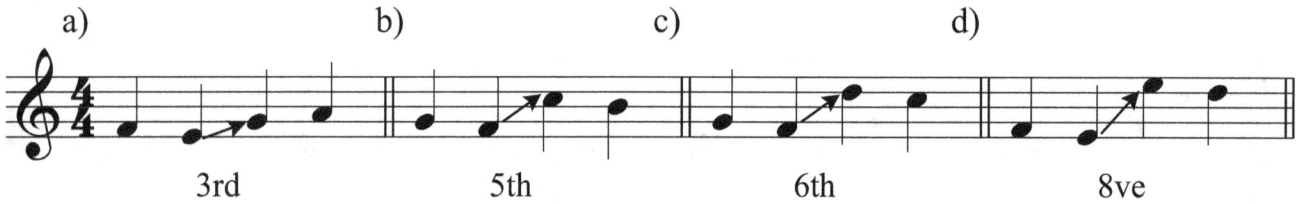

Sometimes more than one leap in a row can be effective. Two leaps in the same direction are acceptable if the intervals combine to form a chord.

Figure 9.4 a) contains two leaps that outline the C major triad. This is good. The leaps in b) work well because they outline a G major triad. The leaps in c) also work because they are notes of the C major triad. Two leaps adding up to the interval of a 7th are poor and should be avoided. In d) the two leaps add up to a 7th and don't outline any chord. This is poor.

Figure 9.4

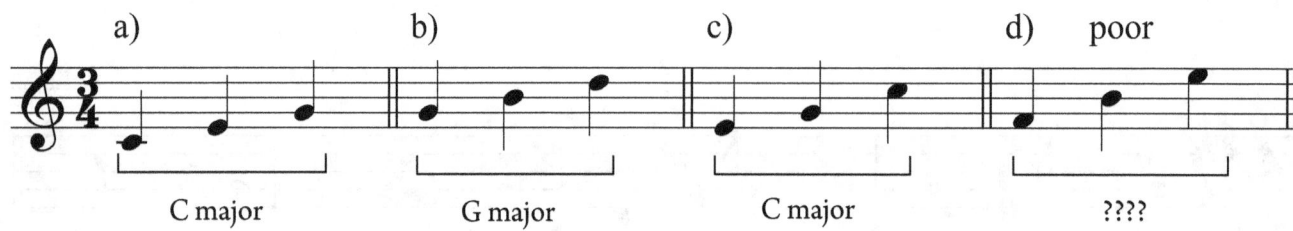

❹ Repeated notes are effective, but too many can create melody that doesn't go anywhere.
❺
❻ Figure 9.5 has too many D's and C's. This is a boring melody that doesn't have any direction.

Figure 9.5

D major

The highest note of a melody can be a climax or high point.

In Figure 9.6, the highest note B♭ appears once and acts as a climax for the melody. The melody moves up to B♭, and then back down to the tonic E♭ in a classic arch shape. This is effective, but not always necessary. Every melody has its own unique character. Different techniques can be used when writing a melody depending on the mood or character that you want to convey.

Figure 9.6

The British Grenadiers
16th century

E♭ major

The melody in Figure 9.7 is a good melody. It contains a motive in measure one that is repeated one step higher in measure two. The leap of a 6th is left with stepwise motion in the opposite direction. The melody ends on the tonic which is the most stable pitch. $\hat{1}$ and $\hat{3}$ are stable pitches. $\hat{2}$ and $\hat{7}$ are unstable pitches. It is very effective to end a melody on the tonic ($\hat{1}$), approached from a step above ($\hat{2} - \hat{1}$), or from a half step below ($\hat{7} - \hat{1}$).

Figure 9.7

D major

1. Compose a melody in G major, using a combination of steps, skips and leaps, ending on a stable pitch. Use the given rhythm. The melodic motive under the bracket should be repeated in the second measure, starting on a different pitch.

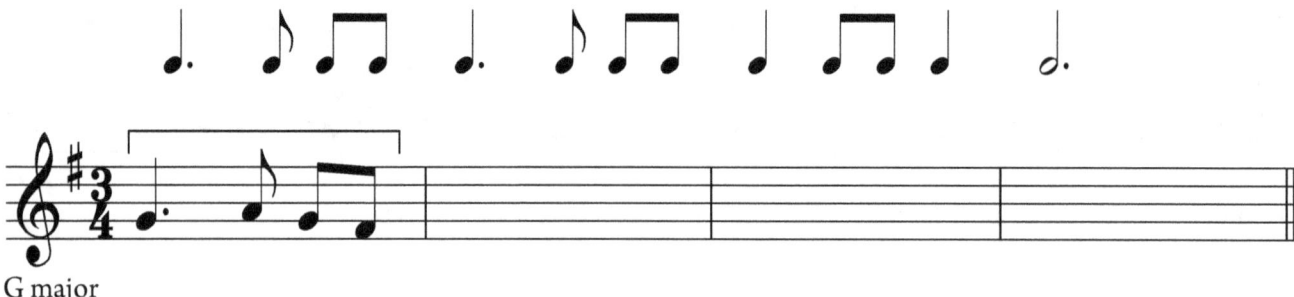

G major

2. Compose a melody in E♭ major, using a combination of steps, skips and leaps, ending on a stable pitch. Use the given rhythm. The melodic motive under the bracket should be repeated in the second measure, starting on a different pitch.

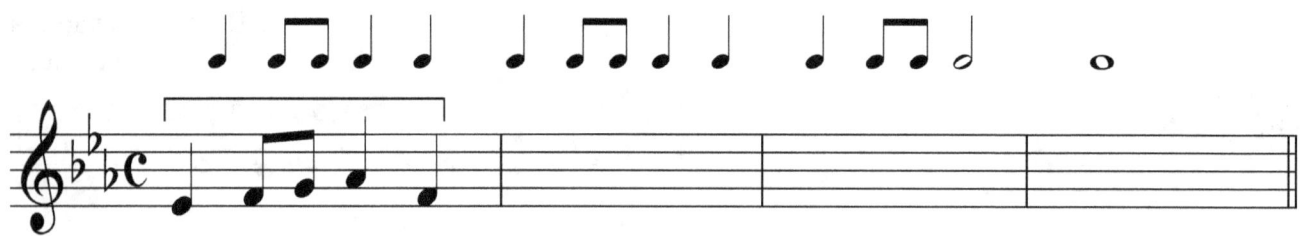

E♭ major

3. Compose a melody in A major, using a combination of steps, skips and leaps, ending on a stable pitch. Use the given rhythm. The melodic motive under the bracket should be repeated in the second measure, starting on a different pitch.

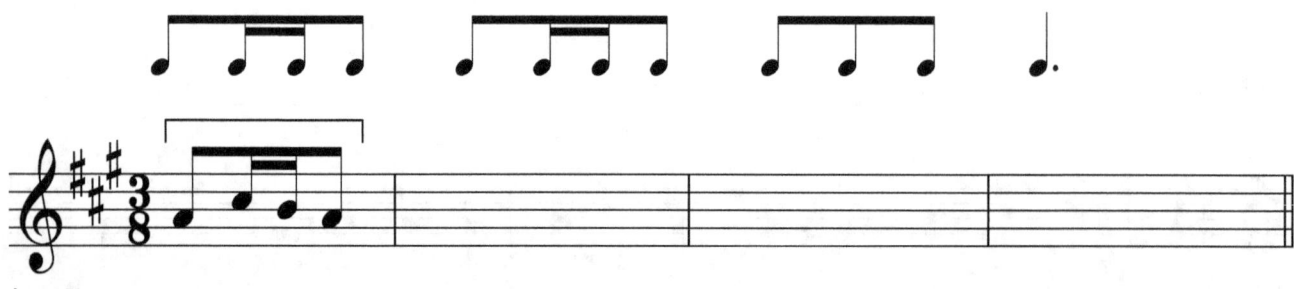

A major

4. Compose a melody in D major, using a combination of steps, skips and leaps, ending on a stable pitch. Use the given rhythm. Write a a motive in measure one and repeat it in the second measure, starting on a different pitch.

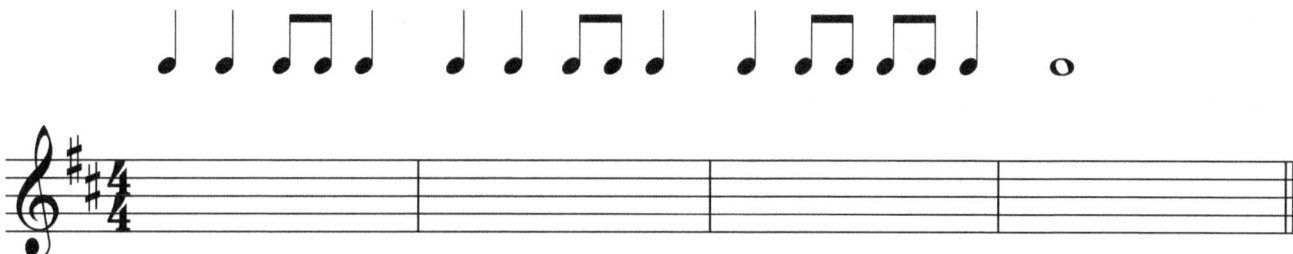

5. Compose a melody in B♭ major, using a combination of steps, skips and leaps, ending on a stable pitch. Use the given rhythm. Write a a motive in measure one and repeat it in the second measure, starting on a different pitch.

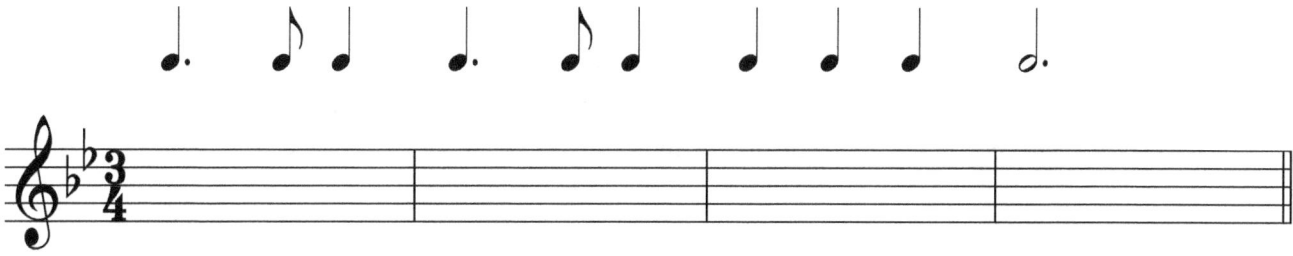

6. Compose a melody in C major, using a combination of steps, skips and leaps, ending on a stable pitch. Use the given rhythm. Write a a motive in measure one and repeat it in the second measure, starting on a different pitch.

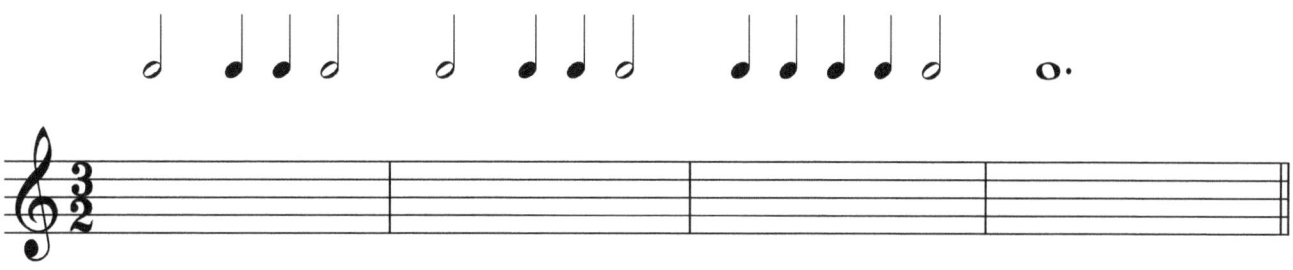

The Motive

Many phrases are built from smaller groups of notes called ***motives***. A motive is a specific pattern of notes and rhythms. Motives can be repeated at a higher or lower pitch.

Figure 9.8 contains a melodic motive in m.1 consisting of a half note, two eighths and a quarter. It skips up a 3rd and then steps down. In the two measures that follow, the motive is repeated a step higher each time.

Figure 9.8

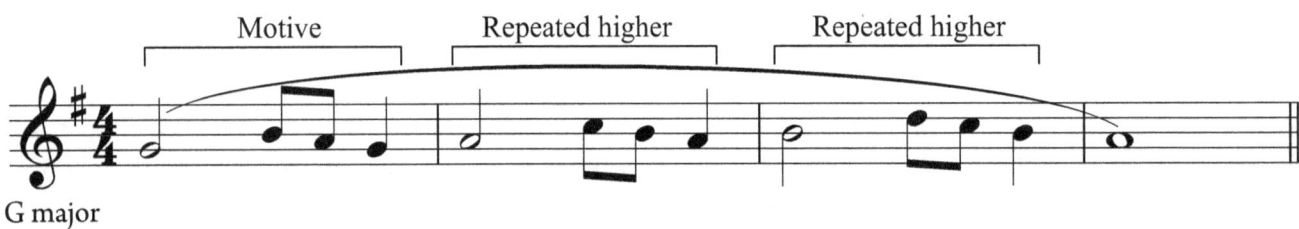

G major

Figure 9.9 contains the famous motive from the first movement of Beethoven's Fifth Symphony (Op. 67). The opening four note motive in mm.1 and 2 is repeated down a step in mm.3 and 4. This motive consists of an eighth rest followed by 3 eighth notes and a half note the interval of a 3rd lower. Beethoven based the majority of this large composition on this 4 note motive.

Figure 9.9

1. Name the major key of each of the following melodies. Circle the melodic motive each time it occurs in each melody.

key:

key:

key:

2. Name the key and find and circle the motives in the following melodies.

key:

key:

key:

🄕🄖Stable and Unstable Pitches

The strongest and most ***stable pitch*** of any key is the tonic ($\hat{1}$). A stable pitch is a note that has strength, finality, and completeness. Many melodies begin and end on the tonic. Another stable pitch is $\hat{3}$. $\hat{1}$ and $\hat{3}$ are the two most important notes of the tonic triad.

Some pitches within a key are considered ***unstable***. An unstable pitch is a note that lacks finality or completeness. A composition would not end on an unstable pitch, but a phrase might. Unstable pitches are found on scale degrees $\hat{2}$ and $\hat{7}$. If scale degree $\hat{1}$ is like a period at the end of a sentence, scale degree $\hat{2}$ or $\hat{7}$ is like a question mark.

The melody in Figure 9.10 ends on scale degree $\hat{7}$. This is an unstable pitch and does not give us a sense of finality or completeness. Play this phrase and listen to this quality.

Figure 9.10

🄕1. Name the major key of each melody. Write the scale degree number for the last note and mark 🄖it as stable or unstable.

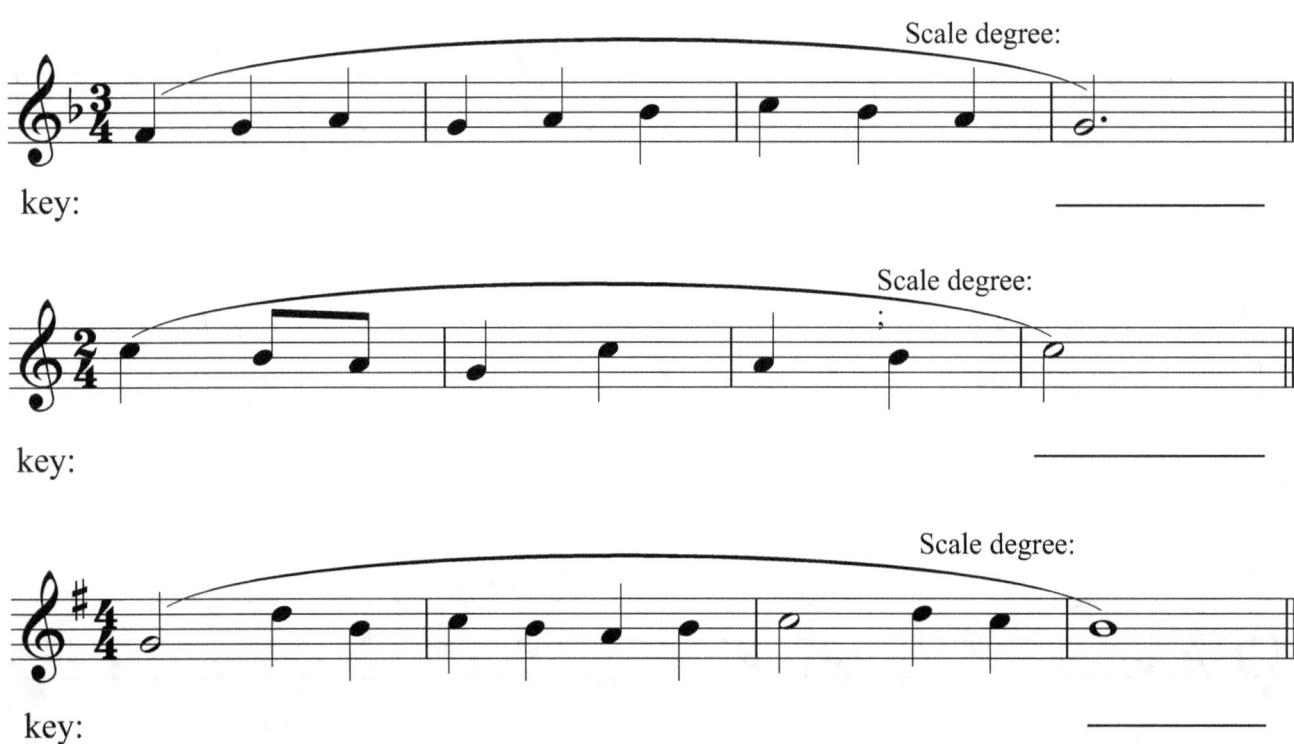

Melody

⑤⑥ Form: Antecedent and Consequent Phrases

Every piece of music has an overall plan or structure, which is the "big picture". This is called the *form* of the music.

Antecedent and *consequent* (question and answer) phrases are common in music. The antecedent phrase acts as a question, often ending on an unstable tone ($\hat{2}$ or $\hat{7}$), which requires an answer. The consequent phrase provides the answer to the antecedent phrase and usually ends on a stable tone ($\hat{1}$ or $\hat{3}$).

We can label music with letters to distinguish the differences within a piece. In this lesson we are going to look at melodies consisting of two phrases, and learn to identify their form and label them with letters.

The melody in Figure 9.11 consists of two phrases that are almost identical. The difference between the first and second phrase is the ending. The first phrase, the antecedent, ends on an unstable tone ($\hat{2}$). The second phrase, the consequent, is a repetition of the first phrase but changes slightly near the end and concludes on a stable tone ($\hat{1}$). Both phrases are nearly the same. We label the first phrase with the letter "**a**." The second phrase is very similar but not exactly the same, so we label it "**a¹**."

Since both phrases are very similar, they form a melodic idea called a ***parallel period***.

Figure 9.11

❺ The two phrases in the melody in Figure 9.12 are different. Unlike the previous example the second
❻ phrase is not a repeat of the first with a different ending, but a completely new musical idea. In this case, we label phrase one "**a**" and phrase two "**b**". The two phrases work together to create a complete section. However, they are different melodically and the labels indicate the difference.

Since the two phrases use melodies that are different they form an idea called a *contrasting period*.

Figure 9.12

❺ 1. Name the key of the following melody. Mark the phrases. Label the first phrase with the letter
❻   **a**. Label the second phrase with the letter **a¹** or **b** to show whether it is similar or different. Circle melodic motive 1 each time it occurs in the melody.

key:

The first phrase ends on: ❏ a stable scale degree   ❏ an unstable scale degree

The second phrase ends on: ❏ a stable scale degree   ❏ an unstable scale degree

This is a: ❏ parallel period   ❏ contrasting period

❺ 2. Name the key of the following melody. Mark the phrases. Label the first phrase with the letter
❻   **a**. Label the second phrase with the letter **a¹** or **b** to show whether it is the same or different.

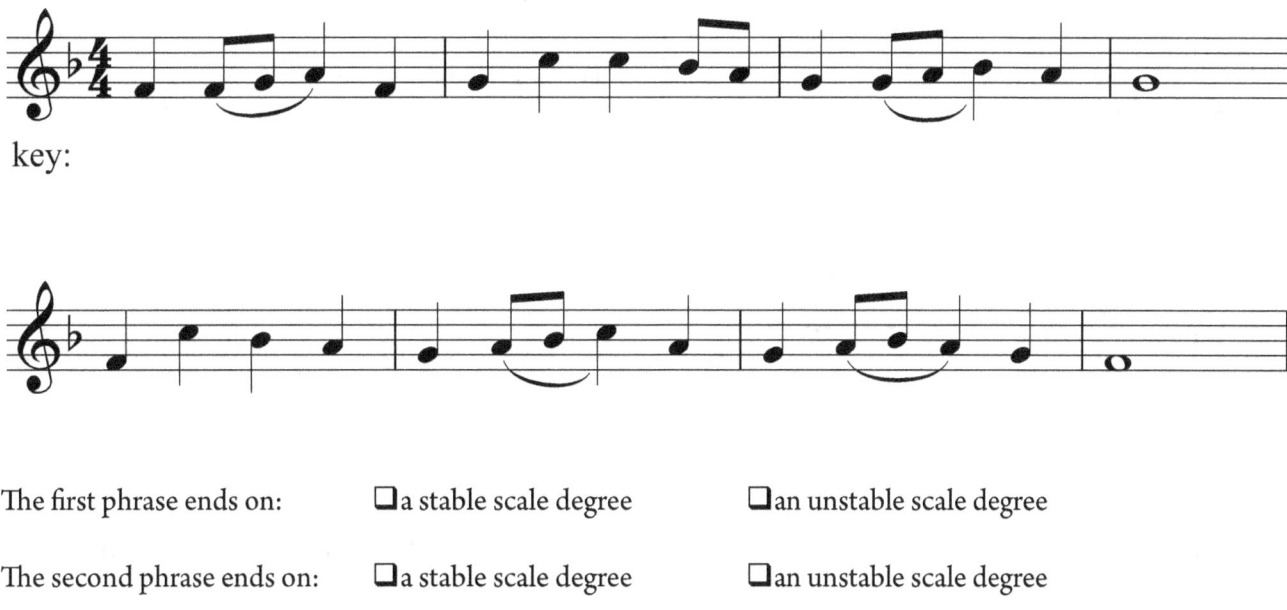

key:

The first phrase ends on: ❏ a stable scale degree ❏ an unstable scale degree

The second phrase ends on: ❏ a stable scale degree ❏ an unstable scale degree

This is a: ❏ parallel period ❏ contrasting period

❺❻ Composing a Consequent Phrase to a Given Melody

You may be asked to create a parallel period by composing a 4 measure consequent or answer phrase to a given melody. Here are the steps for writing this melody.

1. Examine the given melody and decide the key. The melody in Figure 9.13 is in F major.
2. Look at the last note of the phrase. Is it an stable or unstable scale degree? Here, it is $\hat{2}$, an unstable degree.

Figure 9.13

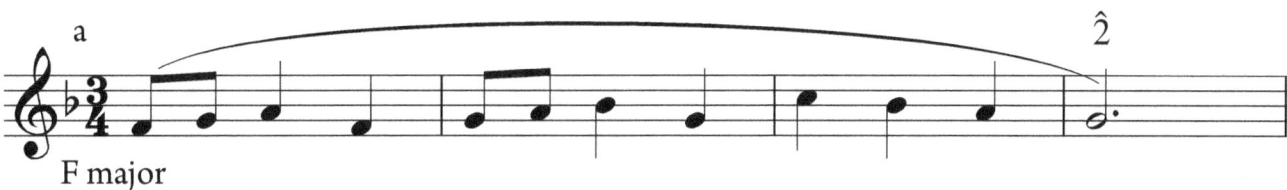

3. Since we are writing a parallel period we want the new phrase to begin the same way as the original phrase. Rewrite the opening phrase and change the ending so it ends on a stable scale degree ($\hat{1}$ or $\hat{3}$). Scale degree $\hat{1}$ is the strongest choice and is especially good if it is approached from a step below ($\hat{7}$-$\hat{1}$), or from a step above ($\hat{2}$-$\hat{1}$). Measure 3 of Figure 9.14 uses the same rhythm as the first two measures. This is good because it provides rhythmic unity. Try not to introduce a new or unusual rhythm when writing these phrases. This phrase concludes by stepping down to scale degree $\hat{1}$.

Figure 9.14

1. Create a parallel period by writing a 4 measure answer to the given question phrase. End your melody on a stable tone ($\hat{1}$ or $\hat{3}$). Mark the phrases.

key:

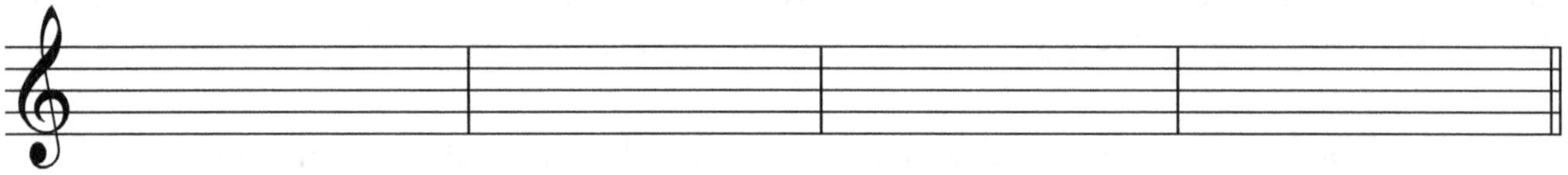

key:

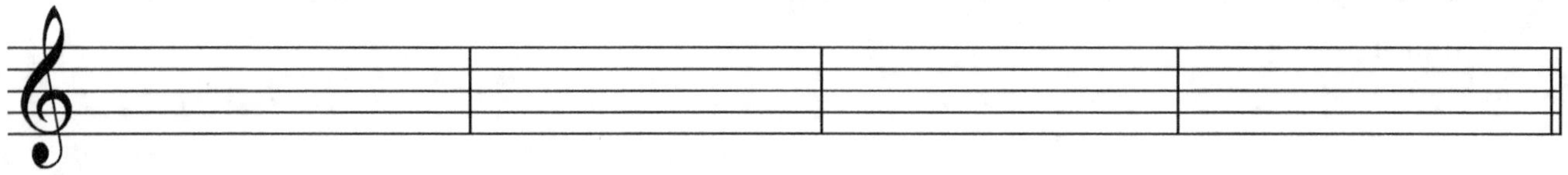

⁶ Form and Melodic Structure

Music can be organized into sections. The overall organization of these sections is called *form*. The form of a composition shows its structure and can help the listener relate to, and understand what the composer is saying.

Once a composer chooses a form, they write musical ideas that eventually become the sections of a piece. These musical ideas are called *phrases*, and they act as musical sentences that help make up the sections of a composition. Much like a paragraph, the sentences contribute meaning to the larger idea of the musical section. Visually, we can identify phrases by counting measures and looking for long notes or rests. Generally speaking, phrases are typically four measures long and end on a long note, like a half note, or on a rest. This acts like the period of a sentence, giving a slight pause between each phrase.

Composers don't usually throw together musical phrases in random order and hope that it works out. Instead, they can plan to have a question and answer type of phrasing structure, where the phrases work in pairs to construct a section of music. This section is called a *period*. A period is usually eight measures long consisting of two four measure phrases.

The first phrase, or 'question,' is called the *antecedent phrase*. This makes sense because the prefix 'ante' means 'before' or 'preceding.' The antecedent phrase usually ends on a note that makes it feel unfinished or makes the listener want more. This could be an unstable scale degree like $\hat{2}$ or $\hat{7}$, leading to a non-final cadence. Half cadences are non-final and leave the music with an open or unfinished sound.

❻ The resolution happens in the second phrase, the 'answer,' which is called the **consequent phrase**. The prefix 'con' means 'with.' This makes sense because the suffix 'sequence' means a 'series' or one thing following another. This phrase usually ends on a stable scale degree like $\hat{1}$ and supports a final cadence.

Study the melody in Figure 9.15. The end of the first phrase feels like the melody is not quite done because it ends on the unstable scale degree $\hat{2}$. The phrase is four measures long and ends on a half note, giving pause before the next phrase begins.

The second phase in Figure 9.15 is very similar to the first phrase. The difference between the two phrases is the ending. The second phrase ends on a stable pitch ($\hat{1}$). Since the second phrase uses the same melody as the first with a slight variation, the two phrases are labeled **a** and **a¹**. This type of melody construction, with two similar phrases, is called a **parallel period**.

Figure 9.15

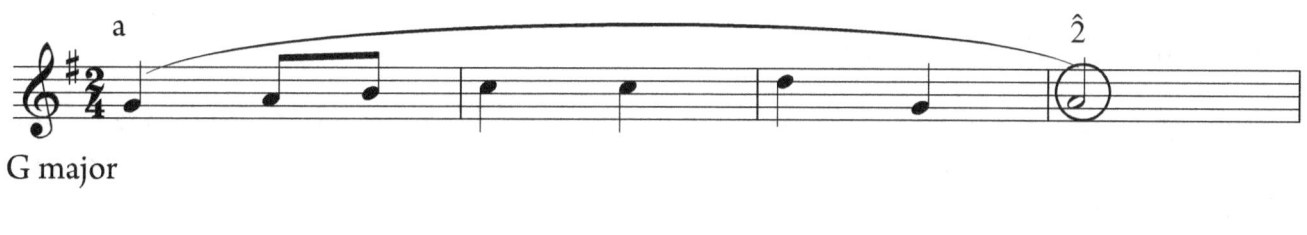

G major

❻ Implied Harmony

The notes of a melody can imply or suggest certain chords that could go along with it. This is called the **implied harmony.** Figure 9.16 contains the I, IV, and V chords in G major.

Figure 9.16

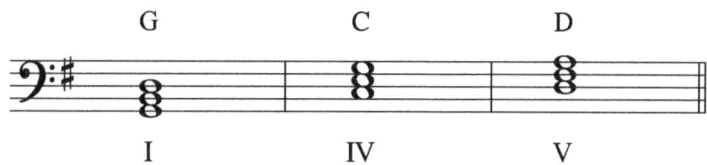

❻ Chords can be used with a melody if they contain the same notes as those found in the melody. The implied harmony for our original melody is suggested in Figure 9.17.

The G and the B in m.1 suggest chord I in G major. It is the opening measure. Most pieces begin with the tonic chord. This helps to establish the key or tonality. The eighth note A in m.1 is not part of the G chord (GBD). This note provides movement to the melody and connects the two chord tones G and B. It is called a *passing tone*. Passing tones are called **non-chord tones**. These are notes that are not part of the underlying chord.

The two C's in m.2 imply the IV chord (CEG) in G major.

The D and G in m.3 imply the I chord, and the A in m.4 implies the V chord.
It is important that the notes at the end of a melodic phrase imply a logical cadence.
Here I - V implies a half cadence. The end of a phrase must have a logical cadence.

The D and the F♯ in m.7 imply V (DF♯A), and the final note in m.8, G, implies I. This implies a perfect authentic cadence in G major.

Ending a phrase on the tonic and approaching it from a step below ($\hat{7}$ - $\hat{1}$) or from a step above ($\hat{2}$ - $\hat{1}$) is extremely strong melodically and tonally. It suggests a perfect authentic cadence and effectively reinforces the key.

Figure 9.17

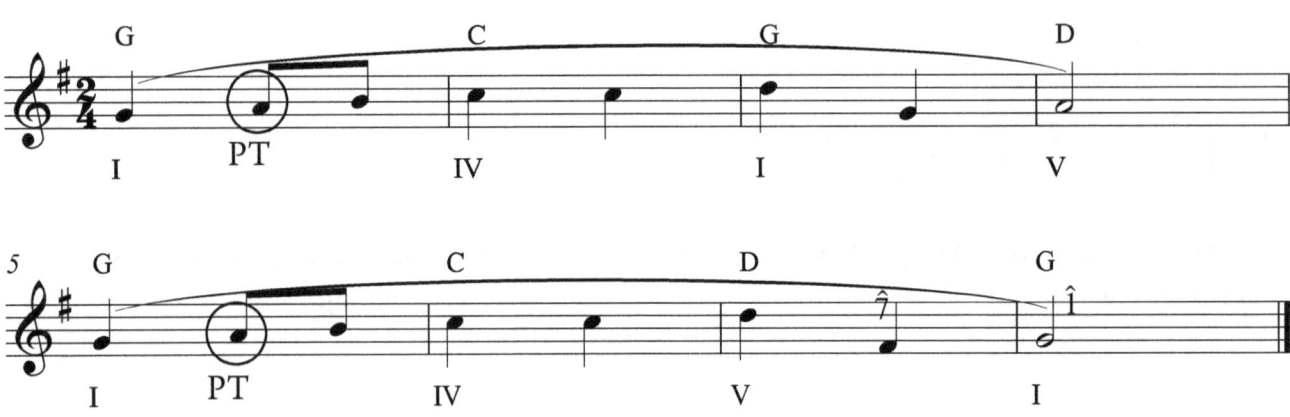

Melody

1. Name the key of each of the following parallel periods. Using Roman numerals I, IV, and V, write the implied harmony under each. Circle and mark any passing tones PT.

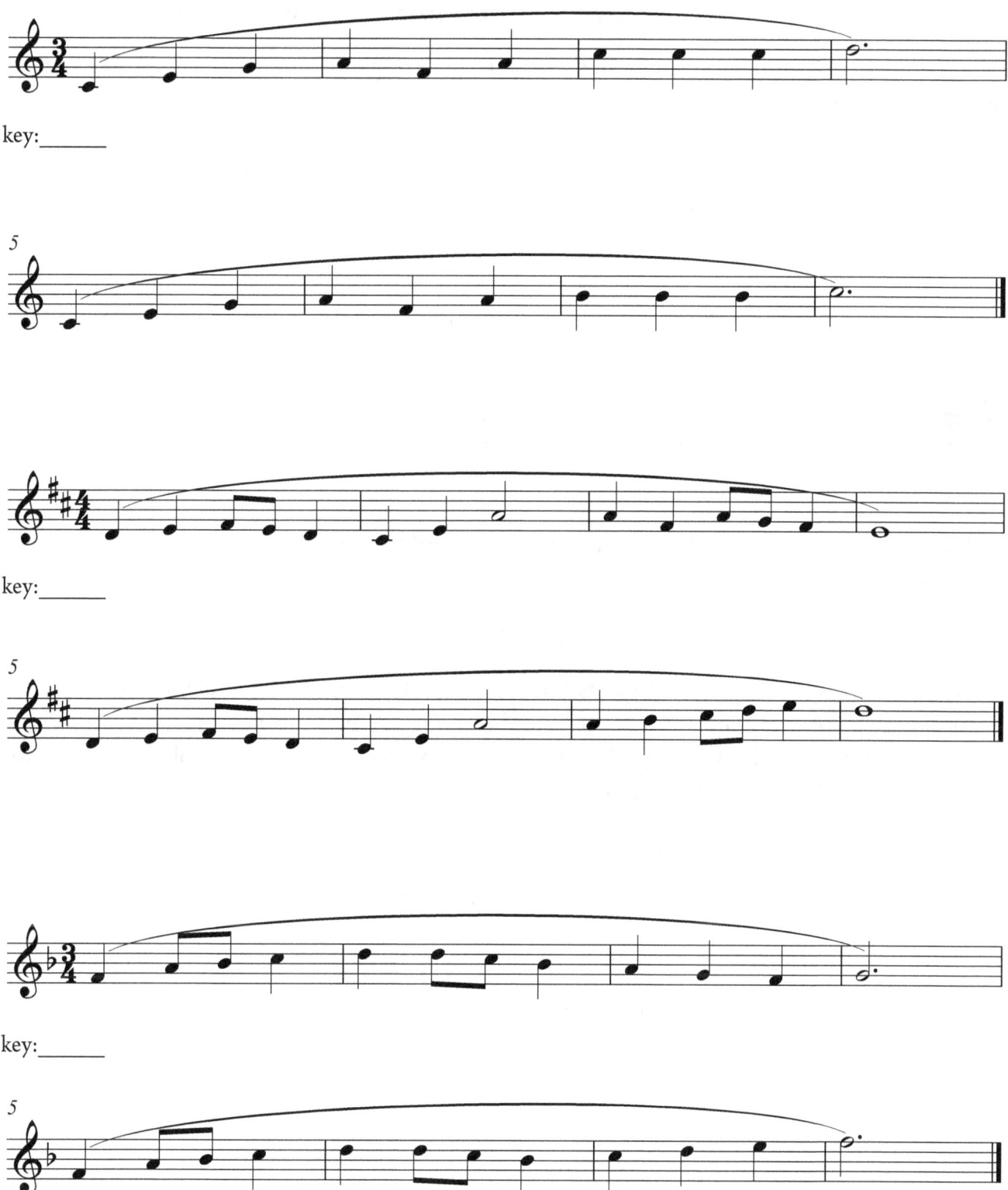

key:_____

key:_____

key:_____

⁶ Writing a Melody

At this level we are going to write a two phrase melody based on two given measures.

Figure 9.18 contains two measures of a melody. Study the steps for writing a two phrase melody based on these measures.

Figure 9.18

1. Name the key. This melody is in D major.

2. Make a structural plan and label the sections "a" and "a¹" to show the question and answer phrases.

3. Decide on the implied harmony for the existing measures.

4. Sketch in the implied harmony for the remaining measures. In this example, I and V are used for mm.3 and 4, implying a half cadence at the end of the first phrase. Since this is a parallel period, the second phrase (a¹) begins with a repeat of mm.1 and 2. The implied harmony for mm.7 and 8 is V - I suggesting an authentic cadence.

5. Add the root/quality chord symbols above the staff.

6. Complete the opening measures of "a¹" by copying mm.1 and 2 into mm. 5 and 6.

6. 6. Complete the first phrase by writing the melody in mm. 3 and 4. This phrase should end on an unstable degree like $\hat{2}$ or $\hat{7}$. Here, it ends on $\hat{2}$. This supports a half cadence which is ideal for the question portion of this melody.

7. This two measure response uses similar rhythmic values to those found in the opening measures. Try to stick to a similar rhythm to maintain rhythmic unity in your writing. The use of an unrelated rhythm may not make sense or seem out of place.

8. The first phrase ends on a dotted half note. This works well since a cadence is a place of rest and requires a slowing of the rhythm. The cadence occurs over the bar with I on a weak beat and V on a strong beat. This is the typical rhythm of a cadence. The second chord of a cadence usually ends on a stronger beat than the first chord.

9. Complete the final two measures of the second phrase. This phrase should end on a stable chord tone. Here, it ends on $\hat{1}$ and is approached by $\hat{7}$. Concluding a phrase with $\hat{7}$ - $\hat{1}$ or $\hat{2}$ - $\hat{1}$ in the melody is extremely strong and supports a perfect authentic cadence.

10. The rhythm of the final two measures matches the rhythm of mm. 3 and 4. Although this is not necessary, it provides rhythmic unity.

11. Indicate each phrase by adding phrase marks.

❻ 1. For the following melodic fragments:

      i.   Name the key.
      ii. Label the formal structure using "a" and "a¹."
      iii. Complete the first phrase according to the given implied harmony.
      iv. If not already given, indicate the implied harmony for the second phrase.
      v. Write the second phrase creating a *parallel period*.
      vi. Add root/quality chord symbols to both phrases.
      vii. Mark each phrase.

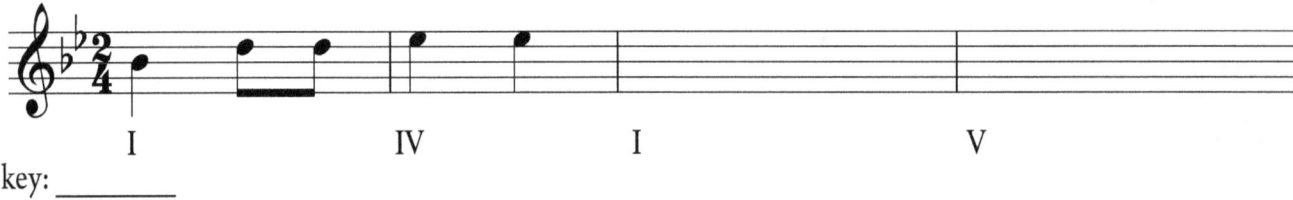

key: _____

key: _____

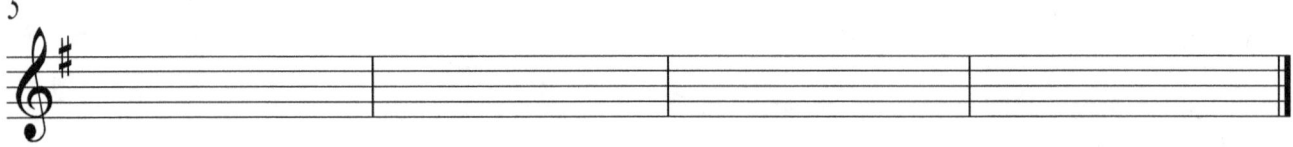

Melody

6

key: _____

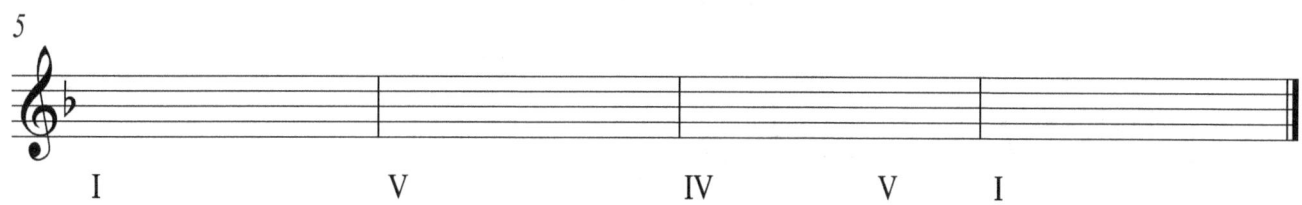

key: _____

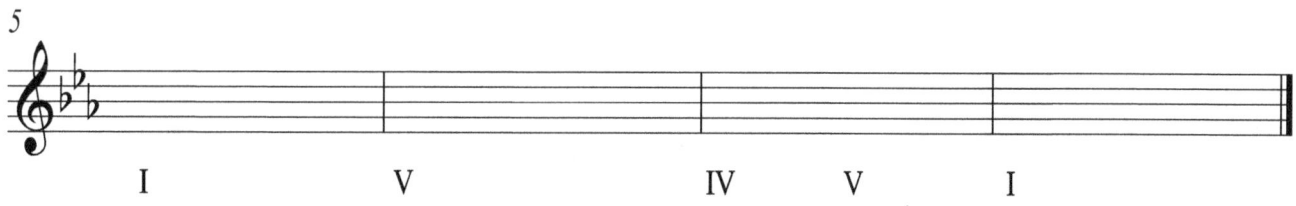

key: _____

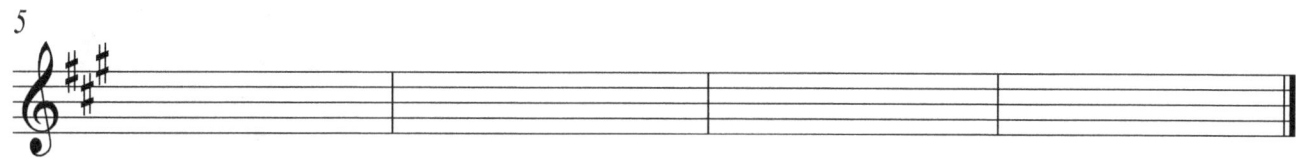

10
History

History Level 4

The Orchestra

An *orchestra* is a large group of musicians playing various instruments. The orchestra is lead by the *conductor*. It is divided into groups of related instruments called *sections*. The four main sections of the orchestra are:

- Strings
- Woodwinds
- Brass
- Percussion

Strings

String instruments use vibrating strings to make sound. The strings are stretched across the hollow body of the instrument and plucked or played with a bow. The string section consists of:

- Violins
- Violas
- Cellos
- Double basses
- Harp

Woodwinds

Woodwind instruments consist of long hollow tubes of wood or metal. The player creates sound by blowing air through a thin piece of shaved wood called a 'reed' or blowing across a mouthpiece. Finger holes on the instruments are open and closed to change the pitch. The woodwind section consists of:

- Clarinets
- Flutes and Piccolos
- Oboes
- Bassoons and Double Bassoons
- Saxophones

Brass

Brass instruments are wind instruments made of metal with a cup-shaped mouthpiece. The player creates sound by pressing his or her lips together in the mouthpiece and pushing air out as if they were making a buzzing sound. This creates a vibrating column of air inside the instrument and produces sound. The brass section is made up of:

- Horns
- Trumpets
- Trombones
- Tubas

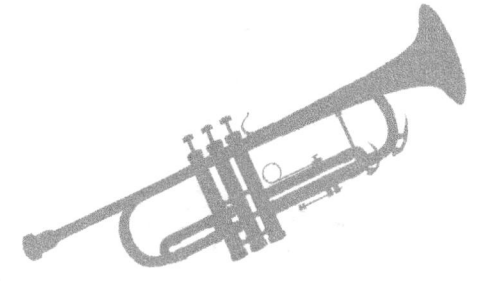

Percussion

Percussion instruments are instruments that are played by being struck or shaken. There are many percussion instruments. Some create specific pitches like the marimba, xylophone, and the timpani. These are some of the instruments of the percussion section:

- Bass drum
- Chimes
- Gong
- Triangle
- Cymbals
- Snare drum
- Tambourine
- Drum
- Timpani
- Xylophone
- Marimba

Figure 4.1 is a standard seating chart for an orchestra.

Figure 4.1

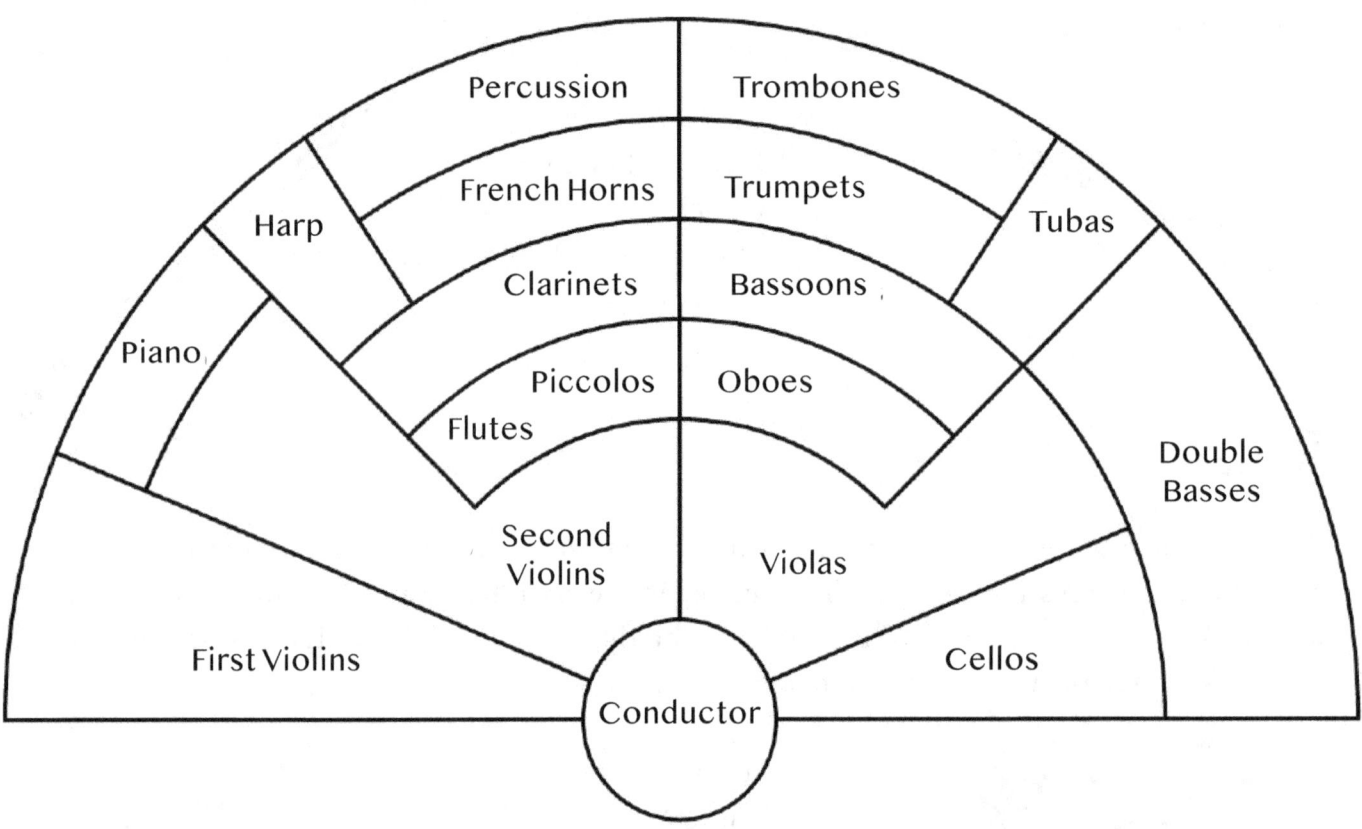

Music Terms

Review the following musical terms from Levels 1 to 4 that are related to style.

cantabile	in a singing style
dolce	sweetly
grazioso	gracefully
maestoso	majestically
marcato	marked or stressed

Benjamin Britten (1913 - 1976) Modern Era

Benjamin Britten was an accomplished conductor, composer, and pianist. He was born in Lowestoft, a town on the English seacoast on November 22nd, the feast day of St. Cecilia, the patron saint of music. Benjamin's mother was a singer and often held concerts in their home.

Britton won a scholarship to the Royal College of Music in London, and his first job was writing music for films.

He did not believe in war and when England decided to go to war with Germany in 1939, Britten left for America. However, he had a great love for the United Kingdom, and in the middle of World War II, he sailed back to his native country.

After the war, the largest opera company in England held a gala and commissioned Britten to write them a new opera. He also composed an opera to honor the coronation of Queen Elizabeth II. Benjamin Britton was the first musician to be gifted with the title of "Lord" by the Queen.

Young Persons Guide to the Orchestra

The **Young Person's Guide to the Orchestra** is a composition for orchestra written in 1946 by Benjamin Britten. It was initially written for an educational film called *Instruments of the Orchestra* featuring the London Symphony Orchestra. It is one of Britten's best-known compositions.

Young Persons Guide to the Orchestra is based on a piece titled *Rondeau* by the Baroque composer Henry Purcell. The form of Britton's composition is *Theme and Variations*. In this form, the theme is stated first, followed by 13 variations. The variations are short pieces based on the theme that vary in mood and sound. Young Persons Guide to the Orchestra is specifically designed to feature the instruments of the orchestra.

The work begins with the theme (based on Purcell's Rondeau) performed by all the instruments of the orchestra. This is followed by each family of instrument: first the woodwinds, then the brass, then the strings, and finally the percussion. Each variation features an instrument in detail and moves through the family from the highest to the lowest sounding. The first variation starts with piccolos and flutes. Following that, each member of the woodwinds gets a variation including the oboes, the clarinets, and finally the lowest sounding bassoons. The variations then go through the strings, the brass, and ends with the percussion.

After the whole orchestra has played through the instrumental sections (13 variations), all of the instruments join together in the final section to perform a fugue* which starts with the piccolo, followed by the woodwinds, strings, brass, and percussion. Once everyone has entered, the brass section is heard again along with a bang on the gong playing Purcell's original melody. Find a recording of Young Persons Guide to the Orchestra on the internet and listen to it.

*A *fugue* is a composition with two or more voices or parts, in which the melody (called the subject), is played by one voice or part and then replayed and changed by the other voices or parts. Fugues contain between two to five parts.

Answer the following questions.

a. Who composed Young Persons Guide to the Orchestra? _____

b. In what country was he born? _____

c. In what era did he live? _____

d. Who composed the theme on which this work is based? _____

e. What era did this composer live? _____

f. How many variations are in Young Persons Guide to the Orchestra? _____

g. What are the four instrument families featured in this composition?

    1. _____

    2. _____

    3. _____

    4. _____

h. What type of piece is the final movement of this composition? _____

Piotr Ilyich Tchaikovsky (1840 - 1893) Romantic Era

Piotr Ilyich Tchaikovsky was born in Votkinsk, a town in Russia's Ural Mountains. His father was a Ukrainian mining engineer. He began piano lessons when he was five years old. In 1850 he moved to the city of St. Petersburg. Here, Tchaikovsky studied law because music was not considered an acceptable profession.

While in law school, Tchaikovsky continued to study music. He attended the opera and theater with his classmates. At age 23 he gave up his legal job with the Ministry of Justice and went to study music full time at the St. Petersburg Conservatory. In 1863, he moved to Moscow, where he became a professor of harmony at the Moscow Conservatory. It is now named after him.

Tchaikovsky wrote six symphonies, the famous Piano Concerto in B♭ major, a handful of operas and three ballets of which, "Swan Lake," "The Nutcracker" and "Sleeping Beauty" are his most famous works. During his life, his music was extremely popular, and he was in great demand as a conductor.

For many years, Tchaikovsky had a patroness named Nadezhda von Meck -- a wealthy widow who supported the arts and artists. She sent him money monthly so that he could concentrate on composing without having to worry about making a living. For 14 years they communicated by letter, but von Meck insisted that they never meet in person. Tchaikovsky dedicated his Fourth Symphony to her.

Tchaikovsky traveled all over Europe for performances of his music. In 1891, he went to America where he was invited to conduct the New York Symphony at the opening of Carnegie Hall.

He died in St. Petersburg on November 6, 1893. The cause of his death was officially declared as cholera; an infection usually contracted from drinking dirty or contaminated water.

The Nutcracker

Piotr Ilyich Tchaikovsky's ballet, **The Nutcracker**, written in 1892, is based on a story by German author E.T.A. Hoffmann. The ballet was choreographed by Marius Petipa and Lev Ivanov. A choreographer designs the dances for a ballet.
In The Nutcracker, a Christmas present, a nutcracker, comes to life as a handsome prince. He takes the young girl who received him as a present on some fantastic adventures. This is one of Tchaikovsky's most famous compositions, and perhaps the most popular ballet in the world.

This is a summary of the story of The Nutcracker.

Act I

It is Christmas Eve and Dr. Stahlbaum and his wife, a former ballerina, are giving a party. Their children, Clara and Fritz, are happy to see the guests. All of the children are given toys. The mysterious Dr. Drosselmeyer is at the party, and performs magic tricks for the children. Dr. Drosselmeyer gives Clara a Nutcracker. She is fascinated by it, and she believes that it has magical powers. Fritz breaks the Nutcracker, and it mysteriously fixes itself. The party comes to an end, the guests depart and the family goes to bed.

Clara is restless and cannot sleep. She sneaks downstairs looking for the Nutcracker. At the stroke of midnight, strange things begin to happen. The room fills with giant mice who attack Clara. The Nutcracker, leading an army of life-size toy soldiers, come to Clara's rescue. The Rat King, who is the leader of the mice attacks the Nutcracker, and Clara hits him with her shoe. The Nutcracker wins the battle and is transformed into a handsome prince.

The Nutcracker Prince turns Clara's house into the Land of Snow. The Snow Queen and the Nutcracker Prince dance with the Snowflakes. Clara and the Nutcracker Prince depart for the Kingdom of Sweets in an enchanted sleigh.

Act II

Clara and the Nutcracker Prince travel across the Lemonade Sea to the beautiful Land of Sweets, ruled by the Sugar Plum Fairy. At the Kingdom of Sweets, the cooks are preparing delicious treats for their visit. The Sugar Plum Fairy welcomes them to her kingdom. In Clara's honor, the Sugar Plum Fairy has her subjects dance for them while they eat. After, the Sugar Plum Fairy and the Nutcracker Prince dance a grand pas de deux.

As the celebration concludes, Clara drifts off to sleep. She awakens at home, but it appears all this was just a dream. Christmas Eve is over. Clara, still thinking of the marvelous dream, is sitting at home by the Christmas tree, with the Nutcracker-Doll on her lap.

Waltz of the Flowers and Dance of the Sugar Plum Fairy

The "Waltz of the Flowers" is a piece from the second act of The Nutcracker. This is one of Tchaikovsky's most well-known compositions. It has been performed and arranged for many combinations of instruments and instrumental groups.

The "Dance of the Sugar Plum Fairy" is a dance from Act 2 of the Nutcracker. The Sugar Plum Fairy dances a pas de deux with her prince. A pas de deux is a dance duet in which two dancers, typically a male and a female, perform ballet steps together. This dance was choreographed by Lev Ivanov.

Choreographer Marius Petipa envisioned the Sugar Plum Fairy's music sounding like "drops of water shooting from a fountain." To achieve this, Tchaikovsky used an instrument called a **celesta**. The celesta looks a little like a piano but has metal plates instead of strings. The plates are hit by hammers, producing a soft, bell-like sound. Tchaikovsky wrote, "The celesta is midway between a tiny piano and a Glockenspiel, with a divinely wonderful sound."

The "Dance of the Sugar Plum Fairy" is one of the ballet's best known musical works.

History Level 5

George Frideric Handel (1685 - 1759) Baroque Era

George Frideric Handel was born on February 23, 1685, in Halle Germany. His father, a barber-surgeon, wanted his son to be a lawyer. However, Handel loved music and practiced on a small keyboard instrument called a clavichord, given to him by his aunt.

In 1693, while visiting the royal court, Handel had an opportunity to play the great organ. When the Duke heard him play, he convinced his father to give him musical training. Handel studied with the organist of St. Michel's in Halle. He learned how to compose, and how to play violin and oboe as well as organ and harpsichord.

In 1702, Handel followed his father's suggestion and entered law school at the University of Halle. After his father's death in the following year, he left his law studies and accepted a position as the organist at Halle Cathedral. The following year, he moved to Hamburg and worked as a violinist and harpsichordist at the opera house. It was there that Handel's first operas were written and produced.

In 1710, Handel accepted the position of Kapellmeister to George, Elector of Hanover, who was soon to be King George I of Great Britain. In 1712, he settled in England where George's wife Queen Anne gave him a yearly income.

Handel wrote operas and oratorios plus music for instruments and ensembles. In 1727, he applied for British citizenship and adopted England as his new home. When King George I died, Handel wrote the music for the coronation of the new king. *Zadok the Priest*, one of these compositions, is still performed today at British coronations.

By 1741, Handel had completed the oratorio Messiah. The first performance of Messiah was given in Ireland in 1742 and was a great success. Many people, to this day, stand during the performance of the "Hallelujah Chorus." Some historians disagree, but the legend is that when the king first heard the "Hallelujah Chorus" he rose to his feet, overcome with emotion. Since the king stood, so did the entire audience. The tradition continues to this day of standing when the "Hallelujah Chorus" from Messiah is performed.

Handel died on April 14, 1759. He was given the honor of a state funeral and was buried in Westminster Abby in London, England. More than 3,000 people attended his funeral.

What is an Oratorio?

An *oratorio* is a large composition for orchestra, choir, and soloists based on a religious theme. Some of the components of an oratorio are:

- *overture* - the musical introduction to the oratorio.
- *recitative* - a kind of musical declamation used during the oratorio, sung in the rhythm of ordinary speech often with many words on the same note.
- *aria* - an accompanied song for a solo voice.
- *chorus* - a large group of singers that performs together with an orchestra.

Messiah

Messiah is an oratorio composed in 1741 by George Frideric Handel. The *libretto,* which is the term used for the text of the oratorio, is based on verses from the Old and New Testaments of the Bible.

It is believed that Handel composed Messiah in only three or four weeks in August and September of 1741. What makes this amazing is the scale of this work. The score is 259 pages, and it takes nearly two hours to perform.

The "Hallelujah Chorus" from Messiah

The "Hallelujah Chorus" is part of Handel's Messiah. It is written for a chorus consisting of soprano, alto, tenor and bass with orchestra. The voices in a four part chorus are:

- *soprano* - sung by womens high voices
- *alto* - sung by womens low voices
- *tenor* - sung by mens high voices
- *bass* - sung by mens low voices

The text for "Hallelujah Chorus" comes from the book of Revelation in the New Testament. The word 'Hallelujah" means praise the Lord and is used in worship as an expression of rejoicing.
Text:
>Hallelujah!
>For the Lord God omnipotent reigneth;
>The kingdom of this world is become the kingdom of our Lord and of his Christ;
>and He shall reign for ever and ever.
>King of Kings and Lord of Lords.
>Hallelujah!

The example below is the opening of the chorus from the Hallelujah Chorus. Each voice part of the chorus receives its own staff line.

Hallelujah Chorus uses a technique called **word painting**. Word painting, sometimes called tone painting or text painting, is the technique of writing music that mirrors the actual meaning of a song.

In Hallelujah chorus low notes symbolize the world while the kingdom of the Lord is sung on high notes. The Hallelujah section has a joyful sound characterized by arpeggios and chromatic notes occurring in a major scale. The line *"for ever and ever"* is repeated over and over.

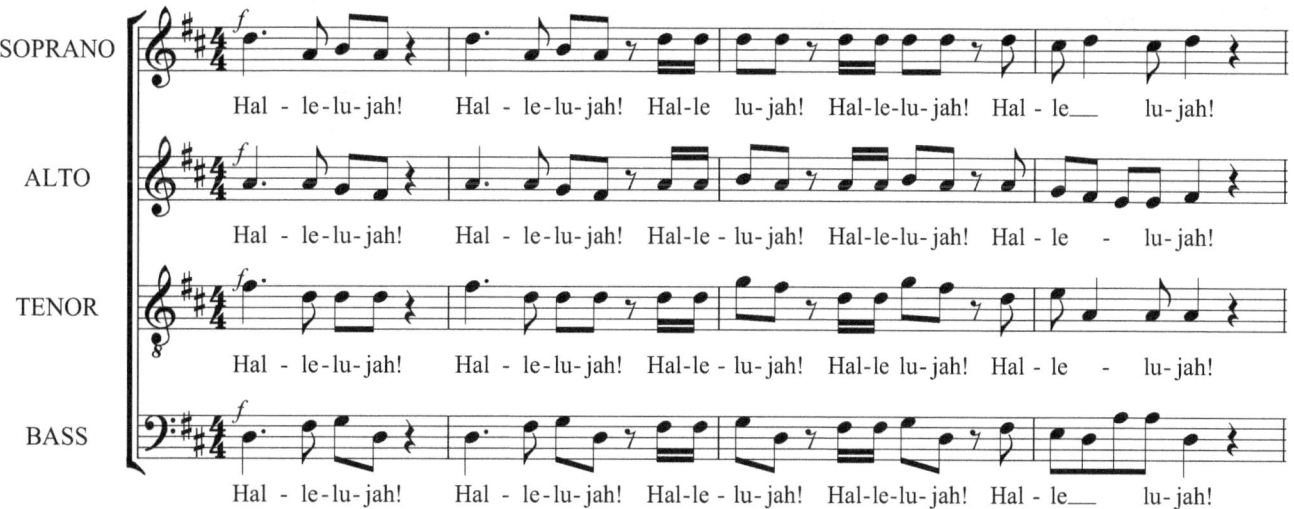

Wolfgang Amadeus Mozart (1756 - 1791) Classical Era

Wolfgang Amadeus Mozart was born in Salzburg, Austria, on January 27, 1756. He was born into a family of musicians and was an incredible child prodigy. Under the strong influence of his father, Mozart began composing music at the age of five! Here is a brief timeline of his life:

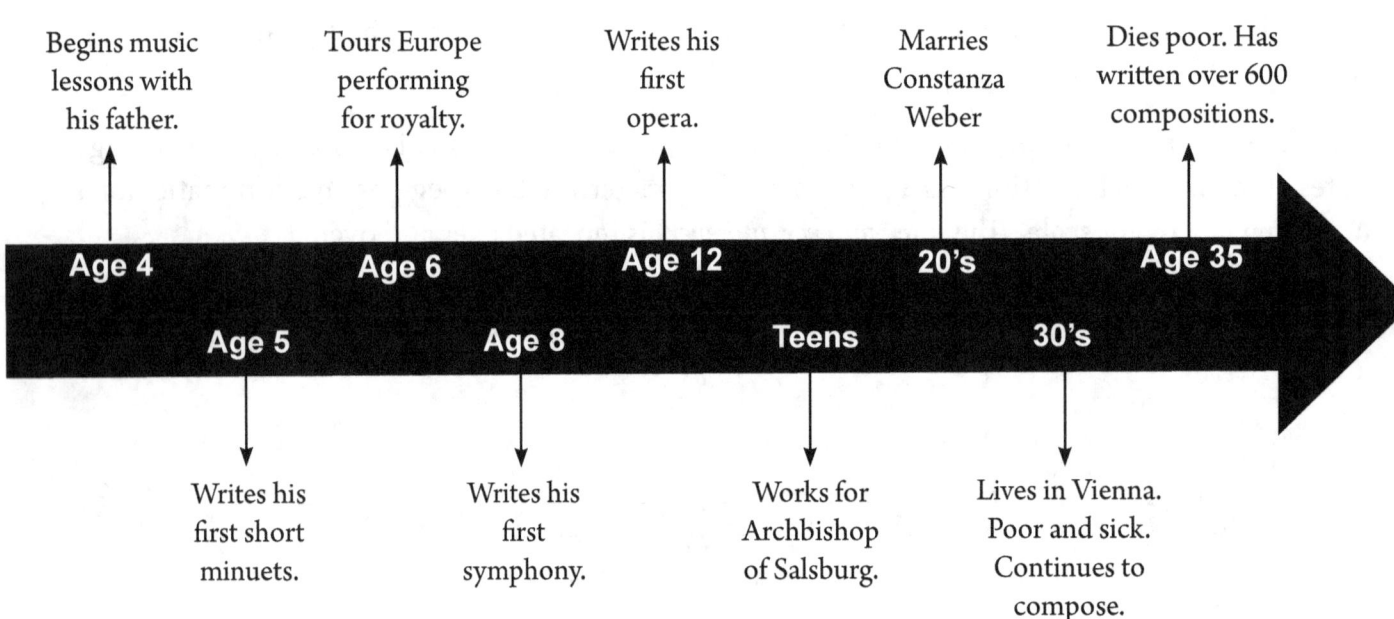

History

Opera

An *opera* is a play with music. The actual word "opera" is Italian for "work" and was first used in England in 1656. The earliest Italian operas were called favola in musica (fable in music) and drama per musica (drama by means of music).

The construction of an opera is like that of a play. It can be anywhere from one to five acts, and last anywhere from 30 minutes to five hours. The average opera is usually about 3 hours long. Like plays, operas are staged and use sets and costumes.

Operas usually begin with an *overture*. An overture is a piece of music played by the orchestra that contains melodies from the main part of the opera. The purpose of the overture is to inform the audience that the opera is starting and to set the mood.

Elements of an Opera

Here are some of the elements that are found in an opera:

Recitatives
Recitatives are simple melodies sung at the speed of normal speech. There were originally accompanied by a harpsichord, and in later operas, by the orchestra.

Arias
Arias are songs that can be taken out of an opera and sung as separate musical performances. Most operas are remembered for their finest arias. Arias are often challenging to perform, and give singers the opportunity to show off their voices.

Ensembles
Ensembles occur when characters in the opera sing together. They range from short duets to long, complex pieces involving many characters. Some of Mozart's ensembles can last for 20 minutes!

Choruses
A chorus is a group of singers, singing together. They supply the crowd scenes and extra characters in the opera, as well as the opportunity for beautiful choral music. Members of the chorus may portray servants, party guests, or other unnamed characters.

The Magic Flute (1791)

Mozart's famous opera, **The Magic Flute, Die Zauberflöte** in German, was composed in 1791. The **libretto** or text of the opera was written by Emanuel Schikaneder. It tells a fanciful and extraordinary story that includes a bird seller, a princess, a young prince who wants to rescue her, an evil Queen of the Night, a wise priest, and of course, a magic flute. The story is very complicated, but the music is beautiful and unforgettable.

The Magic Flute is a genre or type of opera called **Singspiel**. Singspiel (pronounced "zing-shpeel") originated in German-speaking countries and found its roots in comic opera. The translation of singspiel is "sing-play." It includes spoken dialogue between the singing, and often, an exotic or fanciful theme.

The Magic Flute is the most famous example of Singspiel. When Mozart was composing, opera was dominated by Italian traditions and language. Mozart decided to write this opera in German as a way to show pride and love of his country and culture and to connect with the common people, not just the elite. It contains a diverse cast of characters and some of Mozart's most magnificent music.

Queen of the Night Aria from "The Magic Flute"

"Der Hölle Rache kocht in meinem Herzen" ("Hell's vengeance boils in my heart"), is an aria sung by the Queen of the Night, in the second act of The Magic Flute. It is often called "The Queen of the Night Aria." In it, the Queen of the Night, who is in a tremendous rage, places a knife into the hand of her daughter Pamina and demands that she assassinate Sarastro, the Queen's rival.

The Queen of the Night is sung by a *coloratura soprano*. Sopranos sing in the highest range of the four voice parts. However, coloratura sopranos are capable of seemingly superhuman feats. In the Queen of the Night aria, the voice is extremely agile, firing out fast paced notes that ascend as high as the 3rd F above middle C. Coloratura soprano roles have existed from Baroque through 20th century opera.

An amazing performance of this aria by the gifted soprano Diana Damrau can be found on YouTube.

The example below is the opening measures of Der Hölle Rache kocht in meinem Herzen. The piano part is the orchestral reduction. The key is in D minor. **Allegro assai** means very fast.

The excerpt below shows the incredible virtuosity employed by the coloratura soprano in this aria.

This is the text for Der Hölle Rache kocht in meinem Herzen in German with English translation.

Der Hölle Rache kocht in meinem Herzen,	The vengeance of Hell boils in my heart,
Tod und Verzweiflung flammet um mich her!	Death and despair flame about me!
Fühlt nicht durch dich Sarastro	If Sarastro does not through you feel
Todesschmerzen,	The pain of death,
So bist du meine Tochter nimmermehr.	Then you will be my daughter nevermore.
Verstossen sei auf ewig,	Disowned may you be forever,
Verlassen sei auf ewig,	Abandoned may you be forever,
Zertrümmert sei'n auf ewig	Destroyed be forever
Alle Bande der Natur	All the bonds of nature,
Wenn nicht durch dich!	If not through you
Sarastro wird erblassen!	Sarastro becomes pale! (as death)
Hört, Rachegötter,	Hear, Gods of Revenge,
Hört der Mutter Schwur!	Hear a mother's oath!

Harold Arlen (1905- 1986) Modern Era

Harold Arlen was an American composer, arranger, pianist, and vocalist. He worked as a piano accompanist in vaudeville during his early twenties. His first hit song "Get Happy" was composed with Ted Koehler in 1929.

In the 1930's and 40's, Arlen wrote some of his greatest hits including the score to the movie, The Wizard of Oz. He and his co-writer won the 1939 Academy Award for Best Original Song for "Over the Rainbow."

Stormy Weather, It's Only a Paper Moon, and I've Got the World on a String, are just a few of the standards that live on today and make Harold Arlen one of the most celebrated American composers of the 20th Century.

Over the Rainbow

Harold Arlen composed "Over the Rainbow," with lyricist Edgar Yipsel Harburg, for the 1939 movie The Wizard of Oz.

In the movie, it is sung by actress and singer Judy Garland who plays the role of Dorothy Gale. This film introduced Garland's powerful voice to the public. Visit YouTube for a recording of Garland's performance. Over the Rainbow is written for solo voice and orchestra. It follows a type of song form called AABA song form. This was a standard form used during the first part of the 20th century by composers like Harold Arlen, George Gershwin, and Irving Berlin. AABA songs are usually 32 bars in length and preceded by an Introduction.

AABA song form contains an opening section (A), a bridge (B), and a final A section. It is used in a variety of music genres including pop, jazz, and gospel.
The typical AABA song form follows this outline:

(Introduction)   **A** = 8 bars   **A** = 8 bars   **B** = 8 bars   **A** = 8 bars

AABA has no separate chorus, and the title usually appears at the beginning of each A section. In Over the Rainbow, each A section begins with the lyrics "Somewhere Over the Rainbow." The B section is contrasting and brings the listener back to the last A section.

The lyrics to Over the Rainbow help to illustrate the AABA song structure form.

Introduction   When all the world is a hopeless jumble,
and the raindrops tumble all around,
heaven opens a magic lane.

When all the clouds darken up the skyway,
There's a rainbow highway to be found,
Leading from your window pane.

To a place behind the sun,
Just a step beyond the rain.

A   Somewhere over the rainbow, way up high,
There's a land that I dreamed of,
Once in a lullabye.

A   Somewhere over the rainbow, skies are blue,
And the dreams that you dare to dream,
Really do come true.

B   Someday day I'll wish upon a star,
and wake up where the clouds are far behind me.
Where troubles melt like lemon drops,
Away above the chimney tops,
That's where you'll find me.

A   Somewhere over the rainbow, skies are blue,
And the dreams that you dare to dream,
Really do come true.
If happy little bluebirds fly.
Beyond the rainbow,
Why, oh why can't I?

Answer the following questions.

a) Where was Handel born? _____

b) In what music era did Handel live? _____

c) What country did Handel adopt as his new home? _____

d) What is an oratorio? _____

e) When did Handel compose Messiah? _____

f) What voices make up the 4 parts of the chorus in Hallelujah Chorus?

_____ _____ _____ _____

g) What is word painting? _____

_____

h) Give one example of word painting in Hallelujah Chorus. _____

_____

i) What is an opera? _____

j) In what era did Mozart compose? _____

k) What year did Mozart compose "The Magic Flute?" _____

l) What genre or type of opera is "The Magic Flute?" _____

m) What language did Mozart use for "The Magic Flute?" _____

n) What is an aria? _____

_____

o) What type of soprano sings the Queen of the Night aria? _____

History

Choose the correct answer.

The composer of the Wizard of Oz:

❏ Harold Arlen ❏ George Gershwin ❏ Irving Berlin

Harold Arlen was:

❏ French ❏ Russian ❏ American

"Over the Rainbow" was written for:

❏ Bette Davis ❏ Judy Garland ❏ Beyonce

The song form of "Over the Rainbow" is:

❏ AABA ❏ ABBA ❏ ABAB

History Level 6

The Baroque Era (ca 1600 - 1750)

The word **Baroque** is used to describe a style of art from a specific period in history. *Art* can mean a lot of things. Here, it applies to painting, architecture, and most importantly to our field of study, music.

All Baroque art, architecture, and music was created around 1600 to 1750. However, Baroque music is a style of music. It is not an exact period of time.

What is the Baroque style?

Artists of the Baroque period attempted to evoke emotions in the listener by appealing to their senses. A composer could create a piece of music that would make the listener feel a specific emotion (sadness, happiness, etc.). This was known as **the doctrine of the affections**.

Baroque music is tuneful, very organized, and its melodies are often highly decorated and elaborate. This music can be quite dramatic.

A lot of Baroque music is **contrapuntal** or based on **counterpoint**. This means that there can be many different lines of music (or melodies) all going their own way. These single melodies weave together to make a whole piece of music.

The best way to understand Baroque music, is to listen to the great Baroque composers.

There are many great composers from the Baroque era. The greatest one is Johann Sebastian Bach (1685–1750).

Other famous baroque composers include:

Johann Pachelbel (1653–1706)
Antonio Vivaldi (1678–1741)
George Frideric Handel (1685–1759)

Johann Sebastian Bach (1685 - 1750)

Johann Sebastian Bach was born in Eisenach, Germany, where his father, a musician, taught him to play violin and harpsichord. By the time Johann was 10, both his parents had died. Johann was raised by his older brother who was a church organist. Johann also became a very skilled organist.

Bach's life has three major periods.

The Weimar period. Bach worked for the Duke of Weimar. In this period he became an organ virtuoso and wrote many great works for the instrument.

The Cöthen period. Bach worked for the Prince of Anhalt-Cöthen. During this period he composed a lot of chamber music including suites, instrumental sonatas, and the Brandenburg Concertos.

The Leipzig period. During this period Bach became the cantor, organist, and music composer for St. Thomas Lutheran Church in Leipzig, Germany. Bach remained there for the rest of his life.

Bach wrote music for keyboard instruments (harpsichord, clavichord, organ), orchestra, choirs, chamber groups, and many solo instruments. He is considered one of the greatest musical geniuses in history. In fact, he is such an important composer, that the year of his death (1750), is used to mark the end of the Baroque Era.

Two-part Invention in C major, BWV 772 - J.S. Bach

Bachs *Inventions and Sinfonias,* also known as the *Two and Three-Part Inventions* are a collection of thirty pieces for keyboard. There are 15 two-part and 15 three-part inventions in the masterpiece. Bach said that he composed the Inventions "for amateurs of the keyboard to achieve a cantabile style of playing in two and three parts." They were written as musical teaching pieces for his students.
The two-part inventions were composed in the Cöthen period, and the three-part inventions (Sinfonias)were completed at the beginning of the Leipzig period.

Polyphony is the performance of multiple melodies at the same time. It's a little like two people giving speeches next to each other, but the speeches are different. Imagine having four speakers giving four different speeches at the same time. Eventually, rules developed to control these multiple melodies. These rules became known as counterpoint or the practice of controlling the relationship between the different melodies.

Polyphony is one of the musical textures. Texture is how you hear the music. It may sound dense, thick, thin, or a number of different ways. Polyphony is typically described as thick or densely textured, due to the independence of multiple melodic lines.

An invention is a short composition for a keyboard instrument using two-part **counterpoint**. In a two-part invention, there are two lines of music that interweave with one another. As a result, two part inventions are **polyphonic**.

Inventions use techniques we have covered in past melody writing lessons. These are:

- *motives*: short melodic and rhythmic ideas used to create a melody
- *imitation*: the technique of repeating a musical idea (motive) in another voice or part.
- *sequence*: the repetition of a motive or phrase at a higher or lower pitch.

Below are the opening four measures of J.S. Bach's Two-Part Invention in C major, BWV 772. BWV is a numbering system used to identify Bach's compositions. This invention is based on a seven note motive found in m.1. Imitation of the opening motive can be found in the bass clef in m.1. A sequence moving downward can be found in mm.3 and 4.

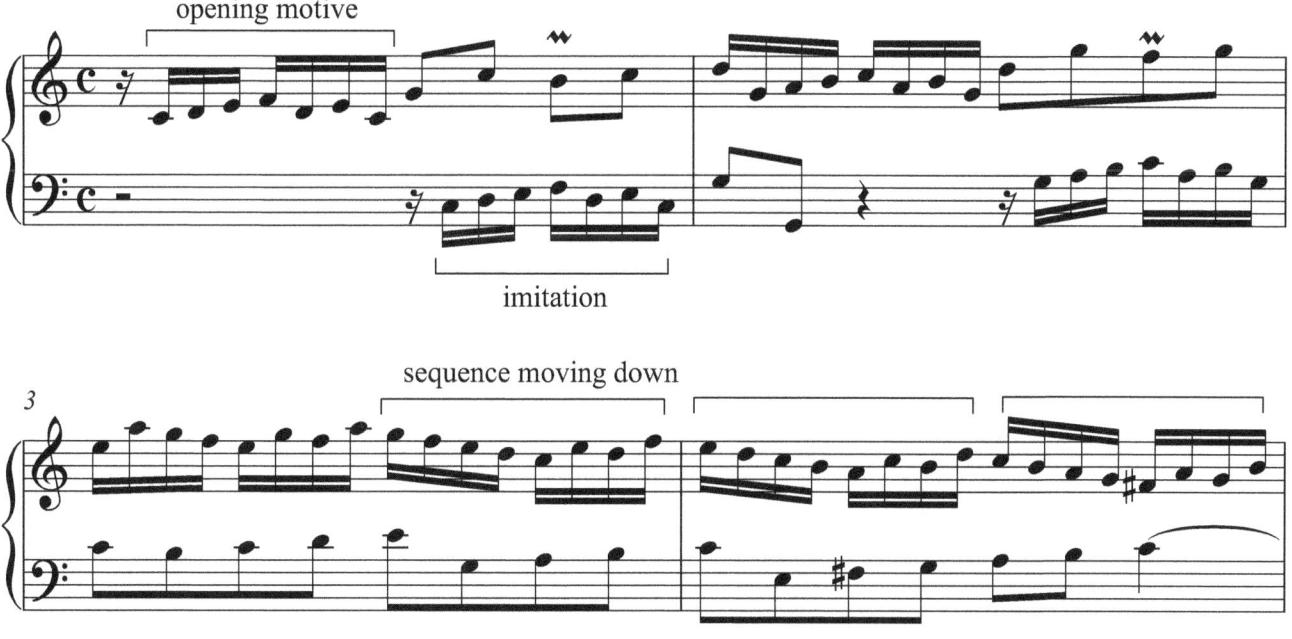

Brandenburg Concerto No. 5 - Johann Sebastian Bach

The six Brandenburg Concerti, BWV 1046-1051, by Johann Sebastian Bach is a collection of chamber music works presented to Christian Ludwig, the Margrave of Brandenburg in 1721. Margrave is a title that used to be given to Governors of German provinces.

He assembled these six *concerti grossi* and presented them, as a type of job application, to the Margrave. A ***concerto grosso*** is a baroque work for orchestra. It usually has three movements and contains a group of solo instruments called the ***concertino*** that contrasts with the full string orchestra which is known as the ***ripieno***.

Bach's title for these works was "concertos for a variety of instruments," since each one uses a different combination of instruments. He tried to use as many different combinations of common instruments as he could. Bach never actually called them the Brandenburg Concertos. The name was given to the pieces by a biographer after his death.

The Fifth Concerto in D major for **violin, flute**, and **harpsichord** makes use of a very popular chamber music ensemble (violin, flute, and harpsichord). These three instruments are the *concertino*. Bach, himself a keyboard virtuoso, included an amazing solo harpsichord cadenza in this concerto.

The first movement of this concerto is in ***ritornello*** form. In this form, a repeated section of music, known as the ritornello alternates with different musical sections.

Below is the opening of the Brandenburg Concerto No. 5. by J.S. Bach. The score below is an *open score*. In open score, each instrument has its part written on a separate staff. Traditionally the instrument names are written in Italian and appear on the left of the score from highest to lowest. On this score, the top line is the flute, and the bottom is the harpsichord, with the string section between them.

The Classical Era (ca 1750 - 1825)

The Classical era follows the Baroque era. Music from the Classical era was composed around 1750 to 1825.

Classical music is clear, structured and balanced. Form is very important, as well as harmony and tonality—that is, the key in which a piece is written.

Classical music uses dynamic contrast to emphasize movement from the tonic to new keys and then a return to the tonic. It is often loud one moment and then soft the next. It changes volume frequently. It is different from Baroque music in that it is simpler in style, without the heavy figurations and ornamentation. It is not polyphonic, that is, there is no weaving together of different tunes like those found in Baroque music.

Classical music often has a clear tune or melody with an accompaniment. Music with a single line of melody and a harmonic accompaniment is called **homophonic music** or **homophony**.

Most classical music is ***absolute music***. This means that it is written specifically for the sake of being music. There are no pictorial or literary associations. It is not supposed to depict or portray anything. It's just beautiful music!

Large forms featured in the Classical period include the solo sonata, symphony, and the concerto. This period also saw a rise in ***chamber music***. Chamber music is composed for smaller groups of musicians. These groups consist of two to ten players, with one player on each part. Examples of chamber music include trios, quartets, and quintets.

The greatest composers of the classical period are:

Joseph Haydn (1732–1809).
Wolfgang Amadeus Mozart (1756–1791).
Ludwig van Beethoven (1770–1827).

The classical period ended before Beethoven died. In fact, Beethoven was the one who ended it. Beethoven's later music was so new and unique that it had to be called something completely different.

Sonata Form in the Classical Era

Sonata form reached its zenith in the Classical era at the hands of Haydn, Mozart, and Beethoven.

Sonata form consists of three main sections:

1. **The exposition**: this is the opening section of sonata form. In this section, the composer introduces themes or melodies. Often there are two contrasting themes in two contrasting keys. Contrasting key or tonality is an essential part of this form.
2. **The development**: this is the middle section, and the composer *develops* the themes stated in the exposition. This developing is often done through movement to different keys.
3. **The recapitulation**: in this section the composer returns to the main themes stated in the exposition. This section does not usually change key and remains in the tonic throughout.

Sonata form was used as the basis for movements of solo sonatas, symphonies, concertos and chamber music.

Eine Kleine Nachtmusik (1st Mvt.) Wolfgang Amadeus Mozart

Wolfgang Amadeus Mozart (1756 - 1791) was one of the most important composers of the Classical era. He composed over 600 works, including some of the worlds most famous symphonies, chamber music, operas, and choral music.

Mozart gave the name *Eine kleine Nachtmusik* to his Serenade No. 13 for strings in G major, K 525. It is one of his most popular pieces, and the opening theme is famous. It was composed in 1787.

The title Eine kleine Nachtmusik means: "A little Night Music." "Nachtmusik" was a title that was given to serenades in the 18th century.

The genre of this work is chamber music. It is composed for two violins, viola, and cello and optional double bass. It can be performed as a string quartet or by a small group of string instruments, with one added double bass.

The first movement of Eine kleine Nachtmusik is in sonata form.

The complete work consists of 4 movements.

Choose the correct answers.

a. The Baroque period occurred approximately:	☐ 1600-1700 ☐ 2010-2015	☐ 1650-1725 ☐ 1600-1750
b. The following are famous Baroque composers:	☐ J.S. Bach ☐ Mozart	☐ Vivaldi ☐ Handel
c. These elements can be used to describe Baroque music:	☐ counterpoint ☐ romantic	☐ doctrine of affections ☐ highly ornamented
d. These are Bach's 3 main periods.	☐ Leipzig ☐ Berlin	☐ Weimar ☐ Cöthen
e. Bach composed for the following mediums.	☐ keyboard ☐ choir	☐ orchestra ☐ chamber music
f. How many 2 part inventions did J.S. Bach write?	☐ 21 ☐ 12	☐ 15 ☐ 6
g. The 3-part inventions are also known as:	☐ sonatas ☐ dances	☐ sinfonias ☐ fugues
h. The 2-part inventions are written for this many voices:	☐ 2 ☐ 6	☐ 3 ☐ 32
i. 3 elements found in the 2-part inventions are:	☐ motives ☐ imitation	☐ sequence ☐ monophony
j. This is the numbering system used to identify Bach's works:	☐ NRA ☐ BVW	☐ BWV ☐ BMW

History

Answer the following questions.

a. Who composed Brandenburg Concerto No. 5? _____

b. What genre is this work? _____

c. What 3 instruments are featured in this work? _____

d. What is this group of instruments called? _____

e. The full string orchestra in a concerto grosso is called a

☐ ripieno   ☐ concertino   ☐ oratorio   ☐ sequence

f. The form of the first movement of Brandenburg Concerto No. 5 is

☐ rondo   ☐ ritornello   ☐ sonata   ☐ binary

Answer the following questions as true (T) or false (F).

a. The classical period occured around 1750 to 1825. _____

b. The 3 major composers of the classical period are Haydn, Mozart and Bach. _____

c. Music with a single melodic line and accompaniment is *homophonic*. _____

d. Most classical music is *program music*. _____

e. Sonata form consists of 3 main sections. _____

f. These sections are: the *exhibition*, the *development* and the *recapitulation*. _____

g. Eine kleine Nachtmusik is *chamber music*. _____

h. Eine kleine Nachtmusisk is written for strings. _____

i. Eine kleine Nachtmusik contains 5 movements. _____

j. The first movement of Eine kleine Nachtmusik is in *sonata form*. _____

Music Terms

Study the following music terms

secondo, seconda	second, lower part of a duet
sempre	always
senza	without
sforzando, sf, sfz	sudden strong accent on a single note or chord
simile	continue in the same manner as has been indicated
subito	suddenly
tre corde	three strings, release the left pedal on the piano
troppo	too much
una corda	one string, depress the left pedal on the piano

11

Music Analysis

Form in Music

Music is often organized into sections. The general organization of these sections is called *form*. The form of a piece of music demonstrates its structure and can help the listener relate to and understand the intentions of the composer.

One way to approach music composition is through form. A composer uses phrases to represent musical ideas. The phrases are like musical sentences that make up the sections of a composition. Like sentences in a story, the individual phrases work together to create a complete paragraph and contribute to the larger musical section. Phrases are typically four measures long and often end on a longer note or a rest. This acts like the period of a sentence, giving a small pause between each phrase.

Phrases help to create sections in music. Composers may write phrases in groups that work together to form a section of music or an entire composition. We can label these phrases with letters to help identify the form and structure.

Study the phrases in Figure 11.1.

Phrase 1:

The letter '*a*' is used to identify the first phrase (mm.1 - 4) and any other phrases that are exactly the same. This phrase ends on scale degree $\hat{5}$, making it feel unfinished. It is four measures long and ends on a half note, giving pause before the next phrase begins.

Phrase 2:

The second phrase (mm.5 - 8) acts as a resolution or answer to the first phrase. It is labeled 'a^1.' 'a^1' is used to label phrases that are very similar to '*a*' but may contain some slight differences. This phrase is the same as '*a*' except for the last note. It is four measures long and ends on a stable pitch ($\hat{1}$). It also ends with a rest, giving pause before the next section starts.

❹ Phrase 3:

❺ The third phrase (mm. 9 - 12) is labeled '*b*' because the melody is different than phrase '*a*.' Music
❻ needs **repetition** so the listener has something familiar to hear, but it also needs **contrast** so it does not become boring. The two elements work together to make great compositions. If '*a*' was stated three times in a row, it might become too repetitive. This new material provides diversity and contrast. Phrase 3 is four measures long and ends on an unstable pitch ($\hat{5}$).

Phrase 4:

The fourth phrase (mm.13 - 16) is the same as phrase two, and like phrase two, it is labelled '*a¹*.' This phrase rounds out the piece and it ends on a stable pitch.

Figure 11.1

1. Answer the questions dealing with the following compositions.

a. Add the time signature directly on the music.

b. Name the key of this piece. _____

c. Mark the phrases with slurs.

d. Label the phrases with *a*, *a¹*, and *b*.

e. Name the chord formed by the notes at A: _____ B: _____

Piano Sonata, Mvt. I

Franz Joseph Haydn
(1732-1809)

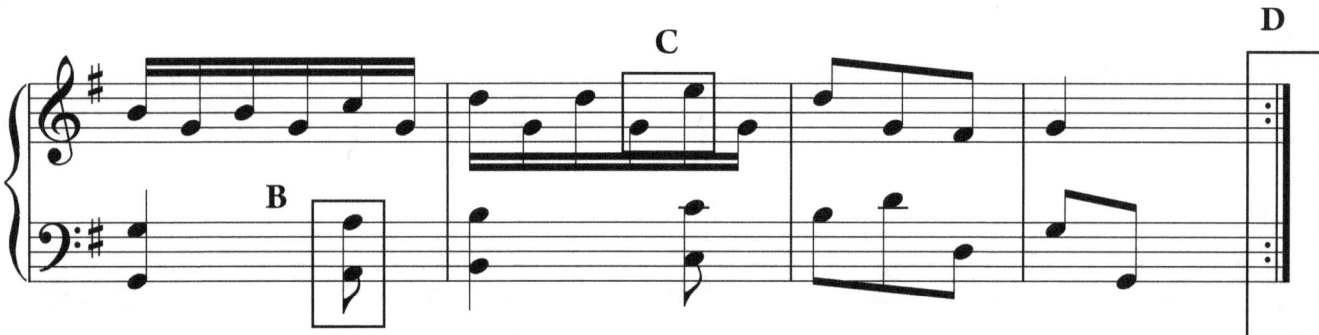

a. Add the correct time signature directly on the music.

b. Name the key of this piece. _____

c. Name the composer of this piece. _____

d. On which beat does this piece begin? _____

e. Name the intervals at: A _____ B _____ C _____

f. Does this piece end on a stable or unstable degree? _____

g. Explain the sign at D _____

h. Define *Presto* _____

i. Find one half step and circle it.

Menuetto

Wolfgang Amadeus Mozart
(1756-1791)

Andante

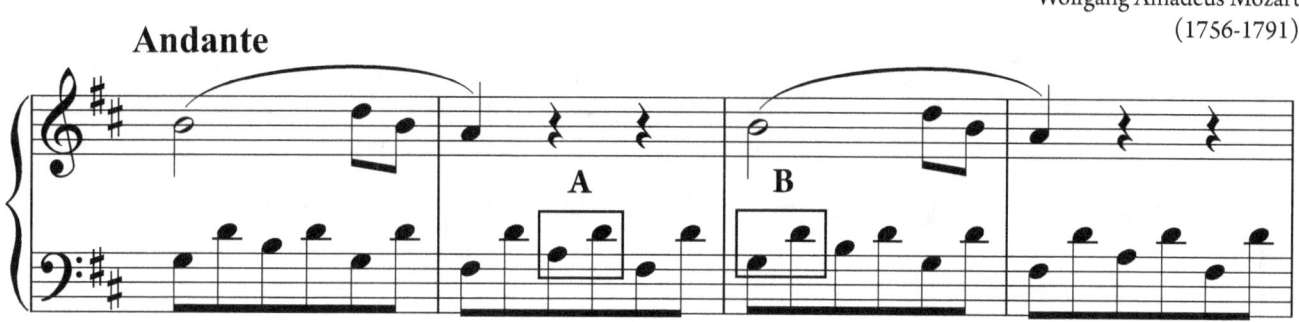

a. Add the correct time signature directly on the music.

b. Name the key of this piece. _____

c. Name the composer of this piece. _____

d. When did this composer live? _____

e. Name the intervals at : A_____ B_____ C_____

f. Explain the sign at D _____

h. Define *andante* _____

i. Does this piece end on a stable or unstable scale degree? _____

j. Name the triad formed by the notes at E: _____

k. In this key, this triad is the: ❏ tonic triad   ❏ subdominant triad   ❏ dominant triad

© San Marco Publications 2023

Music Analysis

❺ Answer questions dealing with the following musical excerpts.

❻

1. Who composed the music shown above?* _____

2. What is the name of the composition? _____

3. What key is it in? _____

4. What four voices are used to sing this piece?
   _____ _____ _____ _____

5. Name the triad formed by the notes at A _____

6. Name the interval at B. _____

7. Name the interval at C. _____

8. Name the interval at D. _____

*See History lessons.

1. Who wrote the above musical example?* _____

2. What musical period was it written? _____

3. What character is singing in this passage? _____

4. In what language is she singing? _____

5. What is the key of this piece? _____

6. Name the triad and inversion at A: _____
                                        B: _____
                                        C: _____

7. Circle one chromatic half step on the score. Label it CHS.

8. Define Allegro assai: _____

9. How many measures are in this example? _____

*See History lessons.

Sonatina

Cornelius Gurlitt
1820 -1901

1. Name the composer of this piece? _____

2. Name the key of this piece. _____

3. Write the time signature on the score.

4. Define "moderato" _____

5. How many phrases are in this example? _____

6. Does the first phrase end on a stable or unstable degree? _____

7. Does the second phrase end on a stable or unstable degree? _____

8. Label the phrases either: (a - a¹⁾) or (a - b) depending on the form.

9. What triad is formed by the notes in the box at letter A: _____

10. What triad is formed by the notes in the box at letter B: _____

11. Find the interval of a melodic minor 3rd, circle it, and label it min 3.

12. Find the interval of a melodic perfect 5th, circle it, and label it per 5.

13. Find two different diatonic semitones, circle them, and label them DS.

14. How many slurs occur in this piece? _____

Muzio Clementi
1752 -1832

1. Name the composer of this piece? _____

2. When did he live? _____

3. Write the time signature on the score.

4. Name the key of this piece. _____

5. Define "allegro." _____

6. Define "dolce." _____

7. For the triad at letter A, name the: Root _____ Quality _____ Position _____

8. For the triad at letter B, name the: Root _____ Quality _____ Position _____

9. How many times does the broken tonic triad occur in the bass clef. _____

10. Find a melodic major 2nd, circle it and label it maj 2.

11. Find a melodic major 3rd, circle it and label it maj 3.

12. Find a diatonic half step, put a box around it and label is DHS.

1. Name the key of this piece? _____

2. Write the time signature on the score.

3. Check the terms that apply to this time signature. ❑compound   ❑triple   ❑simple   ❑duple

4. Mark the phrases with a slur.

5. Label each phrase using the letters *a, a¹* or *b*.

6. Define "andantino." _____

7. Name the triad at letter A.   root: _____   quality: _____

Form - Review

One of the basic units of organization in a composition is the **phrase**. A composer may use groups of phrases to form sections, and the sections may be put together to create specific forms. Like the sentences in a story that work together to create a paragraph, phrases are musical sentences that work together to create a section.

Composers often write pairs of phrases that have a question and answer structure and work together to create a section of music. These are called **antecedent** (question) and **consequent** (answer) phrases.

The two phrases in Figure 11.2 create a section called a **parallel period**. The first phrase (*a*) ends on an unstable scale degree implying a half cadence. The second phrase (*a¹*) repeats much of the melodic material from the first phrase but ends on a stable scale degree implying an authentic cadence. Because the two phrases are very similar melodically, they are given the labels *a* and *a¹*.

Figure 11.2

❻The two phrases in Figure 11.3 create a section called a contrasting period. In a contrasting period, the melodic material is different (or contrasting) between the two phrases. The first phrase (*a*) ends on an unstable scale degree implying a half cadence. The second phrase uses different melodic material than the first phrase and is given the label *b*. It ends on a stable pitch implying an authentic cadence.

Figure 11.3

❻Binary Form

Sections similar to those found in Figure 11.2 and 11.3 can be combined to create larger musical forms. One of the most simple forms is **binary form**. The prefix 'bi" means 'two.' A piece in binary form consists of two different or contrasting sections that are labelled **A** and **B**. Lowercase letters are used to label the single phrases of the parallel and contrasting period. Uppercase letters are used to label the sections in binary form because they are larger.

Figure 11.4 contains the folk song *Greensleeves*. This is an example of a 16 measure piece in binary form. It consists of two parallel periods. The first 8 measure section is given the label **A**. The second 8 measure section is contrasting to the A section, and given the label **B**. The phrases of the A section could be labelled *a* and *a¹* and the phrases of the B section could be labelled *b* and *b¹*. However, when analyzing binary form, the phrases are not always so cut and dry. Binary form is just labelled with A and B to reflect the two larger contrasting sections.

Figure 11.4

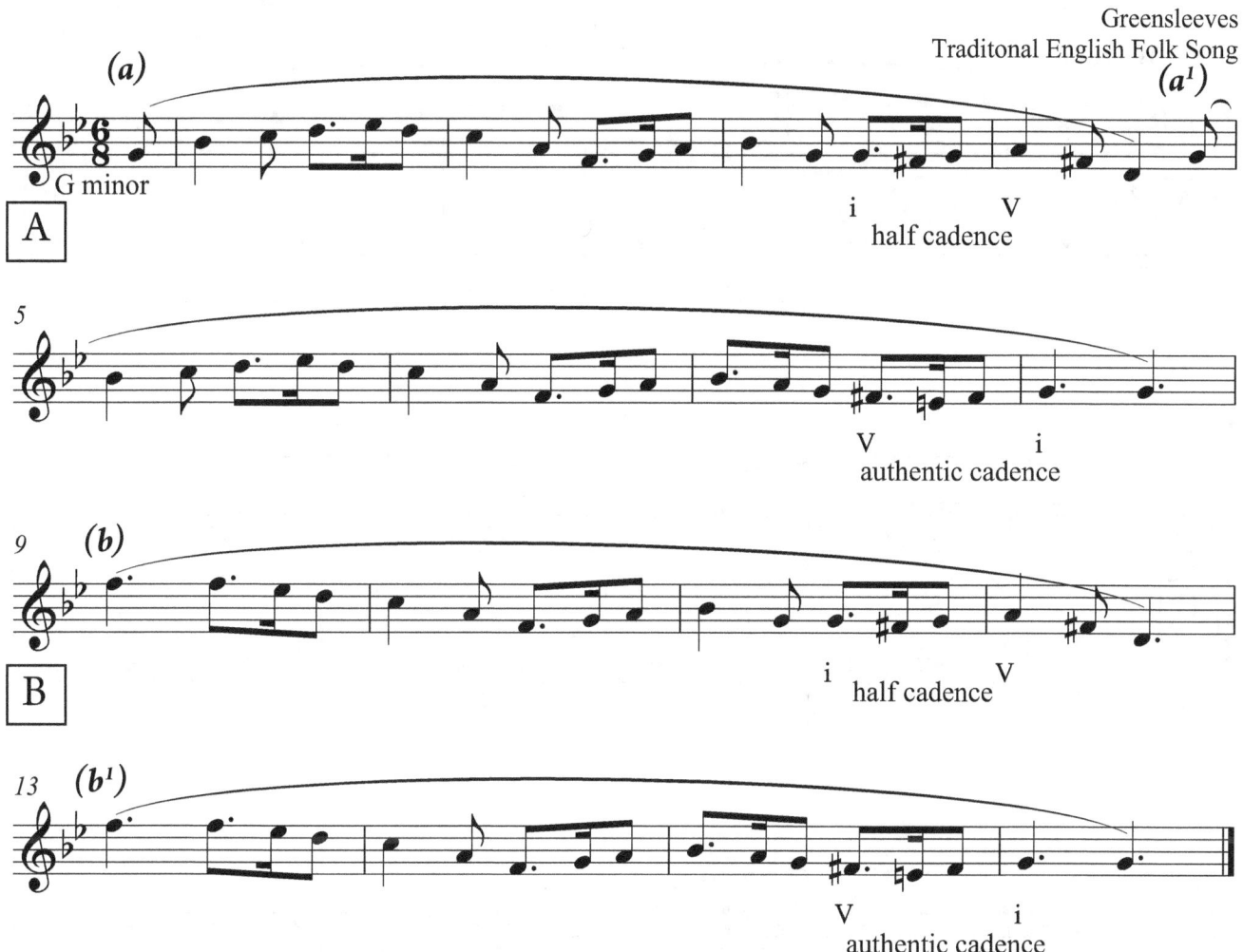

Ternary Form

Study Figure 11.5. This piece is in a three-part form called **_ternary form_** (ABA). The prefix 'ter' means 'three.' This form has three parts labelled A - B - A. In ternary form, the A section always returns after a contrasting B section.

In Figure 11.5 the first section (mm.1 - 8) is labelled A. The second contrasting section (mm. 9 - 16)is labelled B. The final section (mm. 17 - 24) is an exact repetition of the first section, and is labelled A. Sometimes the final A section is not an exact repitition of the first section. The composer may shorten, lengthen, alter the melody slightly, or vary the accompaniment of the final A section. In this case the form would be analyzed as ABA^1 to reflect this variation.

❻ Figure 11.5

Wolfgang Amadeus Mozart
12 Variations on "Ah vous dirai-je Maman"

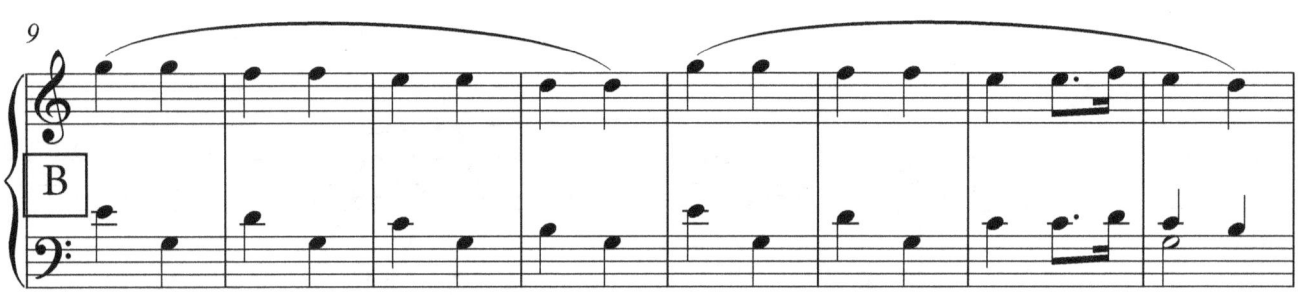

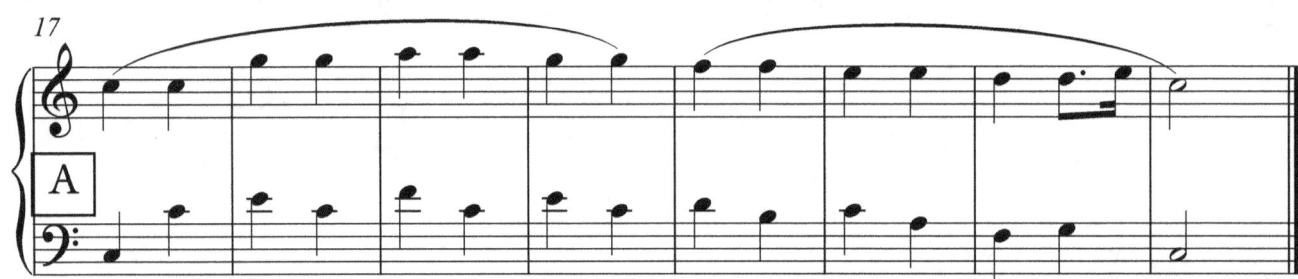

Binary and ternary forms are fairly simple, but they act as a basis for more complex forms in classical music. Phrases are used to organize a piece. Antecedent and consequent phrases are grouped to form periods. The periods come together to make sections, and the sections come together to make a composition. The sections vary by musical idea and are identified and labeled by their contrast or difference from one another. Compositions with the AB structure are in binary form, and compositions with ABA or ABA[1] are in ternary form.

Anton Diabelli
Op. 125. no. 3

Allegretto

1. Name the key of this piece. _____

2. Write the time signature directly on the score.

3. The form of this piece is: ❑ binary   ❑ ternary

4. Label the score by using A, A¹, and B to define the form.

5. Define **Allegretto**. _____

6. Check all statements below that apply to the chord at A:

   ❑ tonic triad   ❑ subdominant triad   ❑ C major triad   ❑ root position   ❑ broken chord

7. Check all statements below that apply to the chord at B:

   ❑ tonic triad   ❑ dominant triad   ❑ G major triad   ❑ 1st inversion   ❑ solid or blocked chord

8. Name the cadence at C:

   ❑ perfect authentic cadence   ❑ half cadence   ❑ imperfect authentic cadence

9. Symbolize the chords of this cadence on the score using functional chord symbols.

❻

Anton Diabelli
Op. 125 No. 4

1. Name the key of this piece. _____

2. Write the time signature directly on the score.

3. Check the words below that apply to this time signature.

     ❏triple ❏compound ❏duple ❏simple ❏quadruple

4. Mark the phrases using a slur.

5. The form of this piece is: ❏binary ❏ternary

6. Label the score by using A, A^1, and B to define the form.

7. Define **Moderato**. _____

8. Name the chord at letter A: _____

9. For the chord at letter B name the: root_____ quality _____ position _____

10. For the chord at letter C name the: root_____ quality _____ position _____

11. The cadence at D is: ❏half ❏perfect authentic ❏imperfect authentic

12. Write the functional chord symbols for this cadence directly on the score.

13. Find and circle a broken dominant triad on the score. Label it DT.

14. Find and circle a broken tonic triad on the score. Label it TT.

6

Joseph Haydn
(1732-1809)
Sonata Hob XVI 34, III

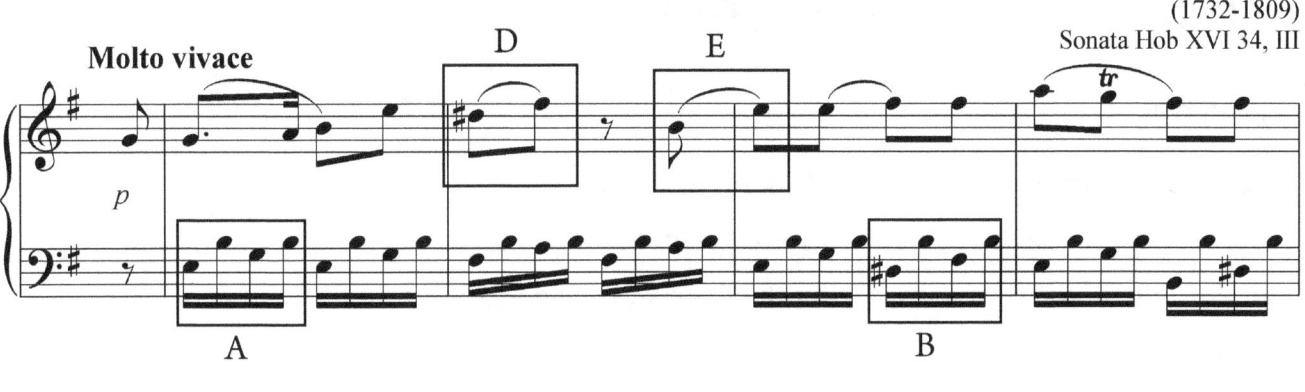

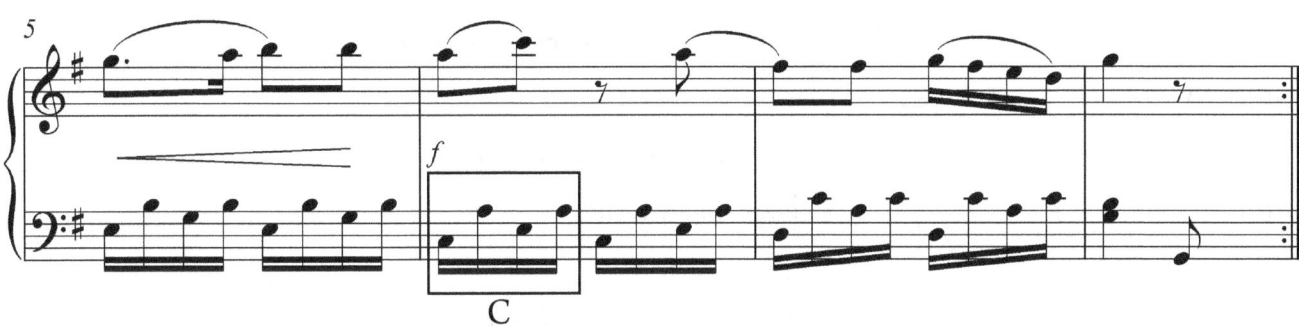

1. Name the key of this piece. _____

2. Write the time signature directly on the score.

3. This excerpt is written for a right hand melody with left hand accompaniment. This is and example of:

   ❑ polyphonic music   ❑ homophonic music   ❑ contrapuntal music   ❑ absolute music

4. What musical era was this piece composed? _____

5. Name the chord at A: root_____   quality_____   position_____

6. Name the chord at B: root_____   quality_____   position_____

7. Name the chord at C: root_____   quality_____   position_____

8. In this piece, chord A is the: ❑ tonic triad   ❑ subdominant triad   ❑ dominant triad

9. In this piece, chord B is the: ❑ tonic triad   ❑ subdominant triad   ❑ dominant triad

10. In this piece, chord C is the: ❑ tonic triad   ❑ subdominant triad   ❑ dominant triad

11. Define *Molto vivace*: _____

12. This excerpt is an example of a: ❑ parallel period   ❑ contrasting period

13. Name the interval at D: _____

14. Name the interval at E: _____

Music Terms and Signs

Terms

accelerando, accel.	becoming quicker
accent	a stressed note
ad libitum, ad lib.	at the liberty of the performer
adagio	slow
alla, all'	in the manner of
allegretto	fairly fast, a little slower than allegro
allegro	fast
andante	moderately slow, at a walking pace
andantino	a little faster than andante
animato	lively, animated
a tempo	return to the original tempo
ben, bene	well
cantabile	in a singing style
col, coll', colla, colle	with
con	with
con brio	with vigor
con espressione	with expression
con fuoco	with fire
con grazia	with grace
con moto	with motion
crescendo, cresc.	becoming louder
da capo, D.C.	from the beginning
D.C. al fine	repeat from the beginning and end at *Fine*
dal segno, D.S. 𝄋	from the sign
decrescendo, decresc.	becoming softer
diminuendo, dim.	becoming softer
dolce	sweetly, gentle
e, ed	and
espressivio, espress.	expressive, with expression

fine	the end
forte, f	loud
fortissimo, ff	very loud
fortepiano, fp	loud, then suddenly soft
grazioso	gracefully
grave	slow and solemn
larghetto	fairly slow, not as slow as largo
largo	very slow
leggiero	light
lento	slow
loco	return to the normal register
ma	but
maestoso	majestically
mano destra, m.d.	right hand
mano sinistra, m.s.	left hand
marcato	play marked or stressed
meno	less
meno mosso	less motion
mezzo forte, mf	moderately loud
mezzo piano, mp	moderately soft
moderato	at a moderate tempo
molto	much, very
non	not
ottava, 8va	the interval of an octave
pedale, ped	pedal
pianissimo, pp	very soft
piano, p	soft
piu	more
piu mosso	more motion
poco	little
poco a poco	little by little
prestissimo	as fast as possible

presto	very fast
primo, prima	first, the upper part of a duet
quasi	almost, as if
rallentando, rall.	slowing down
ritardando, rit.	slowing down gradually
rubato	flexible tempo with slight variations of speed to enhance musical expression.
secondo, seconda	second, lower part of a duet
sempre	always
senza	without
sforzando, sf, sfz	sudden strong accent on a single note or chord
simile	continue in the same manner as has just been indicated
staccato	play short and detached
subito	suddenly
tempo	speed at which music is performed
Tempo Primo, Tempo I	return to the original tempo
tranquillo	tranquil, quiet
tre corde	3 strings, release the left pedal on the piano
troppo	too much
una corda	1 string, depress the left pedal on the piano
vivace	lively, brisk

Signs

  accent - a stressed note

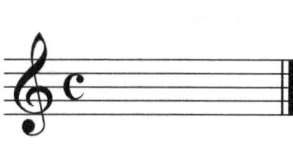 **common time** - symbol for 4/4

 **crescendo** - becoming louder

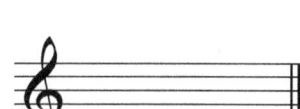 **decrescendo** - becoming softer

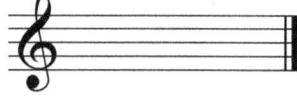 **double bar line** - the end of a piece

 **fermata** - hold note or rest longer than written value

 **slur** - play the notes smoothly (legato)

 **staccato** - play short and detached

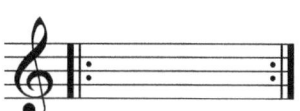 **tie** - hold for the combined value of the tied notes

 **repeat marks** - at the second sign go back to the first sign and repeat the music from there. The first sign is left out if the music is repeated from the beginning.

 **tenuto mark** - when placed over or under a note, hold it for its full value.

 **pedal symbol** - press/release the right pedal.

	**dal segno, D.S.** - from the sign.
	**8va** - play one octave higher than written pitch.
	**8va** - play one octave lower than written pitch.
	down bow - on a string instrument, play the note by drawing the bow downward.
	up bow - on a string instrument, play the note by drawing the bow upward.
,	**breath mark** - take a breath or a small break

Level 5 Exam

1. Name the following notes.

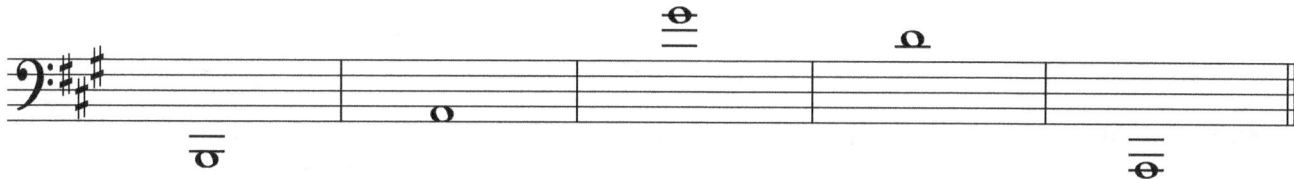

2. Name the following as chromatic half step (CHS), diatonic half step (DHS), or whole step (WS).

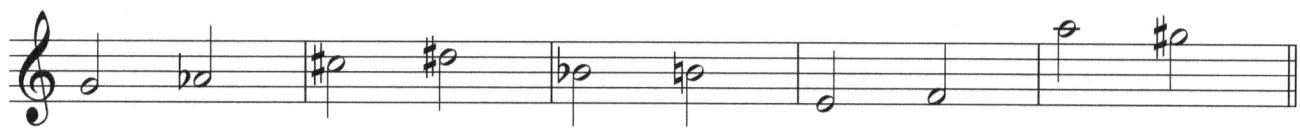

3. Write the following scales in quarter notes ascending and descending using the correct key signature for each. Label the dominant (D), subtonic (ST) and leading tones (LT).

E major

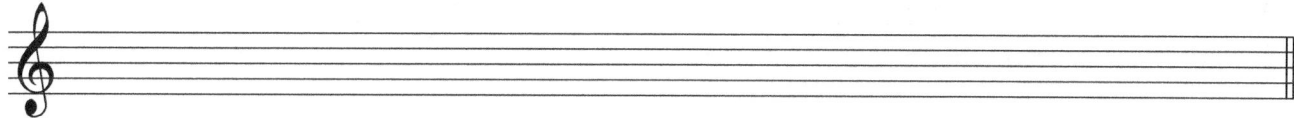

E major's parallel minor, harmonic form

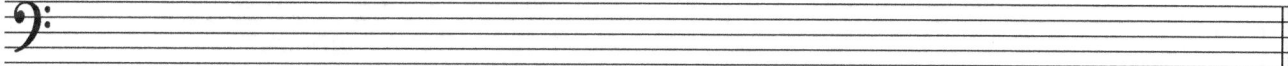

F minor, melodic form

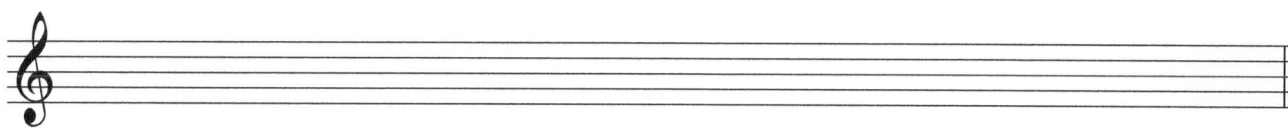

F minor's relative major

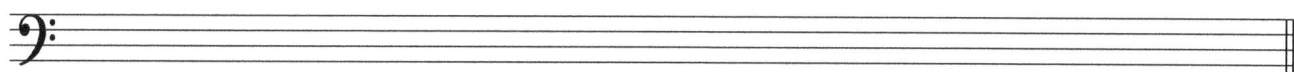

B minor, natural form

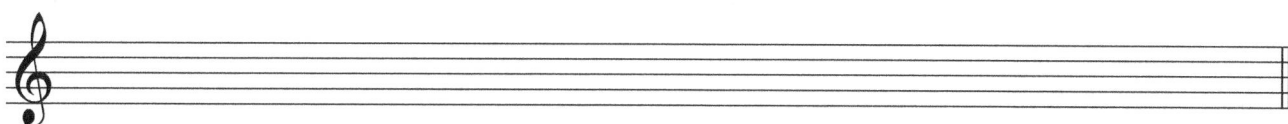

(5) 4. Name the following intervals.

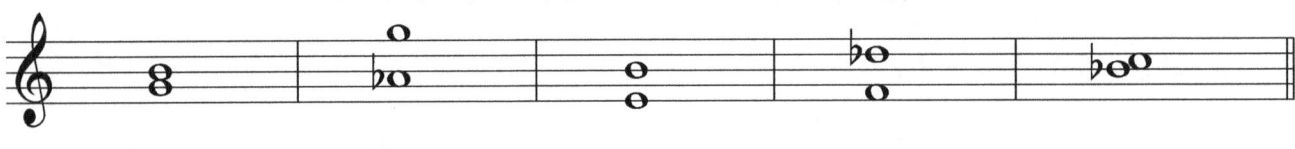

___ ___ ___ ___ ___

(5) 5. Write the following intervals above the given notes.

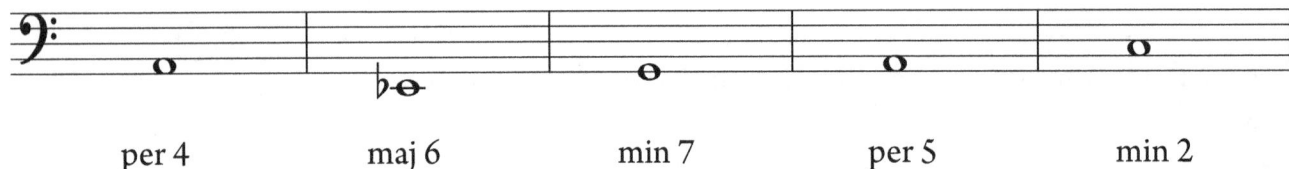

per 4   maj 6   min 7   per 5   min 2

(10) 6. Complete the following measures with rests under the brackets.

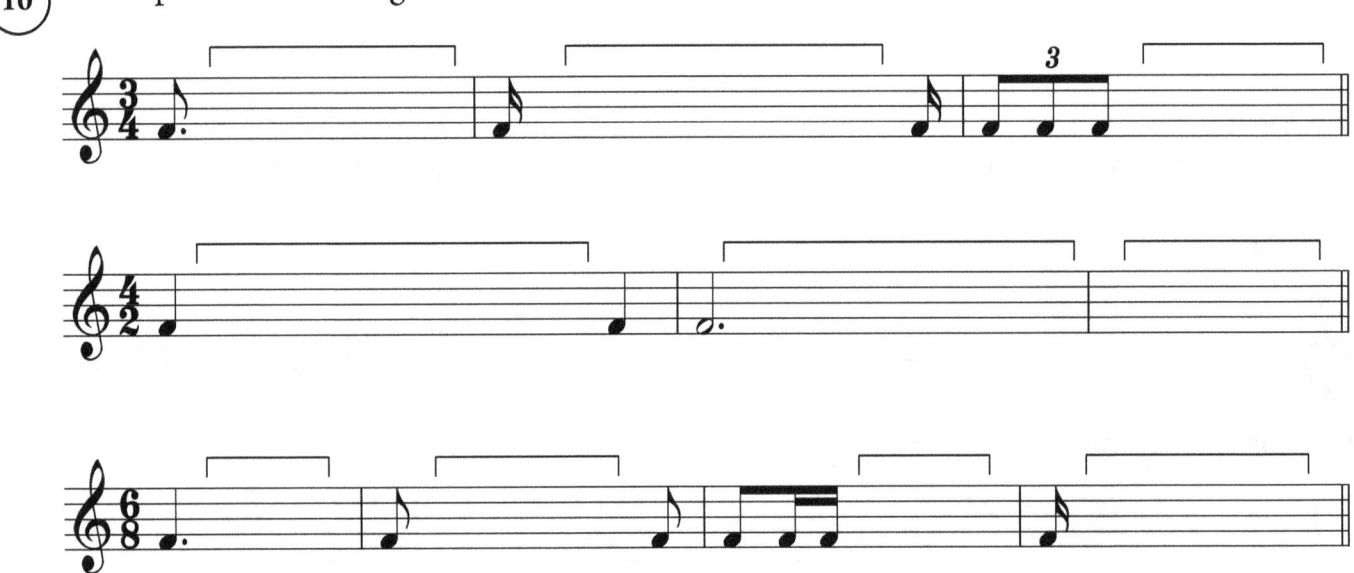

(10) 7. Name the key of the following melody. Transpose it down one octave into the bass clef.

key: _____

8. Name the key of the following melody. Compose an answer phrase to the given question phrase.

key: _____

9. Write the following chords using key signatures for each.

i. the tonic triad of E major in root position
ii. the dominant triad of D harmonic minor, first inversion
iii. the subdominant triad of B flat major in second inversion
iv. the dominant 7th of G major
v. the tonic triad of F natural minor, second inversion

i. ii. iii. iv. v.

10. Match each statement with its correct answer.

_____ Composer of "The Wizard of Oz"	a) Dorothy
_____ "Der Hölle Rache kocht in meinem Herzen"	b) "Over the Rainbow"
_____ Oratorio by Handel	c) Singspiel
_____ Opera by Mozart	d) Hallelujah Chorus
_____ Virtuoso female singer	e) Messiah
_____ Sings "Over the Rainbow"	f) The Magic Flute
_____ German born English composer	g) Handel
_____ Uses word painting	h) Queen of the Night aria
_____ Song in AABA form	i) Harold Arlen
_____ Name for German comic opera	j) Coloratura soprano

11. Define the following terms.

andantino _____

larghetto _____

rubato _____

largo _____

mano destra _____

poco _____

lento _____

pedale _____

spiritoso _____

marcato _____

prestissimo _____

tranquillo _____

dolce _____

leggiero _____

molto _____

espressivo _____

vivace _____

fine _____

marcato _____

adagio _____

12. Analyze the following musical excerpt by answering the questions.

(10)

Muzio Clementi
1752-1832

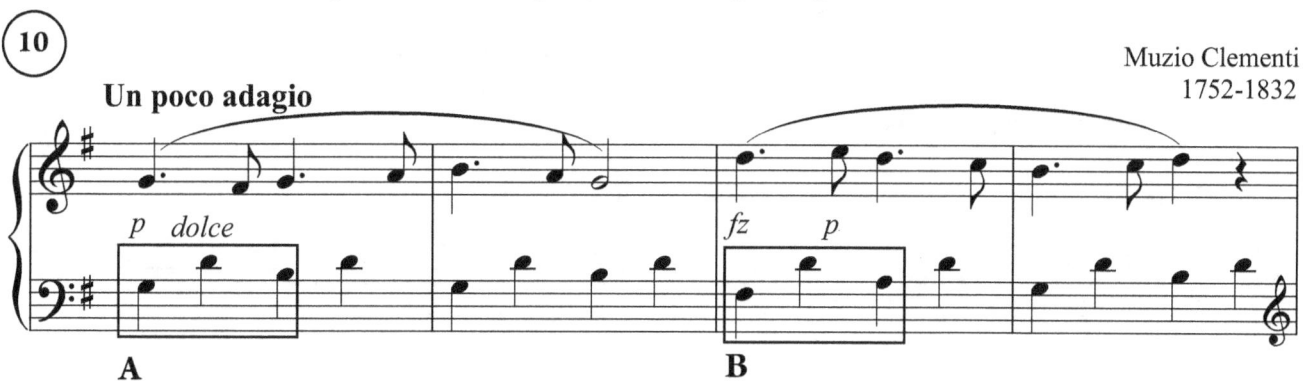

1. What is the key of this piece? _____

2. Write the time signature on the score.

3. Define **dolce** _____

4. Define **Un poco adagio** _____

5. Label the two phrases as: a - a¹ or a - b.

6. For the triad at A, name the: Root: _____ Quality: _____ Position: _____

7. For the triad at B, name the: Root: _____ Quality: _____ Position: _____

8. Find a chromatic half step in the score. Circle it and label it: CHS.

9. Find and circle a G major scale on the score. Label it: G major.

10. Name the highest note in this piece. _____

Level 6 Exam

1. Name the following intervals.

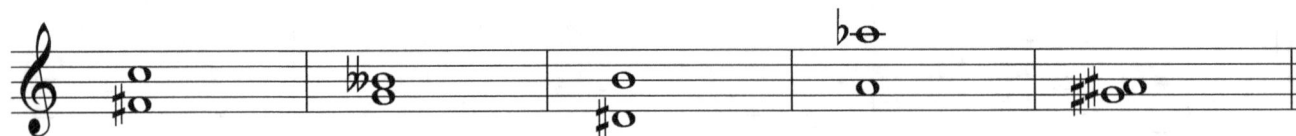

2. Write the following intervals above the given notes.

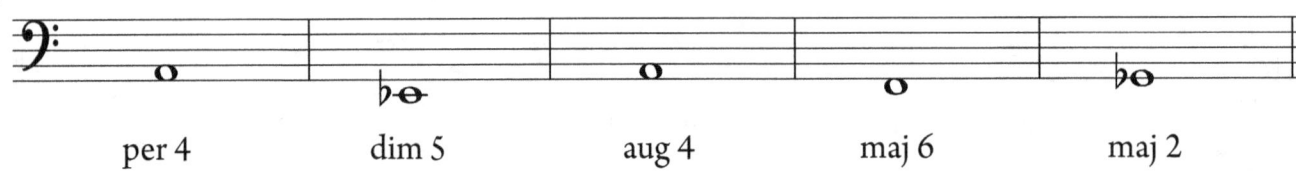

per 4   dim 5   aug 4   maj 6   maj 2

3. Name the key of the following melody. Write the root/quality and functional chord symbols implied by the melody.

key: _____

4. For the following melodic fragment: Name the key. Complete the first phrase according to the given chord symbols. End this phrase on an unstable scale degree. Write an answer phrase creating a parallel period and ending on a stable degree. Mark the phrasing.

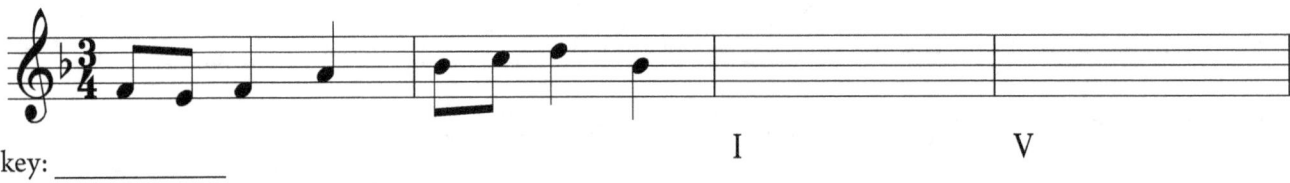

key: _____

5. Complete the following measures with rests under the brackets.

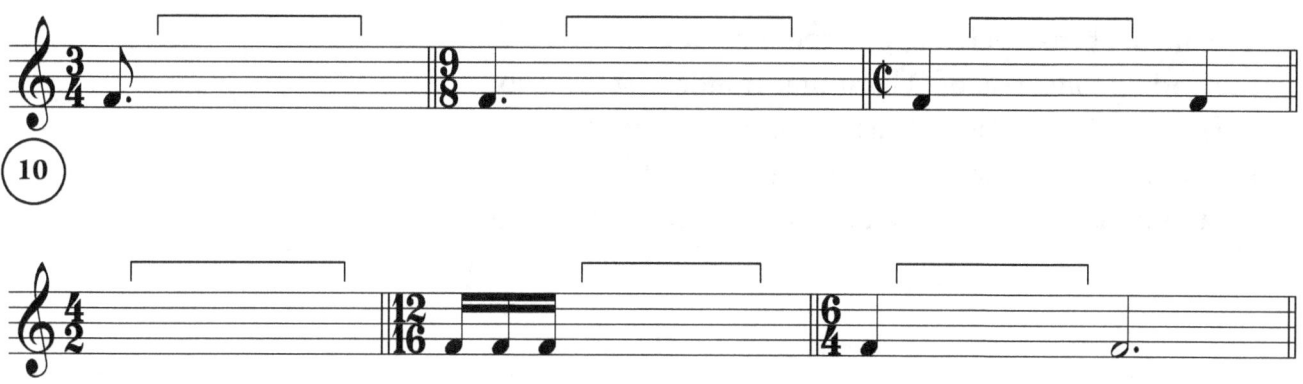

6. Name the key of the following melody. Add the time signature at the beginning of the score.

Key: _____

Transpose it up an augmented 4th using a key signature. Name the key.

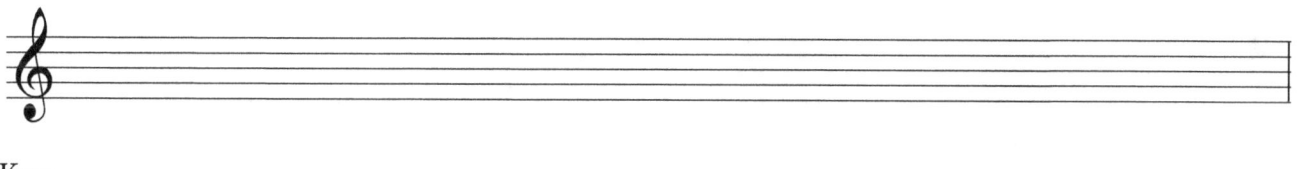

Key: _____

Transpose it **up** into the key of G major. Name the interval of transposition.

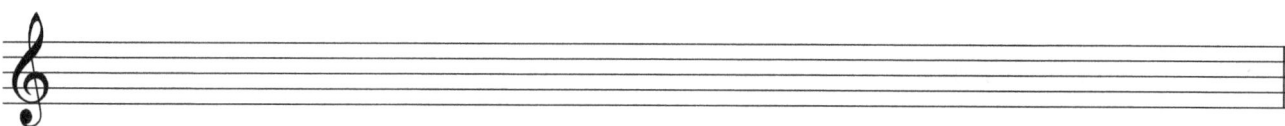

Interval of transposition: _____

7. Write the following chords using key signatures for each.
   i. the mediant triad of E major in root position
   ii. the leading tone triad of D harmonic minor, first inversion
   iii. the subdominant triad of D flat major in root position
   iv. the dominant 7th chord in A flat major in root position
   v. the tonic triad of C sharp natural minor, second inversion

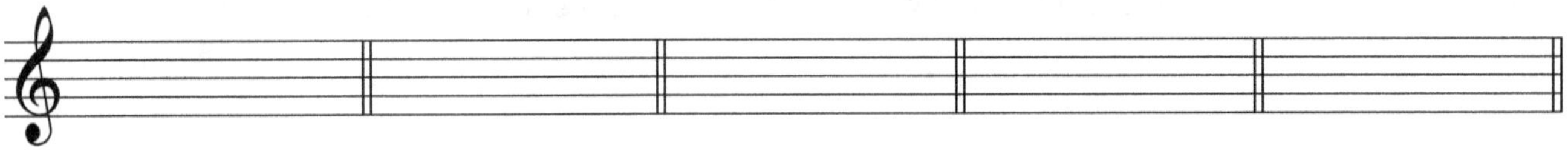

8. Write the following scales ascending and descending in whole notes using a key signature for each.

G flat major

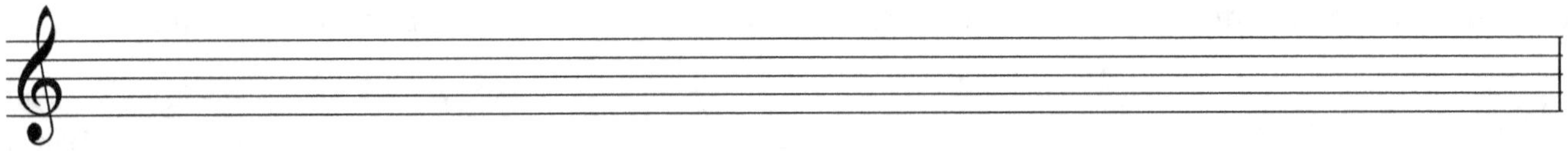

F minor, melodic form

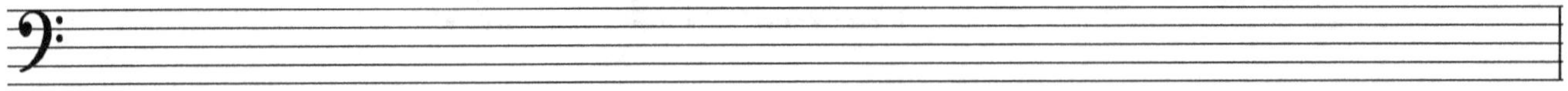

B flat minor, harmonic form

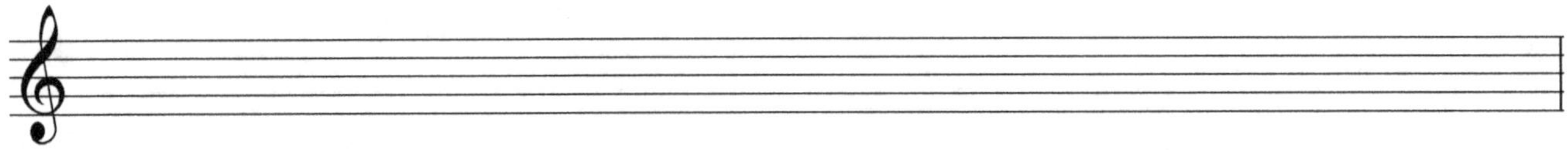

F sharp major

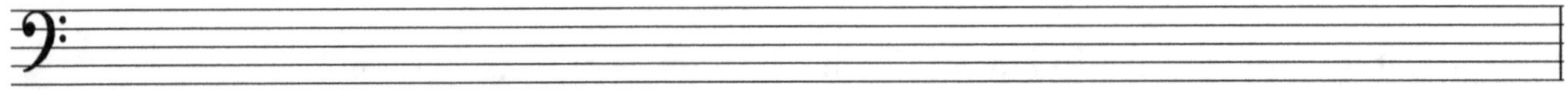

The enharmonic tonic major of C sharp major

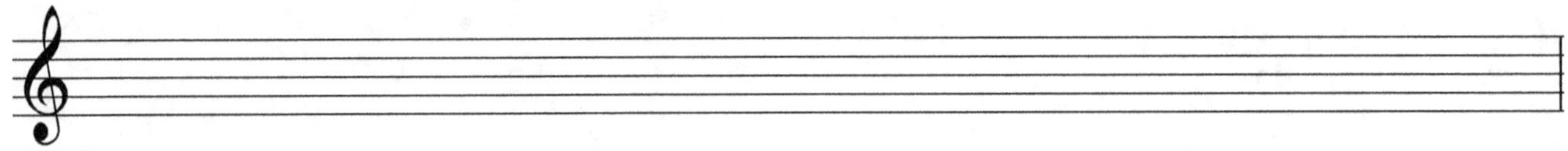

9. For the following melody: Name the key. At the end of each phrase write the functional and root/quality chord symbols and name each cadence as half, perfect authentic, or imperfect authentic. ⑩

key: _____   Cadence: _____

                                  Cadence: _____

10. Match each statement with the best answer. ⑩

   a. Composer of Brandenburg Concerto No. 5   ____Motive
   b. Classical Period   ____Brandenburg Concerto No. 5
   c. Also known as Serenade No. 13 for strings   ____Wolfgang Amadeus Mozart
   d. Composer of Eine kleine Nachtmusik   ____ca. 1600-1750
   e. One of the sections found in Sonata form   ____Invention in C, BWV 772
   f. Compostion using 2 part counterpoint   ____Eine kleine Nachtmusik
   g. Genre of this work is Concerto Grosso   ____Development
   h. Short melodic or rhythmic idea   ____ca. 1750-1825
   i. Baroque period   ____Johann Sebastian Bach

11. Define the following musical terms. ⑤

   a. *animato* _____
   b. *con fuoco* _____
   c. *piu mosso* _____
   d. *senza* _____
   e. *subito* _____

©San Marco Publications 2023

12. Analyze the following musical excerpt by answering the questions.

Ludwig van Beethoven
(1770- 1827)

1. What is the key of this piece? _____

2. Write the time signature on the score.

3. In what era was this composed? _____

4. Define *Allegretto espressivo* _____

5. For the triad at A, name the: Root: _____ Quality: _____ Inversion: _____

6. For the triad at B, name the: Root: _____ Quality: _____ Inversion: _____

7. Find a diatonic half step in the score. Circle it and label it: DHS.

8. Find a broken C major triad on the score. Circle it and label it: C major.

9. Name the interval at C. _____

100

www.ingramcontent.com/pod-product-compliance
Lightning Source LLC
Chambersburg PA
CBHW081615100526
44590CB00021B/3445